BETWEEN THE FOLDS

Published with the support of
the School of Hawaiian, Asian, and Pacific Studies,
University of Hawai'i

BETWEEN THE FOLDS

STORIES OF CLOTH, LIVES, AND TRAVELS FROM SUMBA

JILL FORSHEE

University of Hawai'i Press
Honolulu

To Pierre

This publication has been supported in part
by the Australian Research Council.

© 2001 University of Hawai'i Press

Printed in the United States of America

06 05 04 03 02 01   5 4 3 2 1

Library of Congress Cataloging-in-Publication Data
Forshee, Jill.
  Between the folds : stories of cloth, lives, and travels from Sumba / Jill Forshee.
    p. cm.
  Includes bibliographical references and index.
  ISBN 0–8248–2288–9 (cloth : alk. paper) — ISBN 0–8248–2346–X (pbk. : alk. paper)
    1. Sumbanese (Indonesian people)—Costume.   2. Sumbanese (Indonesian
people)—Industries.   3. Sumbanese (Indonesian people)—Commerce.   4. Textile fabrics,
Sumbanese.   5. Textile industry—Indonesia—Sumba Island.   6. Textile
designs—Indonesia—Sumba Island.   7. Sumba Island (Indonesia)—Social life and customs.
I. Title.

DS632.S89   F67   2000
305.89'922—dc21   00–033781

University of Hawai'i Press books are printed on acid-free
paper and meet the guidelines for permanence and
durability of the Council on Library Resources.

Designed by David Alcorn, Alcorn Publication Design,
Red Bluff, California.

Printed by The Maple-Vail Book Manufacturing Group.

CONTENTS

Color plates follow p. 130.

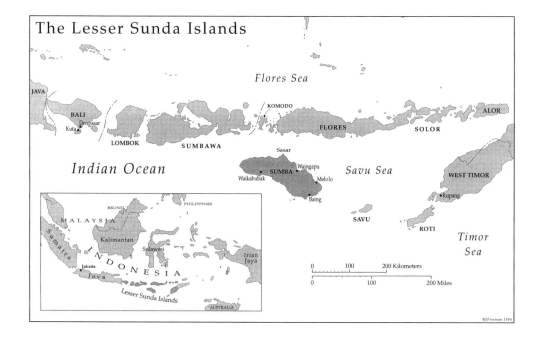

The Lesser Sunda Islands

Flores Sea

JAVA

BALI
Denpasar
Kuta

LOMBOK

SUMBAWA

KOMODO

FLORES

SOLOR

ALOR

WEST TIMOR

Kupang

Sasar

Indian Ocean

Waikabubak
SUMBA
Waingapu
Melolo
Baing

Savu Sea

SAVU

ROTI

Timor Sea

BRUNEI
PHILIPPINES

MALAYSIA
Kalimantan
Sulawesi

Sumatra

I N D O N E S I A
Jakarta
Java

Irian
Jaya

Lesser Sunda Islands

AUSTRALIA

0   100   200 Kilometers
0   100   200 Miles

©JFreeman 1996

PREFACE
ENTERING THE FIELD

My interest in eastern Sumba developed by chance encounters, as do most turns in life. On visits to the Indonesian island of Bali during the 1980s, I noticed panoramic "Sumba cloths" displayed in numerous shops lining the lanes of tourist enclaves. Like many other foreigners, I was drawn to the strikingly bold designs on the cotton fabrics and wondered about their place of origin. During July of 1990, in Central Java, I attended a special exhibition of textiles at Gadjah Mada University; it contained highly decorative cloths peculiar to the eastern coastal region of Sumba. Standing before hanging fabrics, alive with rampant creatures and intricate patterns, I spoke with a number of people who were displaying their cloth. Most had come to Java, by plane or by ferry, from their distant homes in eastern Sumba expressly for the event. While the vigorous beauty of their fabrics engaged me, the vivaciousness and savvy of the people who had produced them interested me even more. I decided to go to the island a few months later, to look at this tradition firsthand.

Boarding a small bus at the East Sumba airport destined for the main town of Waingapu, I sat behind a driver wearing an Australian rancher's hat, a vest of local *ikat* fabric, jeans, and American cowboy boots. He drove into town to the tunes of a Hawaiian ukulele (from a cassette deck) while occasionally beating on a small water buffalo hide drum held between his thighs. Along the way, we passed several houses where I briefly glimpsed women at looms on verandahs. As we entered Waingapu, a brightly painted concrete statue of Jesus, clad in Sumba fabrics, beckoned by the side of the road. The hotel we arrived at was fenced by men unfurling colorful textiles. In the lobby, an attentive mix of tourists and locals was watching Elvis Presley on television.

I realized by this time that being "modern" or "traditional" was not an either/or proposition, but rather, conceptual moves in a process by which people account for themselves—in times, in places, in the world. From what I had seen thus far in Southeast Asia, a certain playful unruliness seemed to erupt at the edges of so-called modern and traditional spaces—evident in metropolitan centers or regions accommodating tourists. These were compellingly *un*defined areas, in a cultural-anthropological sense of the "indigenous"—rife with peculiar creations stemming from wide-ranging sources. In Sumba, I soon came to realize that actions and inventiveness surrounding cloth had sources in any number of social and imaginative fields.

In January of 1994, a few years after my first visit to Sumba, I followed "Luka" on a mile-long detour through an immense field of high maize to circumvent the village of a powerful female black magician. On this particular day, we were going to see indigo dyeing in a neighboring village. By this time, I had been carrying out research in the eastern coastal region of Sumba for ten months, focusing on local textiles and the social phenomena surrounding them.

My traveling companion had refused to walk through the first village on route to the village of our destination because much of his family had been plagued with bad health from the resident sorceress' evil workings. As we began our detour he removed his white T-shirt, to be less visible from a distance, and led the way through the high stalks of maize. From the waist up, with his brown complexion, long black hair, and face quickly turning in response to every sound, Luka resembled a stereotypical, anthropology textbook illustration of an equatorial hunter-gatherer. From the waist down, he sported baggy, khaki trousers, a madras plaid belt, and trod through the muddy maize fields in high-tech hiking sandals—a sort of casually fashionable internationalist gone tribal.

What occurred to me as I simultaneously attempted to maintain my balance in the soggy field and keep sight of the man leading me through it was how I was crossing another field between my own (sometimes ludicrous) projections and those of the people I had come to study. Along with whatever ironies were emerging in my eyes, being in a "traditional" culture had continued to lead me through numerous local mazes filled with surprises. What happened over my research stay in Sumba did as much to convolute any former ideas about the boundaries or certainties of "culture" as it did to compel me to continue to follow the meandering routes of the people I had chosen as "subjects."

The eastern Sumbanese for centuries have been producing, using, and trading uniquely pictorial cloth, which is extremely complex in the making and historically has been a major prestige marker for the noble caste. Although collected by Dutch colonialists before Indonesian independence and long prized in international textile collections, in the past couple of decades, world demand for Sumbanese fabrics has increased immensely as a result of a flourishing international tourist trade in Indonesia—a trade largely centered on the island of Bali, but spreading across the archipelago to islands such as Sumba. In recent years the fabrics have become commodities in a global "ethnic arts" market. New forms of prestige have joined the tableau of Sumbanese status symbols, and these manifest through connections with outsiders and traveling away from the island (most frequently to the other Indonesian islands of Bali and Java, several hundred miles to the west of Sumba) to participate in the internationalized textile trade in urban and tourist centers.

My friend who traversed the field of maize to avoid the menacing gaze of a village witch is also a traveled man. A talented textile designer with some command of English, he has often functioned as a tourist guide in East Sumba, has designed and sold many textiles to incoming foreigners, and has acquired a global market savvy by visiting Bali and Java on textile-selling missions. His panoply of personal prestige markers is selected from a range of international fashion trends, available to him through his access to cosmopolitan urban culture and to foreigners. While often wearing Western clothes and feeling at ease trading with tourists, he is at the same time a believer in the powers of local sorcery (and a follower of the Sumbanese animist belief system, Marapu) and plans his periodic commercial ventures away from the island by first killing a chicken and examining its entrails. In my view, he is not caught between cultures or times. Rather, he is interpreting and reflecting aspects of his culture at this time—recreating and maintaining his social identity in a changing world, using the implements at hand.

When my companion and I emerged from our field trek to arrive at the village of our destination, we encountered a scene that typifies much of East Sumba textile production. Several women of all ages were sitting on the porch of a high-peaked ancestral house, weaving cotton threads colored with local plant pigments, or binding yarns with strips of palm frond to resist certain dyes, and occasionally taking breaks to chat and chew betel nut. Within spitting distance of the house were large stone funerary megaliths carved with animals, human figures, and geometric symbols often seen in local textiles. As is customary, the area for indigo dyeing was isolated well away from the house, and two women (one very old) were engaged in the dyeing process, their arms stained a dark blue to the elbows as they lifted skeins of cotton threads from the dye baths. My male friend held back from approaching the dye area, following the gendered prohibitions and fears that are part of the lore and alchemy surrounding the indigo plant and its liquids.

Along the paths of the production and trade of textiles of eastern Sumba, one can get a palpable sense of what have been historically male and female domains, as well as the role gender plays in determining mobility. Women often appear in Sumba as relatively stationary fixtures on porches or in household kitchens and, indeed, have been traditionally discouraged from venturing outside family compounds unescorted or without specific family business to attend to, such as going to market. Villagers widely believe that women traveling alone are potential carriers (or victims) of black magic. Indeed, as my escorted sojourn through the maize field illustrates, people will sometimes go to great lengths to avoid a woman given to sorcery.

Much of the everyday discourse of local life goes on between women in their domestic spaces, often as they engage in weaving and dyeing. Men have long held the role of forging trade links, involving their frequent traveling between village domains and beyond. While this difference in mobility and activity is still the norm in Sumba, women have begun to enter the commercial textile arena in recent years, with the expanded social networks and travel this implies. In some villages, transformations are emerging, not only in designs and destinations of woven fabrics, but in social interactions and identities that are beginning to challenge gendered roles in Sumbanese communities.

Some months after returning to the United States, I received a fax from "Biba"—sent from Jakarta—in which she expressed her excitement at being able to send a letter to America instantly. She was on a textile-selling mission (her second to Java) and had flown from East Sumba with a large box of fabrics, woven by her and some of the other women of her village. On an earlier trip, she had contacted a circuit of galleries willing to take her pieces on consignment and was now collecting money owed to her and supplying new textiles to the shops. My friend had become successful at designing, producing, and marketing vibrantly complex fabrics admired by Westerners and Javanese living in Jakarta.

Like my male friend, she also had acquired a cosmopolitan fashion sense. In 1993 she had her traditional, tightly bunned hair cut short and colored to cover the gray, but she continued to wear her ancestral jewelry and made no attempt to hide the numerous tattoos of animals that ran up her arms. She wrote me of the things she had done in Jakarta: seen an American adventure film, gone on shopping trips to immense malls, and eaten at Pizza Hut. She then related that the most startling thing about being in the metropolis (more than a thousand miles from her home) was that the sun actually rose from a completely different direction than it did in Sumba—this was how she realized that she was in another world.

x

The following chapters will attempt to give glimpses into the various "worlds" that make up social realities of a region of East Sumba. The parallels, intersections, digressions, and collisions of these worlds are indicative of the nature of the lives of people represented in this text—as well as the conditions under which I passed through them. These conditions were tinged by certain relations of power, not only playing out between residents of Sumba, but inherent in the very presence of a Western ethnographer encountering, observing, interpreting, and (especially) depicting people of a non-Western region. Yet Edward Bruner's assessment that "there are no naive ethnographers—but neither are there naive informants" (1993:330) reasonably rounds out the power equation, in admitting to a two-way street of agendas and vulnerabilities.

I made two initial visits to East Sumba (in 1990 and 1991) and each time stayed for a period of two months. During my first stay I lived with a family in one village and learned something of the process of creating textiles. On my second visit, I moved around the region, establishing the perimeters of my research project. For the greater part of an extended fieldwork period of fifteen months (1993–1994), I rented a small house near the main town of Waingapu, where I occasionally resided. I spent most of my time, however, in the three village regions I describe in this book, routinely lodging in several different households. I circulated between these areas, stopping from a few days to a few weeks at one site, then traveling to another. Thus, moving about became as much a part of my methodology as did staying in place. This presented problems as well as advantages—my shifting of locations sometimes interrupted sustained ethnographic probing, but it permitted me to maintain the scope I wanted for this account. Travel also took me away from Sumba for a few weeks on three occasions, to Bali and to Java, where I met up with several Sumbanese along their textile trade routes.

I initially communicated in Sumba using solely the national Indonesian language (Bahasa Indonesia), in which most Sumbanese I met were fluent. Gradually, I learned the regional language of Kambera and eventually listened and spoke employing both languages, often in mixture. Throughout this book I will translate from both.

ACKNOWLEDGMENTS

I am deeply grateful to many people in Sumba for the help they have given me over the years and for the persistent beauty of their fabrics, which initially drew me to their island. Most of the information in this book was gathered during a fifteen-month doctoral research period in 1993 and 1994, supported by the Fulbright Foundation and the Wenner-Gren Foundation for Anthropological Research, under the auspices of the Indonesian Academy of Sciences (LIPI) and the Textile Museum of Jakarta. Preliminary research periods (1990, 1991) were funded by Luce Grants through the Center for Southeast Asia Studies at the University of California at Berkeley and by Lowie Grants from the Department of Anthropology at Berkeley. In 1998 I returned for a two-month stay in Sumba, supported by a Postdoctoral Research Fellowship at Northern Territory University, Darwin, Australia. I completed a final revision of this book as a fellow at NTU in Darwin, affiliated with the Centre for Southeast Asia Studies. In the last stages of writing, I also benefited from the support of an Australian Research Council Large Grant. I wholeheartedly thank all of these programs and institutions here.

Of the people who read this manuscript in various stages, I particularly benefited from the comments of Herbert Phillips, whose intellectual astuteness and limitless generosity will always be remembered. I am greatly indebted to Marie Jeanne Adams, whose work inspired my original interest in Sumba. Her commitment to sharing knowledge and her enthusiastic helpfulness were invaluable throughout my research and writing. I also owe much to Nelson Graburn's lively inquisitiveness, keenly insightful criticisms, and ongoing encouragement. Sylvia Tiwon added to this book, through her knowledge of Indonesia and her elegance of thought. Sandra Cate made immensely helpful comments on many versions of what follows, as colleague and friend. Throughout my research and writing, Eric Crystal and the Center for Southeast Asia Studies at Berkeley provided assistance, which I deeply appreciate. Albert Wahrhaftig provided inspiration early on in my studies related to art and anthropology. Maria Massolo helped on an early draft of this manuscript, and I thank her for her generosity and incisiveness. I must also thank Chris Healey and Ian Walters for their kindness and support at NTU in Darwin. I am grateful to the two anonymous readers from the University of Hawai'i Press and to the immediate interest and support of Pamela Kelley as editor, to Masako Ikeda's helpfulness as managing editor, and to the professionalism of Joanne Sandstrom as copyeditor. My most constant encouragement and criticism have come from Pierre Horn. His insights and friendship made this a much richer work, and I dedicate this book to him.

In Sumba I owe much to the kindness and assistance of Tamu Umbu Ndjaka, Tamu Rambu Margaretha, Umbu Melki Kapeta, Dovianus Yan Kila, Umbu Pullu Maramba, Rambu Ana Intan, Rambu Anamotur, Rambu Ataleu, Rambu Pakki, Rambu Yohana, Ngabi Mau Amahu, and Martha, to mention just a few.

I also want to thank my family, which includes my parents, Harold and Erma Forshee; my husband, Pierre Horn; Christophe and Chieko Horn; and Jacques and Mathilde Horny. Despite the meanderings my work has necessitated over the years, they all in some way have assured me a sense of place in the world.

PART ONE: FABRICSCAPES

CHAPTER 1
INTRODUCTION

This book is a wide-ranging ethnographic journey, contoured by people who create and trade a kind of cloth through which they interweave and convolute the traditional and the modern, blurring such definitions. I will trace how engagements with cloth motivate, facilitate, and implicate people in far-reaching connections with one another and how these links affect lives and the fabrics that surround them. In *Cloth and Human Experience,* Jane Schneider and Annette B. Weiner (1989) emphasize that the human actions that make cloth politically and socially salient are as important as the material properties and symbolic potentialities contained in fabrics. As a social, economic, and aesthetic medium—an art[1]—cloth is a channel for passions that underlie people's endeavors. Cloth in Sumba, moreover, excites elusive realms of the imagination. In current times, designs in fabrics reveal profound shifts in the perspectives of those who create them.

Vital Designs of East Sumba

In eastern Sumba, movements of cloth—through designs and exchanges—colorfully map processes of cosmopolitanism and of conservatism, shaping historical and recently shifting divisions in the worlds of men and women. The stories surrounding this cloth are varied and include those of animists, Christians, and Moslems; Sumbanese, Indonesian Chinese, and Westerners; inventive geniuses, master artisans, and exploited weavers; rogues, entrepreneurs, nobles, and slaves.

This is not an account of an all-encompassing globalization or a culturally neutralizing modernity, nor is it an exhaustive ethnographic study of a discrete locale. Rather, it explores moments of possibility in the lives of some people as they respond to choices in their environments—in the last decade of the twentieth century, in a peculiar textile economy. I present something of the nature of personal ambitions and entanglements (cf. Thomas 1991) with wider worlds in a region of Indonesia that has been studied generally in terms of internal social organization. I do not set out to diminish these tremendously important analyses, which largely have made my own work possible. But I will shift the emphases, from kinship, local exchange relations, and (largely male-centered) public ritual acts to include alternate routes of identity in eastern Sumbanese life.

Accenting recent phenomena in the provenance of textiles, my study incorporates those who comply with and those who elude or challenge traditional modes of practice and exchange. While ethnographic accounts of eastern Indonesia generally have considered the basis of social organization to be in the out-marriage of women between clans—a "flow of life" (Clamagirand 1980; Fox 1980a) that continues to form cores of alliance in this region—there are notable pauses and swerves in this flow in eastern Sumba. New forms of commerce, education, and social interaction are facilitating broadened spheres of exchange and circulation involving men and women. People now envision themselves in the world in ways not possible a decade ago.[2] Sometimes, as we will see, their visions produce visible, lyrical moments, as they re-create imagery to reorder their places in the world. Art culminates in form, which reveals something of the conditions of its own discovery.

That tradition is not static is no longer a revelation in anthropology. However, little has been written of the recursive effects of people knowingly exploiting others' illusions of their "timeless pasts."[3] In international contexts, eastern Sumbanese concoct traditionality and re-create archaisms to fit the cultural stereotypes of outsiders. A spirited tension between models of traditional forms and the schemes of those who produce and trade them is a recurrent theme in this book.[4]

Cloth in Times and Places

In the eastern coastal portion of Sumba, vibrantly pictorial cloth (*hemba maramba*) long has been a medium for identification, marking social rank through motifs and colors. Textiles historically have identified clan groups in the alliances indexed by their circles of exchange. In the caste-based communities of the region, cloth is one element in a centuries-old system of conspicuous consumption that visibly communicates authority and place—through high-peaked ancestral homes, funerary megaliths, and elaborate fabrics. The quantity and quality of local textiles enfolding the dead upon burial or accompanying a bride as she settles in her husband's village assert social status in a persistent and strikingly visible aesthetics[5] of power and identity.

Susan Rodgers notes that history often has a physical, tactile form in Southeast Asia (1995:27), and this is eminently so in eastern Sumba, as history is enfolded in cloth. Through time, the region's textiles have been transformed consistently in their designs and uses, in response to influences within, between, and beyond village realms. Marie Jeanne Adams (1969, 1971a, 1972) has given accounts of how the aesthetic and symbolic fields of East Sumba's fabrics have reflected local intellectual order while dynamically chronicling historical relationships with powers beyond Sumba's shores.[6] In this way, Dutch colonialism, Chinese trade, prestige goods from India, and numerous other imported influences have been recorded visually in Sumbanese motifs and woven into village cloth. Thus, local textiles came to embody and emblemize social connections with the rest of the world, as valued and interpreted by various people in Sumba.

As people in eastern Sumba have been drawn into a larger political and cultural economy, following a commodity flow of a global arts market for their textiles, tensions and ironies arise between the conservative and the innovative. Indeed, new forms of capitalism have challenged if not completely altered former domains controlling production and uses of cloth. As a result, textiles once the exclusive regalia[7] of Sumbanese nobility have become another kind of regalia in farther reaches of the world—signifying the wealth, travels, and sophistication of their new owners. There is an ironic reflexivity in this, revealing multiple appropriations and vicissitudes in cloth and lives. The byways of Sumbanese fabrics are riddled with gossip, boasts, myths, and contentions—often beginning from the village porches of their creation and carrying through the traders and merchants who expedite the textiles' flows as international commodities that ultimately adorn walls and bodies in regions remote indeed from their sources.

A world market for Sumbanese fabrics provokes local dilemmas involving gender, rank, and ethnicity. As textiles increasingly have been designed for and sold to various outsiders—shop merchants, tourists, and middlemen—the privileged control over the production, use, and trade of such goods (and the symbols they contain) has eroded. Things of value now more easily get away from their owners, who are powerless to recapture them.[8] New commercial routes and relations have circumvented what was once a sovereignty in control of cloth as a prestige symbol. A sense of loss pervades many Sumbanese discussions of fabrics, not only of the authority to command them, but of the knowledge, skills, and commitment required to produce textiles as splendid as those of the past.

5

Currently, through interactions with foreigners, villagers in East Sumba have come to possess glossy museum catalogues from places like Los Angeles, Geneva, and Melbourne. In such publications, they see themselves depicted in the context of a (largely) Western, institutionalized aesthetic system—an alien "art world."[9] Such imported representations (of themselves and of numerous other ethnic groups around the world often termed in the West as "tribal") have informed Sumbanese devices toward interacting with a global audience and gaining in the bargain.

Moreover, "ethnicity" has come to be a crucial means of identity for indigenous Sumbanese, and one notably stimulated by market forces. Not only are people self-conscious of the value of ethnic difference through their encounters with an international market, but the stakes involved in this commerce have instigated fierce competition among ethnic groups living in Sumba. Chinese, Arabs, and entrepreneurs from other Indonesian islands now vie for profit in a flourishing fabric trade.

Eastern Sumbanese villagers cleverly play with notions like "ethnicity," "tradition," "primitivism," and "authenticity" as they fashion culture in meetings with outsiders.[10] The sound of an approaching tour bus often sends men racing to change from modern slacks to traditional *hinggis*, which colorfully wrap their bodies as they welcome awestruck foreigners to their homes. Women present *"antik"* textiles to tourists, while anticipating and often capriciously responding to their demands for "meanings" in designs. T-shirts now flaunt motifs formerly the prerogative of village-woven fabrics, asserting an ethnicity with a stylishly modern cachet. And people sometimes plot themselves in the symbols and stories their textiles convey, affecting social schemes in the spaces surrounding cloth.

Such plots proceed along expanded exchange routes and new meeting grounds for many in eastern Sumba. Men now regularly journey to the island of Bali, approximately four hundred miles to the west of Sumba, to sell textiles in bustling tourist centers. Joining in the trade diasporas of entrepreneurs from around Indonesia and the world, these travelers partake of the cosmopolitan popular culture of tourist enclaves, frequenting discotheques and interacting with foreigners and Indonesians from many regions. Such venturing has become an ongoing, consequential phenomenon in the lives of the textile traders of East Sumba, whose far-reaching experiences contrast with those of the women who largely remain in households and produce the widely traded cloth. This disparity stimulates conflicts and intrigues, some of which animate the stories in this book.

Cloth-based activities thus vividly accentuate matters of gender and power in eastern Sumba, evident in the contrastive (but contested) roles between men and women. I will demonstrate how world demand for fabrics has affected the ways they are produced and valued locally and how (following Weiner 1994:395) production and control of objects might limit or expand the possibilities for gender-based hierarchy. Rather than reproducing formerly imposed, hierarchical centers and peripheries, I will allow various reckonings of selves, times, and places to emerge in their own terms, as closely as I am able to translate them here.

Arts and Lives

Fabrics created in eastern Sumba contain meanings on numerous levels, reflecting the ways and reasons people are involved with cloth. Where individual grappling and inventiveness surface in designs, there is a visible resonance between life and art that reflects something of a specific place and time and sometimes wider reverberations in a world context. Levi-Strauss writes that art lies halfway between scientific knowledge and mythical or magical thought (1966:22). Fabric arts in this account often straddle concrete and metaphysical realms in the thoughts and emotions of those who create them and in the conditions of their value.

Informed by studies of the salience of textiles in cultural life across Indonesia, and within a context of global systems of exchange and transnationalism, this book brings into focus specific lives in eastern Sumba and very personal depictions of the provenance of cloth in contemporary settings.[11] There is no ultimate "conclusion" to the lives I describe, but rather, significant moments and reflections in their ongoing processes. Movements in this account trail perambulations in the present world. Instances of spontaneous creativity or deeply personal, calculated actions defy glosses of Westernization, globalization, or capitalism that "modernity" might imply.[12] I convey something of the disputes and shifts that develop through people's deeds and experiences over time—and how these might be glimpsed in words, actions, and fabrics. All such phenomena involve a reflexivity regarding the near and the far—both separate and entwined conditions in eastern Sumba. Incorporating a small portion of such a scope, this book is a (sometimes slippery) "multi-sited ethnography."[13]

Cultural transformations are processed on two-way streets. Not only are villagers affected by international influences, but elements gleaned from vastly different sources are transformed in Sumba's locales. Public buses crisscrossing the island now accommodate ancillary cultures, kaleidoscopically mixing recorded rock music with live folk revelry. Passengers clad in locally dyed and woven fabrics and imported polyester all experience increasingly overlapping and mobile social lives. Posters from Rambo films or American boxing matches or gynecological charts from Indonesian Family Planning clinics mark entrances to eastern Sumbanese houses, claiming and reframing concepts and symbols from distant places.

7

Ethnographies of the Personal in Global Contexts

Recent scholarship has reconsidered ethnographic positions toward "globalization" (in its variously interpreted manifestations) within distinctly personal dimensions of experience, probing beneath the often overdetermined positions of "victims" in a world economic system.[14] This book follows a number of ethnographies that have attempted to describe life in communities in non-Western or "marginal" areas in a contemporary global context—while maintaining proximity to specifically situated lives.[15] My account especially accents individual responses as people experience various pressures of change. Through attention to ambiguity and contingency, such studies disrupt a certain essentialism that has characterized many anthropological portraits of "natives" in the past.[16]

Recently, "interstitial" or "borderzones" have become important social arenas for analysis.[17] Sumbanese cloth moves through certain "hybridized" places, such as Bali, linking people from around the world. Stakes involved in cross-cultural commerce incite struggles and audaciousness among Sumbanese participants as desires and illusions of a wide range of people converge on uncertain grounds. Regions in which these people interact, nonetheless, are occupied places, no less significant than other more "real" areas of dwelling. If James Clifford's claim that "people and things are increasingly out of place" (1988:6) is in fact a condition in much of the world, then we must try to account for how people and things reoccupy the places they move to. Various interpretations of what is "in place" might then come into question, especially as we attempt ethnographies of people and objects in motion.[18]

Representations

International audiences and consumers demand and affect "Third World" arts on a massive scale,[19] from Thai "modern" (Phillips 1992) to West African "primitive" (Steiner 1994). This has been the case for some time. But more recently scholars have regarded the social and historical environments surrounding the production and exchange of arts intentionally produced for foreign audiences as important areas in processes of cultural change. These processes lie beyond the nagging art historical or ethnological predicaments of authenticity or cultural appropriation.[20] Responses of individuals in this book demonstrate how and why recent fabric arts stimulate and reflect their own dialogues between the global and the local, enmeshing complex social and aesthetic worlds.

A recognition of implicated worlds contributes to a current paradigm of reality beyond an ethnographic present (Fabian 1983). Over the past two decades, anthropologists have been increasingly talking about peoples with an integral past, present, and future. Repetitive cultural patterns— "traditions"—while indicating pasts, are constantly prone to innovations reflecting specific presents and anticipated futures.[21]

A call to reflexivity and "rediscovery" in anthropology (which includes a necessarily critical stance toward modes of representation) underscores a large body of literature at this point. My purpose here is to convey, tangibly, a processual human condition that is more than a "post-condition" of a previously intact or pristine reality.[22] People have always lived in the wake of events and circumstances, and while those of the

8

modern era may be much more penetrative than those of the past, the lives affected are not lived in terms of an aftermath.[23] Rather, living proceeds contingently through a present that the ethnographer is challenged to at least glimpse, if not wholly define.

Uncertain Boundaries

Regarding methods and focus, I agree with Fredrik Barth that if we have to construct an initial situation, we should not choose the fiction of a perfect structure but rather the fiction of an initial amorphous lack of order (1993:7), which then might take shape through processes.[24] The "amorphous lack of order," in the case of my field choice, takes form in textile circuits formed by the people I engaged with during my research. Serendipitous paths—much like stray threads—often produced an unwieldy tapestry of human desires, events, and differences within a region, rather than a bounded community sustaining predictable behavior.

I encountered widespread ethnographic self-consciousness immediately in Sumba; people wanted me to depict them in a publication related to textiles, hoping that would certify them to the outside world as "authentic" Sumbanese producing "real" Sumba cloth. People's awareness of potential benefits (economic and social) involved in foreign representation infused much of the interaction I experienced in Sumba. I knowingly participated in this undercurrent of the conditions of my fieldwork. Two years after completing my research, I curated a photographic exhibit at the Hearst Museum of Anthropology at the University of California, Berkeley, that also included fabrics and artifacts from eastern Sumba. Although I did not have such a display in mind at the time of my fieldwork, I nonetheless eventually fulfilled what eastern Sumbanese people regard as a foreign researcher's tradition of depicting Sumbanese culture in literary and museum contexts.[25]

9

Whether in the face of Indonesian state rule or local social hierarchies, foreign alliances—with researchers, art dealers, or tourists— seemed all the more valued in eastern Sumba because of the self-empowering postures of autonomy they often permitted to local people. A woman might transcend her ascribed low-caste status through trade relations with a European "ethnic arts" gallery owner. A man might increase his chances of sexual adventure with foreigners through the clever use of imagery in international contexts. Through displays of cloth, Sumbanese relentlessly enacted new postures in meeting places between the local and the foreign.

Brian Spooner (1986) has written of gaps in knowledge (between producers and consumers from vastly different social worlds) as areas that necessarily give rise to interpretive narratives. Much of the intrigue and lore of Sumbanese textiles generates from such chasms—with many people ingeniously manipulating relationships, artistry, and stories to benefit from opportunities within the social frontiers of transnational commerce. Moments of wonder or insecurity impel the creation of concepts and forms (in art, belief, myth making, an altered self-awareness) that serve people to explain the world to themselves and others.[26] In this book, creative gestures of diverse people will illuminate their attempts to secure ideal or at least manageable senses of their worlds and their places within them.

Moreover, explaining one's place in the world is also motivated by emotionality,[27] which excites many Sumbanese endeavors, most vividly those connected to issues of rank and representation. Perplexities of social lives find emotional release in aesthetic expressions, such as in designs of cloth. For example, we will see a religious conversion reasserted in images of woven angels, an overwhelming rage at a neighbor inspire a cloth-bound depiction of animal sacrifice, and even a moment of mirth in the face of a ridiculous European tourist eventually become rendered into fabric as novel designs.

A language of internal argument—through people contesting historical social conventions and cultural norms—frequently has eluded studies of textiles and societies, which perhaps have collapsed too much into all-encompassing indigenous social and cosmological systems (crucial as such systems may be).[28] Unsettling shifts in representation and alternate routes of action, as I will show, often define the recourse of malcontents— who inflict a certain wobble upon these systems.[29] In exploring the importance of material culture in societies, we need to account for the fervor of individuals—who often push cultural boundaries and defy social rules, endowing objects with fluctuating meanings in turbulent living contexts. As Daniel Miller argues, culture is always a process; it is never reducible to either its object or its subject form, and it should always be evaluated as a dynamic relationship, never of mere things (1987:11). Arts proclaim a kind of "knowledge" that can translate passions into intelligible, social forms (M. Rosaldo 1980:38). Such forms are elucidated in this book, much as "cultural artifacts of the moments that produced them" (Dening 1996:43), partially illustrating what becomes historically notable among people in eastern Sumba and consequential for the provenance of images in cloth.

Unfolding Passages

Much of this volume proceeds in narrative form, through a series of vignettes. These short episodes form a larger story of individuals and communities and their relations to a wider world. My interaction with people in East Sumba often proceeded through the exchange of personal stories.[30] What Kamala Visweswaran calls "an anthropological self that took pleasure in the plots and twists that structure drama as life" (1994:6) was what I, often indeliberately, deployed during my fieldwork period. While this distracted me from theory and quantification, it permitted my engagement with human situations, which usually enveloped my own.

Although I knew many people and experienced a number of village environments in Sumba, I ultimately limited my study to what I considered a cross-section of people and places reflecting a currently representative social scope of eastern Sumbanese cloth. My analysis focuses on a collection of individuals who differ drastically from one another and in their relationships to me. Certain people were eager to be "subjects," and a few were tenacious in giving me accounts of themselves. Others were less compliant; one woman in particular resisted most of my attempts at depicting her life. Although she usually avoided answering questions and always refused to be photographed, this woman's personality in some ways emerges more poignantly than others', as her story unfolds close to her terms of expression, through the artistry of her cloth.

Photographs in this book are meant to illuminate the text. The distance created by my camera and position are counteracted, I believe, by the expressiveness of those whose images and creations are "captured." So too with their words and actions in my ethnographic account. Although I have changed the names of people (and certain villages) to protect the privacy of individuals, I have not fabricated their words and the incidents in the lives I describe. I employ a narrative mode of description, yet it is faithfully based in empirical data. It is, of course, my own compiling and retelling of such data—an obvious mediation—which I have crafted from actual events, historical records from diverse sources, a multitude of fabrics, and the statements and actions of various people.

I have structured this book into three parts. Part 1, "Fabricscapes," includes the first three chapters, intended as orientations to eastern Sumbanese social life and cloth. The ethnographic body of the study unfolds in parts 2 and 3: in selected village areas of East Sumba, in the main commercial and administrative town of Waingapu, and in a tourist region of the island of Bali frequented by traders from Sumba.

Chapter 2, "Locations, Histories, Identities," provides a context and overview for aspects of social organization, beliefs, and history in East Sumba, along with observations and arguments regarding current transitions in the region.

Chapter 3, "Enfolding History and Flux," presents cloth in terms of its value in social analysis and its historical place and import in East Sumba.

11

This chapter describes elements of the production of cloth and selected "meanings," which resonate with fabrics and characters to emerge in subsequent chapters. I lay the grounds for considering cloth production and trade as communicative arts and commodities that—while profoundly integral to social organization and ritual practices—also travel well beyond them.

Part 2, "Between the Folds," enters villages and lives, through a series of individual portraits. What surfaces are the protean senses of place and identity people maintain and the idiosyncratic ways these materialize. This section characterizes gender, ethnic, and caste-based identities in the region as they overlap and intersect in the lives of a number of people involved with cloth.

In all villages, complicities as well as resistances follow the demands of a global textile market, and sometimes both responses are enacted by one individual. Not only are people to emerge in these chapters defiant of simple categorization as typical villagers, but their distinctive personalities and social worlds also resist unified analysis. Indeed, they carry out multiple, situationally contingent identities and inhabit dramatically contrasting realms of existence.[31] Some dwell in spirit-inhabited worlds bounded by nearby rivers, others revel in the far-off frontiers of Balinese nightclubs, and still others embrace a recent Christian cosmology in Sumba that recasts moral, geographical, and aesthetic worlds.

12

Chapter 4 describes aspects of the lives of particular people in "Wandi," the first of three villages in this book. Characterized by a relative openness of its inhabitants and a frequency of foreign visitors, Wandi generates a voluminous commercial textile trade. Moreover, as a hub of novel fabric design for several decades, Wandi produces cloth ingeniously reflective of larger trends in Sumbanese social environments. Simultaneously, the village issues a plethora of mass-produced, low-quality fabrics and has recently experienced a surge as well as a glut in its textile industry. Wandi bustles with intense rivalry between its inhabitants, which crests in the context of the tourist and textile trades. Distinctive pasts and personal perspectives give rise to unforeseeable moments of creativity, visible in fabrics from this village.

Chapter 5 enters "Parai Mutu," the second village of the study. In eastern Sumba, this village is among the most conservative and caste based, with particularly rigid restrictions upon women. Parai Mutu produces some of the finest textiles on the island, and people from this village resourcefully manipulate their social worlds through cloth-based endeavors. This chapter emphasizes the ploys of individuals—particularly women—who push conventional boundaries or inhabit their environments to their fullest abilities.

Chapter 6 explores the ways some people of the "Hawewa" region have responded to textile production and modern life. In this particular area, contrasting locations and behaviors demonstrate how tendencies can vary drastically within what is generally considered one village domain. These contrasts include explicitly different views on what constitutes authority and how certain individuals have attempted to claim control in their lives through involvements with cloth.

In part 3, "Shuttling between Worlds," I shift to a dialogic view of Sumbanese-Other encounters. People engaged in such meetings come from dizzyingly multiple backgrounds and positions, and the "foreigners" in my accounts are as wide-ranging as the Sumbanese described in preceding chapters. Through a multi-sited ethnographic scope, these chapters shuttle back and forth between very different characters, places, and kinds of experiences.

Chapter 7, "Worlds Converge," conveys events surrounding a *pameran* (I.; exhibition), a local village festival of dances and textiles constructed toward tourist audiences that draws in participants from throughout East Sumba. These festivals (which were occurring biweekly in the region in 1994) condense an international market engaging people from Sumba. I describe the self-conscious performances of particular people introduced in earlier chapters, the significance of certain textiles they try to sell, and what occurs in the intersections between and among locals and foreigners.

13

Chapter 8, "Village Encounters," emphasizes individual foreign visitors to Sumba villages and the predicaments and lore these visits generate. In such instances, wants and deeds of outsiders sometimes conflict with those of local people. When a lone Danish backpacker insists upon sleeping in her tent on the grounds of a village while ignoring its inhabitants, she incites a pervasive terror among people who suspect her of madness or sorcery. When two sophisticated Berliners convince a village entrepreneur to remodel the central room of his clan house into an art gallery, the results demonstrate something of the gap between worlds involved and the ultimate power of immediate social exigencies—as the impending death of an elder disrupts the pristine gallery space.

Chapter 9, "On Other Islands," follows some villagers to expanded arenas of social life and commerce in cosmopolitan centers in Bali and Java. The multicultural environment of a Balinese tourist region situates experiences of Sumbanese (introduced in previous chapters) traveling to the island. A venture to Jakarta by a trio from Sumba also unfolds. This chapter examines how individuals renegotiate personal status while away from their island, with sometimes dramatic results involving personal gain or loss.

In the same chapter, I portray quests for an elusive status—involving "authenticity" and "distinction"—as many international tourists also attempt to transcend limits by seeking out the exotic or the primitive. Drawing from various theorists, I characterize convergent searches for value and prestige on the part of people from Sumba and their international clients in the tourist and textile trade—with each one imaginatively enhancing the other.

Chapter 10, "Unfolding Passages," examines reentries of villagers into their households following the adventures of preceding chapters. Stories people tell, tales told about them by others, and tensions within (and reevaluations of) social lives surface, along with shifting identities, realliances, and prestigious display. I reconsider the specific, yet multivalent, nature of the human network involving textiles and society in East Sumba.

In chapter 11, "Conclusion," I reflect on how people engaged in textile production and trade contour their social lives, tenaciously maintaining or re-creating identities through designs both social and artistic. I reiterate theoretical issues constructed through the narrative of the book, involving gender, status, artistic imagination, identity, and what individuals from a so-called traditional society and their (many forms of) artistry might express as they occupy places in the present world. I conclude with recent glimpses (1998) of a few memorable individuals from the book, illustrating how their stories and creations go on as they move through what are always modern times.

14

CHAPTER 2
LOCATIONS, HISTORIES, IDENTITIES

In the southernmost region of Indonesia, Sumba sits askew from the sweeping arch of islands forming the province of Nusa Tenggara Timur (the Lesser Sunda Islands). Much of the eastern coastal portion of the island (of this account) appears as a largely uninhabited open range—a monotony of savannah etched by gullies—lacking the rich volcanic soil and rainfall of the more verdant Indonesian islands.[1] Livestock grazes on eastern Sumba's sweeping grasslands, and crops along rivers provide patches of greenery. Within the most arid region of Indonesia, Sumba (along with neighboring islands of Savu, Roti, and Timor) slips into the climatic and geographical categories of Australia rather than those typical of Southeast Asia.

Indeed, the late dry season (*ndau wandu,*[2] between October and December) in eastern Sumba prompts rain prayers *(hamayangu wai urangu),* ritual processions of chanting men calling down the long-awaited monsoon. Rivers to the sea might be impregnated by mythical red crocodiles *(wuya rara)* at this time, signaling that rains are imminent. Such images of potency and penetration as well as danger, borne through passages and undercurrents, reflect exigencies of life in Sumba as beings move between realms.

East Sumba

In international tourist guidebooks, as well as scholarly publications, Sumba is often located three or four islands to the east of Bali or Java, a "marginal" place to the rest of Indonesia when considered in relation to the heavily populated central islands. Although incorporated into an Indonesian nation in the 1950s, the island is distant from Jakartan centers of power and public awareness. In fact, Javanese and people from western Indonesia often confuse Sumba with the island of Sumbawa, which sits to its northwest.

Sumba is not known to have possessed a writing system until the arrival of Dutch mission schools in the late nineteenth century. Material cultural records of the past (accessible to outsiders) exist in the stone funerary megaliths occupying most villages and in older textiles and artifacts that have for the greater part been exported and preserved in foreign collections.[3] Yet despite extensive world collecting, objects of value remain hidden in village households or lie buried in Sumba's graves.

In East Sumba as in other regions of the island, male ritual specialists *(ratu)* recite accounts of regional history *(lii ndai)* as part of ritual oratory. Myths in the region generally relate that Sumba's first inhabitants arrived by boat, or sometimes from the heavens, at the northernmost peninsula (Cape Sasar), and dispersed into clans *(kabihu)*, which migrated and populated the remainder of the island.[4]

Ancient forebears established the numerous political districts of eastern Sumba, centered in capital villages *(paraingu)*. Such village centers continue to anchor origin myths that legitimize noble families still claiming sovereignty in their domains. People from lower-ranking lineages generally inhabit villages *(katoku)* outlying the noble settlements. Although currently people are far more dispersed from their ancestral regions than in the past (through occupations brought about by modern economic changes),[5] attitudes of many people in the region of my study echo what Marie Jeanne Adams concluded thirty years ago: "the Sumbanese individual is primarily conscious of his identity as a member of a household, *uma,* linked with a localized lineage, *kabihu,* while at the same time his loyalties and duties are organized in complex ways within a territorial unit, the *tana,* or district" (1969:22–23).

The indigenous eastern Sumbanese maintain a basically three-tiered caste system, composed of nobility *(maramba)*, commoners *(kabihu)*, and slaves *(ata)*. Following Sumba's incorporation into an Indonesian national system, the nobility no longer has legal control with which to enforce customary law *(uku marapu)*, but it nevertheless retains considerable social control. The *maramba* caste still possesses extensive resources, especially in terms of land *(tana)* and livestock *(banda luri,* 'living wealth'), and persists in demonstrating status through display. Social power has manifested visibly through time in large, often elaborately carved funeral megaliths *(reti)*, strikingly graphic textiles *(hinggi maramba)* worn as clothing, and clan homes *(uma kabihu)* with immense, high-peaked roofs *(ndidung)*. Through such display, Sumbanese elites assert—visibly—status and dominion.[6] In current times, however, systems of local power are challenged by forces such as Indonesian national law and ideology, religious conversion, public education, increased ethnic pluralism in Sumba, general access to print media and television, and growing local interaction with foreigners through the tourist and textile trades.

"Ethnicity" as a category in Sumba has taken on more definition as people have been more exposed to Indonesian state discourses about it,[7] to migrations from other islands of the archipelago, and to foreign visitors.[8] Social rank, however, seems to be as important to Sumbanese notions of identity as are other "ethnic" markers such as language, dress, and beliefs—all of which signify status. As Rita Kipp has written, "ethnicity is not so much something we determine by noting the differences

16

Figure 1. Nobleman, megaliths, and clan home.

between people . . . but rather something we discover by finding out which differences, if any, matter to people" (1993:19).

17

Undoubtedly, differences always have mattered in Sumba, but the means for asserting them have diversified in recent decades. Modern institutional changes have led to reevaluations of "history" by many Sumbanese, who reconstruct their pasts using an altered *bricolage* of political or mystical powers.[9] People will now often claim that their ancestors descended from aristocracies of other lands (such as Java or India), rather than from mythical realms. Through such claims, they situate themselves within an earthly, historical context.

Beliefs through Time

People in eastern Sumba presently live with a multiplicity of moral standards and juggle social and religious systems that shift between a modern, state-promoted, moral universalism of monotheistic religion (*agama,* I.) and local, customary ideas of the right ordering of the world (*huri,* often also referred to by the Indonesian term *"adat"*). Between this balancing of a morality introduced by forces away from their island and particularities enforced by beliefs and phenomena that thrive on its land-scape, Sumba's people evince a multidimensionality to their ways of living and thinking that can only be modestly revealed through my account.

The animist belief system historically general to Sumba is called

Marapu (which means "the roots" in the Austronesian language of
Kambera). Of the population of 165,00 within the district (*kabupaten*, I.)
of East Sumba (which is divided from the district of West Sumba by a
border running north and south through roughly the center of the island),
I estimated in 1994 that currently half was still within the Marapu fold.[10]
Many Christian converts in the region continue to practice Marapu
rituals and express pre-Christian beliefs, particularly involving death
rituals, marriage alliances, and honoring ancestral and supernatural
powers that be.

Funerary rites *(lii taningu)* exalting ancestors are central in Sumbanese social and ritual life.[11] Stone grave markers (often dragged for some
distance by large groups of people to loom as monuments of important
individuals or families) are imposing features in most villages of Sumba.
Rites honoring the dead—involving ritual oratory, material offerings,
animal sacrifices, and large attendances—are essential in maintaining the
ongoing goodwill of ancestors and ensuring health, fertility, and prosperity
among their living descendants.

Marapu is a conceptual system of parallel, often gendered dualisms
found historically throughout eastern Indonesia.[12] Expressed in opposing
concepts, such as male *(mini)* and female *(kawini),* hot *(mbana)* and
cold *(maringu),* wet *(mbaha)* and dry *(madu),* these dualisms take form
in Sumbanese social organization, ritual speech, architecture, textile
designs, and numerous other cultural expressions.[13] The opposing concepts that characterize cosmology and expression in eastern Sumba do
not always secure harmony in society or balance in individual lives.[14]
An unresolved nature of complementarity, with unpredictable poles
and routings, stimulates departures from "norms" in eastern Sumba
communities.

Within Marapu cosmology, supernatural fields of power inhabit particular landscapes, legitimizing clans and households in primordial terms.
Geographical fields are animated by earth spirits *(ndewa tana)* and sometimes visited by ancestral spirits *(ndewa marapu),* who many people
believe directly affect their daily lives, in positive and negative senses.
Eastern Sumba has been historically organized socially around a type of
system that Levi-Strauss (1969) typifies as a "house society," with clan
homes and their ancestral spirits as central cosmological forces in
people's lives—irrefutably establishing their senses of place in the world,
their travel routes and stays, and a shared sense of propriety.

This concept of the "house" as a central social category was earlier
taken up by van Wouden (1935) in a specifically eastern Indonesian
context and further developed by Fox, ed. (1980) and others in studies
throughout the region. Marie Jeanne Adams considers that in East Sumba

the concept of "place" is paramount in people's thinking, with references to place providing a consistent and meaningful grid for ordering and expressing people's thoughts, much as do time units for European thought (1979:89). Gregory Forth notes the particular value the eastern Sumbanese attach to place and to staying in place, and how this is consistent with the highly ascriptive nature of their society (1991b:72). Such ideas of place persist with many villagers; yet as people increasingly move about the island by way of public transport, travel away from Sumba, or encounter foreigners, their "grids" become less consistent. Although affiliation to place persists among people in eastern Sumba, alternate locations loom larger in their experiences and imaginations than ever before.[15]

Nonetheless, there is tenacious conviction among people in East Sumba in the powers of specifically local spirits and natural omens, as well as ubiquitous fear of malign magic *(mamarung)* inflicted by mortals. Insidiously afflicting people's lives, such human spells are often borne by liquids and powders. A village girl can be pulled under water by a vengeful ghost inhabiting a river. A man may fall ill from a poison mixed in powdered lime offered with betel nut. Body substances or liquid indigo dye might pollute the food offered to an unwitting victim, causing certain malaise or death. In my experience, such fears are part of the lives of all Marapu followers in eastern Sumba and of many Christian (and Muslim[16]) people. In fact, such beliefs have tenaciously persisted, despite extensive Christian conversion[17] on the island, and continue to shape sensibilities of the world, as will become apparent as we follow people through this book.

A form of Dutch colonial administration came comparatively late to Sumba, as a police garrison and customs office in the eastern port town of Waingapu in 1912. The colonists largely continued a policy of controlling the region through the various rulers on the island. Indeed, the Dutch often established compliant local elites as *rajas* (kings) in various regions, and their lineages continue to be influential in parts of eastern Sumba. The colonial administration supported the Christian mission school system (in particular that of the Dutch Reformed Church) as a force that might subdue the fractious native population by educating the Sumbanese nobility and inducting them into a colonial civil service. Prone to internal warfare and headhunting between village domains, Sumbanese were often bellicose to foreigners entering their realms and had been hostile to some of the initial missionary efforts.

Mission schools initially attracted members of the noble class (Kapita n.d., Wielenga 1913). Hoskins (1987b) has considered that the Sumbanese of the Kodi region of western Sumba were drawn to Christianity

19

because it offered them an avenue to literacy—something they perceived as being the source of an inexplicable and supernatural power for the invading Dutch. In this way, some of the nobility began to "convert" to the new religion, following a historical inclination toward forming alliances with outside powers in order to maintain and expand its own control.[18] Such motivations behind conversion also seem probable regarding the population of East Sumba, where there is a strong historical tendency on the part of the *maramba* caste to maneuver politically for its own social benefit and status and to use opportunities for increased power introduced by foreigners.[19]

What is more, Christian biblical parables emphasizing supernatural providence (such as the tale of the dividing of the loaves and fishes and the turning of water into wine) likely "went down well" with Sumbanese. Conferred abundance at a public festival—through divine intervention— resonates with a conceptual system that emphasizes material wealth, large followings, and links to higher powers. Conversion from animism to Christianity also occurs through fears of a loss of recourse to supernatural assistance following the death of Marapu ritual specialists in some village areas where (for whatever reasons) there is no one trained to replace them. Many in Sumba look to the metaphysical, medium power of trained ritual authorities for protection from malevolent, supernatural forces.

20

Joel Kuipers (1990b) has discussed how, in the Wéyewa area of western Sumba, calamities *(podda)* often reinforce convictions in the importance of ritual obligations. Injurious falls, strikes of lightning, or serious illness are consequences of an individual's deviating from needs of the clan and ancestors. In eastern Sumba as well, misfortunes befall those who break essential bonds and sometimes motivate people to religious conversion in search of alternative powers.

Another compelling pressure for conversion to Christianity is the pervasive notion of *maju* (from *kemajuan,* meaning "progress" in Indonesian),[20] which flows through much of the Indonesian national government discourse of modernization, including the ideal of monotheism.[21] Following this, many Sumbanese converts express a sense of modern accomplishment in no longer being "behind" *(la kajia,* often voiced in Indonesian as *terbelakang),* but instead being part of the contemporary world and the technological and ideological "sophistication" *(yang canggih,* I.) it promises. Balancing concepts of *maju* with historical ideology and social practice can be a demanding task in East Sumba—and people tackle this in diverse manners, as we will see. In terms of religious affiliations, eastern Sumbanese distinguish themselves as *da tamaka la karenja* (those having entered the church, as converts) or as *da palatangu Marapu* (those following the way of Marapu), yet there is much overlapping of Marapu ideology and actions among Christian converts.

Since the 1970s, evangelical Protestantism, mostly promoted by the Bethel Church, has augmented East Sumba's religious diversity. The sect from the United States enjoys growing appeal in Sumba; its charismatic preaching and lively singing are in stark comparison to the staid, Dutch-imported Calvinism. Moreover, a capitalistic ethos emphasizing industriousness and abundance in this life appeals to many Indonesian Chinese merchants in Sumba.

Modern Contexts for Identities

The Jakarta-based national government of Indonesia professes Unity in Diversity as a nationalistic slogan designed to exemplify its democratic principles (and largesse) in acknowledging an amount of cultural autonomy of diverse peoples across the archipelago. The concept of "unity" in this case also advances an encompassing authority over the hundreds of ethnic groups across Indonesia.[22] Thus, in regions such as Sumba, the national government has established school systems, public health facilities, government offices, commercial districts, federal laws, and forms of taxation.

Within this larger, imposed system, many Sumbanese feel an ambivalence in participating in a "modern" political-economic order while still maintaining ethnic and rank distinctions.[23] Because ideas of social superiority and entitlement are based on local notions of history and geography, people (especially elites) of the island seem able to reassert such distinctions in a politically influential sense only within their regional enclaves.

21

Identity and Trade

Until into the twentieth century, established marketplaces were not part of East Sumbanese social life. Exchange of goods (produce, cloth, tools, livestock) was carried out between kin groups—involving wife-givers *(yera)* and wife-takers *(ana kawini)*—or between castes in a system of obligations. Village nobles sometimes created trade links with foreign missionaries or colonial officials on the island. Because there were no true market centers (as had long existed in Java), there was no large-scale folk economy involving vast networks of people and goods—which Alexander (1987), Dewey (1962), Clifford Geertz (1963), and others have noted as important historical structures in Javanese cultural settings.

Through the twentieth century, Sumba gradually developed into a far more heterogeneous island than in the past. The Dutch colonial administration, in its goal of pacification, facilitated the influx of other peoples upon Sumba even before it opened a post on the island. In the nineteenth century, Arab traders settled the town of Waingapu as agents in the horse trade—a commerce greatly stimulated by Dutch demands for cavalry animals.

This trade in horses set a positive precedent among the eastern Sumbanese, following increased personal wealth through the gold coins the Dutch injected into the region's economy—which were often melted down to form articles of jewelry. These riches fell mostly to the *maramba* caste and stimulated an elaboration of prestige goods in the region, including textiles. Thus the association of commerce with foreigners (especially Europeans)—as an avenue to affluence—entered Sumbanese social imaginations.

Arab settlers in East Sumba also traded in human slaves, a centuries-old export system responding to demands of a number of off-island markets and also, for a time in the eighteenth and nineteenth centuries, involving the Dutch.[24] Indeed, the slave trade pervaded coastal regions of Sumba for centuries, often resulting from raids from the neighboring island of Flores, but also involving the eastern Sumba nobility in an established commerce in human beings.

Termed *"tau ata,"* such people were often the unfortunate captives of internal warfare and were regarded as without rights within the local political order. Emerging from a history of slave trade, issues of rank seem to be of more crucial concern to people in the eastern and northern coastal areas of Sumba than in other regions of the island. In many households of high-caste eastern Sumbanese, hereditary dependents (*anakeda kuru uma,* 'children of the house') currently carry on domestic duties in exchange for basic sustenance.

Muslims from Sulawesi, Flores, and Sumbawa (and other islands of what later became the Indonesian nation) also settled around the end of the nineteenth century in the area of Waingapu, which became the largest trade and colonial administrative center on the island and the port from which the Sumbanese textile trade was launched to foreign lands. In the same period, a number of people from the small island of Savu, to the east, were installed in East Sumba as a police force, their immigration facilitated by the Dutch in an effort to settle an island plagued with warfare.[25] Ethnic Chinese from other islands also arrived and, eventually surpassing Muslims in commercial holdings, became established as the primary merchant class of East Sumba.[26]

In recent times, Chinese merchants, who possess the business experience, investment resources, and trade connections away from Sumba through which to profit, also have become prominent in the marketing of local textiles. Many Chinese families in the town of Wain-

Figure 2. Women entering a clan home at a funeral.

gapu regularly ship textiles to shopkeeping relatives in Bali or Java for
resale. Chinese middlemen frequent a number of weaving villages in
eastern Sumba, buying or commissioning work from villagers. Between
these merchants and the indigenous Sumbanese is an economic inter-
dependency as well as a fierce business rivalry. Although many Sumbanese supply Chinese merchants with fabrics for resale, elite village families frequently seek to retain some control over the current market by
guarding their most prized designs. Rivalries persist between ethnic
groups in Sumba as they carry out specific roles along textile trade
routes.

23

Mobility and Gender

James Fox states that "in Eastern Indonesia a common organizing
metaphor for any elaborate sequence is the 'journey'—an interposed
movement through time or space" (Fox, ed. 1988:21). Such sequences
mark eastern Sumbanese lives in numerous ways, from the narrative
structure of ritual speech, to everyday gossip, to far-flung travels, to pictorial designs. Modern journeys elaborate and transform former notions
of place and mobility.

The movement of men and women of eastern Sumba reflect social
and ideological boundaries and various flows between existential realms.
Tensions between people and perplexities of life play out in a shuttling
between worlds most differentially marked by gender. There is poten-

tial power in mobility, in securing or altering one's place in the world by extending influence within it. Yet there is also power in resisting unwanted shifts in location and controlling limits that others might not violate. Adventure threatens to bring pollution or destruction, and human mobility challenges the stability of social life in Sumba.

Echoing tendencies throughout much of Southeast Asia, men of East Sumba—especially young, elite men—have long been the sojourners of their societies. Although historically not seafaring to any extent, they have often forged alliances with external powers in Sumba and traveled between village regions for political reasons, in the process enhancing their own prestige *(marihi)* and becoming—in the oft-quoted phrase of O. W. Wolters (1982)—"men of prowess."[27] "Prowess" as applied to men might be referred to by the eastern Sumbanese as *"haumini,"* which translates as "masculinity" in terms of its display through bravado. Whereas the mobility of high-ranking men is a kind of inalienable right, women largely produce the textiles behind men's business ventures.[28] Elite men in Sumba usually possess motorbikes and can readily ride off to villages at some distance or to the commercial town of Waingapu for entertainment. Many spend much of their time visiting and gambling.

Although travel marks male privilege and a growing worldliness has become a Sumbanese prestige symbol, attachment to ancestral place creates a tension in the wanderings motivated by trade and status seeking. Travel entails tremendous risks, which may result in the worst sort of annihilation—the loss of body and soul. People in East Sumba speak of fearing "bad death" *(meti mbana,* literally "hot death") resulting from violence or dying away from one's home.[29] As long-distance travel has become a regular practice for many (and a symbol of modern mobility), serious perils threaten these ventures. For those removed from their families and protective spirits, potential misfortunes *(hanggamar)*[30] are causes for anxiety. Death abroad will result in a lost soul, an eternally roaming *ndewa,* deprived of the proper death rites from ritual specialists and clanspeople. With whatever celebrity sojourning from Sumba may promise, a haunting tension between moving about and staying in place disturbs people who leave the island, stretching beyond local spaces. Sandra Pannel notes that "space is produced when place is risked or activated in practice" (1997:163). In some cases, the element of risk in particular seems to fuel a kind of island-hopping "deep play" (to extend a concept by Clifford Geertz, 1973a), as men attempt to gain in prestige while chancing destruction. And perhaps therein lies the pleasure.

While many men from Sumba now routinely venture to the island of Bali to trade textiles in tourist areas, their strategies and actions often produce unanticipated results as the entrepreneurs become mired in the vicissitudes of international trade. Against the renown that travel and commerce might offer are tales of men gone astray, squandering money, falling into debt, and sometimes stealthily selling family heirlooms. Modern travels contrast with those of the past in their protracted and exclusionary nature. Where women once sang as men went off to seek food or wage war, they now often resent their prolonged absences in unimaginable places.

Indeed, narratives of theft and loss, as well as of meteoric gain, frequently follow Sumba's worldly traders. Thus does one enterprising nobleman eventually experience financial ruin and public humiliation (chapter 10), while a lower-ranking villager enjoys personal and monetary profits from his interactions with an international market, attaining a certain status with foreign audiences not possible for him with local ones (chapter 4). Foibles and gains play simultaneously through the lives of these traders, illustrating the unpredictability of travel, trade, and social interaction.

Historically, social conventions have determined women's proper places to be within family compounds. In villages of eastern Sumba, loom-bound women sit on verandahs or in the cool recesses under homes. Weavers are embodied by their looms—their extended legs providing the tension of the warp, their backstraps securing them to the entire apparatus. In stark contrast to the men of their families, women often sit rigid and, except for the continuous movement of their arms and hands, stationary at one spot for hours.[31]

In village environments, for women to venture beyond the home, especially alone, is cause for concern. Men often express that women are incapable of controlling their passions and will easily be victimized by the sexual advances of men. What is more, "love magic" *(muru kawini)* is a feared threat-at-large in the region, and many believe that women wandering freely might easily fall prey to it. As Anna Tsing has noted in the Meratus region of Kalimantan, a traveling woman is a disorderly woman (1993:219), and in Sumba this stigma also applies. A woman "going about alone" *(halaku meha)* is not only prone to victimization by malevolent forces, but potentially carries such forces through witchery *(mamarung).*[32] People express the belief that women disrupt the balance of life through infidelities, magic, or the negative feelings they cause through unorthodox behavior.[33]

Sumbanese noblewomen, theoretically, live exclusive social lives. They generally marry through family arrangements within the *maramba* caste[34] and do not travel in numbers away from the island to university or on business as do their male relatives. In East Sumba's textile-producing villages, women most often spend their days within family compounds, helping in the production of fabrics.

Women do, however, control certain modes of prestige, such as pro-

25

ducing fine textiles that will command high market prices and attract local acclaim. What is more, while binding, dyeing, weaving, and chewing betel nut, village women tell tales, joke, complain, pontificate, and create the tone of everyday social life in eastern Sumba. Women's discourse often reshapes forces as they play through communities.[35] Although women are generally less physically mobile than men, their talk often travels, flowing influentially between social worlds. As Kuipers shows in western Sumba, women's speech expresses and evokes personal feelings (in contrast to the ritual speech of men, *panawa tanda,* directed at the ancestors) and is aimed at a human audience (1990b:156)—often grounded in intimacy. Moreover, women's commentaries—in the form of tales and jests—often become a kind of "backtalk"[36] to the postures of entitlement assumed in the unfettered travels of men.

As this gendered warrant is challenged by women who follow their own travel routes—carrying textiles around and away from the island—fabrics facilitate linkages with a world beyond the village and often beyond Sumba, generating knowledge, experience, and lore along their paths. In navigating trade routes, women simultaneously comply with and sidestep the social order.[37] When a lower-caste woman forges prestigious and highly profitable links with wealthy Americans living in Jakarta (chapter 10) or when a high-caste woman enjoys secret trysts under the subterfuge of going to market (chapter 5), they follow the expanded avenues of textile trade to overstep limits locally ascribed to their gender and castes. An economy of cloth stimulates and brings into focus an economy of experience.

Marrying out to other clans is a fundamental movement in women's lives, dislocating them from their natal villages. Living among husbands' kin, women then create their own families in new locations and carry on society based in clan alliances. As Hoskins has noted in West Sumba (1989:145), feelings of separation and detachment characterize expressions in women's lives. Yet there are other avenues that women might choose in the region I examined, and some resist marriage. I knew of numerous situations in eastern Sumba where women willfully remained in their parental homes. While families (and the unmarried women themselves) would often claim that they stayed because a proper marriage partner had not yet been found, certain women doggedly refused marriage despite all opportunities and pressures involved. Each maintained identities and exercised control by refusing to move from a familiar place, yet they were not static in their ideas and actions. In chapter 6, the authority of an unmarried woman as an architect of her own life course emerges. A devoted textile artisan, this woman is also an incisive interpreter of conditions in and beyond her family compound. A number of women in this

26

account command their lives by means of commentary and cloth. This command may or may not involve traveling away from their villages, but it entails authoritative postures in their worlds.

Expanded Alliances, Expanded Worlds

The commodification of textiles—traditional prestige markers of the East Sumbanese nobility—through the general population has motivated the regional elites (or those wanting to elevate their lower prestige) to seek other status symbols not available to most people in Sumba. As discussed, currently an important status symbol involves "traveling afar" *(palaku la mamaliru).* This venturing has activated and intensified the historical tendency to value alliances with outsiders and the material indicators of them. As in times past, such alliances have been forged largely through the mobility of young, elite men. These travels, moreover, echo the custom of traveling at the end of the dry season in Sumba, when people in the parched regions of the island were critically in need of food. Such historical sojourns *(mandara)* took men in search of provisions in areas remote from their villages. While fraught with mortal and supernatural dangers, these quests resulted in much-needed exchanges and sometimes created alliances with better-off people. Currently, trips away from Sumba will often coincide with this time of the year, with men boarding boats to other islands in October or November, after the harvests and before the annual rains.

In the world surrounding vivid textiles, men are increasingly taking advantage of opportunities provided by "women's work" to expand their own economic and social alliances, thereby gaining prestige locally and in wider social arenas. They accomplish this by becoming merchant bridges to an international market, while often locally reasserting women's historical social boundaries. Tourism and the first-world demand for "ethnic art" have provided thresholds for growing mobility (in both a spatial and social sense) for a number of Sumbanese men while at the same time accentuating an increasing gap in mobility between local men and women.[38] "Traditionality," an asset in commerce with foreigners, thus becomes reinscribed in local life.

New tensions arise as people overstep former gendered roles, and what results from this is a push and pull of conservatism and innovation —the acquiescence to community norms while asserting individual desires—that reflects ongoing disruptions within exchange circles, families, and the complementarity that might be seen as structuring eastern Sumbanese life.

27

CHAPTER 3
ENFOLDING HISTORY AND FLUX

*All social groups experience contradictory yearnings—for circulation
and permanence, for expansion through alliance and conquest, and for
rootedness through an internal deepening of authority. Precisely
because it wears thin and disintegrates, cloth becomes an apt medium
for communicating a central problem of power: Social and political
relationships are necessarily fragile in an impermanent, ever-changing
world.*

—Jane Schneider and Annette B. Weiner, *Cloth and Human Experience*

As chronicle of history and communication medium among people
in Sumba, cloth has been a visible indicator of comings and goings,
asserting identities, conveying meanings, and tracing diverse social intersections throughout the island's past. Within all of this, "contradictory
yearnings" are inevitable, as is cloth's value in communicating the impermanent nature of power.[1] Whether or not cloth functions as universally as
Schneider and Weiner's statement implies, it is highly relevant within an
ongoing tension between circulation and permanence that characterizes
social life in East Sumba.

Circling through Time

There is an integral circularity to the makings and movements of
Sumbanese cloth. Initially, it is woven as a continuous warp on a loom
(like a conveyer belt in appearance), wrapping around and moving
between two end beams. Moreover, stages of the production of fabrics
(such as dyeing or weaving) historically have occurred within specific
seasons of the annual agricultural cycle (see M. Adams 1969; Geirnaert-
Martin 1992; Hoskins 1990). Further, cloth passes between clans and
wider alliances, delineating spheres of exchange and obligation. In
present times cloth maps out global circles, traveling out to distant
centers of trade.

While Forth considered that "eastern Sumba generally can be
described as mainly verbal as opposed to visual culture" (1981:20), I
suggest that such focus on the primacy of verbal culture exclusively
foregrounds public male activities (such as ritual speech) and unduly
marginalizes visuality and female endeavors.[2] Ritual oratory is crucial
in displays of authority throughout Sumba, and this importance has
been emphasized in a number of richly informative studies.[3] But other

sorts of authority can be read against those dominating the sites of ritual actions.

To the present, locally woven fabrics are integral to rituals of the region, enfolding and identifying people as they move through life's passages. Numerous fabrics accompany a bride as part of her marriage contract and incorporation into her husband's village. In fact, skill at creating textiles has long been a requisite for women marrying into numerous eastern Sumbanese villages.[4] Sumba's social structure has manifested historically through exchange, and the movement of brides between villages substantiates this on a basic level.[5] Marriage negotiations generally entail the exchange of textiles by a woman's family for gold items and livestock from the family of the groom. The importance of such exchanges (and the quality and abundance of the goods involved) persists to the present.

Upon death, a high-ranking Sumbanese may be buried in well over a hundred textiles, which protect the soul from malevolent forces and identify the deceased (by motifs, color, and quality of the outermost fabric) to ancestors in the next world. Howard Morphy describes paintings on coffins of the dead among the Yolngu of Australia as part of a process by which the soul of the dead person is transformed back into ancestral substance (1991:108). Pictorial cloth wrapping bodies in Sumba also assists in transformations to ancestral substance. Symbolic fabrics outlast the flesh of the dead they enfold, ushering a soul through transposition to another state of being. Cloth signifies identity through its imagery and hues while protecting the enshrouded along an episodic journey (see M. Adams 1969). The substance of the deceased eventually passes through a fabric and resubstantiates in the ancestral realm.

Often a body will remain in a household for months or even years, awaiting an auspicious time and the accumulation of family resources for burial. Much of social life in East Sumba revolves around funerals (apparently no

29

Figure 3. Mourners at the side of a fabric-draped coffin.

less so currently than in the descriptions by Adams of life in the 1960s). People frequently attend rituals honoring the dead, ensuring safe passage to the next world and goodwill toward the living after arrival. A funeral *(taningu)* in Sumba may draw hundreds or even thousands of guests, with the women of each kin group bearing textiles to offer to the family of the deceased. Quantities and quality of such fabrics vary, depending upon relationships between people. Cloth received may eventually be traded or sold to partially offset costs of a funeral, which is an expensive endeavor in terms of rice and sacrificed livestock needed to feed guests and to honor ancestors. Attendance at funerals and associated presentations of fabrics are essential in maintaining social harmony in East Sumba—in everyday and supernatural senses.

The Substance of Cloth

For centuries Sumbanese have been producing a type of cloth now known worldwide as *ikat,* yet origins of this technique are uncertain. Knowledge of its use throughout the Indonesian archipelago is based on other historical conjunctions such as trade and migrations. Heine-Geldern (1937) believed that this method of resist dyeing originated with the Dongson culture of northern Vietnam in the Southeast Asian Bronze Age.[6] The art of *ikat* was probably known in Java since at least the ninth century (Groeneveldt 1877:46, cited in Bühler 1959:23) and was likely diffused to eastern Indonesia through trade links. Many Sumbanese insist that when their ancestors arrived on the island in ancient times, they brought knowledge of producing textiles with them.[7]

Before the appreciable import of factory-spun cotton yarns in the earlier part of the twentieth century (facilitated by Dutch colonial production on Java and trade between islands), Sumbanese fabrics were likely woven exclusively with handspun local cotton.[8] After imported yarns became available, however, there

30

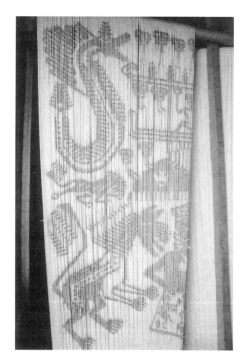

Figure 4. Dark areas of warp bound with palm leaf strips to resist dye.

was a tremendous increase in output of fabrics (M. Adams 1969), stimulated by the shortening of production time facilitated by the ready-made yarn and the increased demand of Dutch trade for Sumbanese cloth.

The word *"ikat"* (*hondu* in Kambera) means "to tie" or "to bind" in the Malay-Indonesian language and describes the basic technique involved in the creation of such textiles. Portions of vertical threads—the warp—are bound in a patterned way, using strips of dried *mburungu* (*gewang,* I.; palm frond), before a fabric is actually woven. The bound sections of the warp resist the dye. A warp is bound and unbound as many times as there will be colors in the finished cloth.

In East Sumba, basic colors employed are blue *(kawuru),* from leaves of the indigo *(wora)* plant (L. *Indigofera sumatrana*), and a rust red *(rara),* achieved through the pulverized inner bark of the roots of the *kombu* or *mengkudu* (I.) tree (L. *Morinda citrifolia*). A yellow-ochre hue *(wingiru* or *koha),* extracted from a variety of plants (frequently from a wood called *ai wingiru* or *ai iju;* L. *Cudrania spinosa*), is also applied; this color has long been hand-painted onto the design after the fabric has been woven, as a sort of highlight. In addition, various tones of black, purple, dark red, and brown are achieved by over-dyeing. In some regions, finished cloths are soaked in a mixture of tobacco juice and water to lend them a tan caste.

In contrast to the schematically patterned and generally smaller designs found in the fabrics of neighboring islands of Flores, Savu, Roti, or Timor or the striped and far less graphic fabrics from western Sumba (see Geirnaert-Martin 1992), eastern Sumbanese textiles are boldly pictorial.[9] For this reason, they appeal to foreigners, who enjoy the discernible, dramatic motifs of the fabrics, such as crocodiles, warriors, skulls impaled upon spikes, horses, deer, lions, and sea creatures. These images have been rendered and combined in seemingly infinite manners, and although "typical" Sumbanese aesthetic principles guide fabric design, many textiles are rich in visual surprises.

31

Figure 5. Dyed, unbound warp ready to be woven.

Gender and Production

Historically, women have been the primary producers of textiles—although new design motifs apparently often came about through the suggestions of high-ranking men. As men encountered new images through interactions with outsiders, they introduced novel design ideas to makers of cloth. Thus motifs from a variety of foreign fabrics, pottery, jewelry, printed matter, and coins were adopted into Sumbanese textiles. In present times, men increasingly create designs for fabrics, continuing their historical influence upon imagery.

The production of cloth substantiates a general disposition of women in Sumba, in physical, metaphysical, and moral senses. Birth, movement, and placement in the world—a circularity of the life cycle—is metaphorically contained in the continuous warp of becoming cloth. The tautness or laxness of this "becoming" is embodied in the posture of a weaver's body. Just as women affect the balance of social life, the weaver engaged in the production of smoothly woven cloth is an exemplary model for female conduct in general. And as a consistent focal point of their vision, dexterity, and imagination, cloth becomes a "canvas" for expression, devotion, and even passion for many women.

Women enjoy authority through using indigo dye. Liquid indigo evokes feminine fluids and the perils or moral symbolism involved with them.[10] The elusiveness of fluids characterizes elements that might uncontrollably flow between realms, penetrating earth, air, and water. This fear of pollution across boundaries (like the violation of definitions of "purity" discussed by Mary Douglas 1966) reverberates through modern notions of propriety in eastern Sumba and the actions that challenge them.

Although men now take part in drawing designs onto warps, binding warps to resist dyes, and the actual dyeing with other pigments, they avoid processes involving indigo because this potent and odorous color bath carries certain dangers. Men tell

Figure 6. Finishing out a fabric.

stories of diseases or madness falling to those who came in contact with the liquid, often as victims of sorcery.[11] For such reasons, an indigo dye pot is usually kept well away from the other work areas of a yard and is avoided by many.

Pregnant women I knew in Sumba expressed fears of miscarriage through contact with indigo fluids. One woman, who often colored warps with the dye, blamed the liquid for her too-frequent menstrual cycles and her failure to maintain a pregnancy. Both ominous and essential, indigo dye sits in womb-like clay vessels with mouths as small as practically possible, containing palpable qualities of an intense and mystical substance. The odor *(wau)* of the fermented dye suggests rotting flesh or blood, and women often compare it to blood of the womb in consistency and scent. An uncolored bundle of yarns soaked in the dye emerges a sea-green; it takes on the desired blue tones when hung to oxidize. Powers of metamorphosis are borne out visibly in the alchemy of dyeing, as the indigo dye responds to elements of water and air, aided by the earthly substance of lime *(kapu)* as a mordant. A volatile pigment in relation to humans, indigo is sensitive to sex, age, and bodily conditions, and people explain the inefficacy of a dye batch in ways that relate to these. Contents of an indigo pot afford a patent power to the generally older women who manipulate the pigment.

33

Janet Hoskins (1989) discusses how in the Kodi region in western Sumba, the liquids of indigo relate to a certain quality of "blueness," an exclusively and mystically female realm, and indigo dyers can be regarded as powerful in positive and negative senses, as both healers and sorcerers (see also Rens Heringa's account of indigo dyeing in Java, 1989). Initial indigo baths are most often created by women past child bearing age. Dried cakes from these baths are then obtained by younger women, who take them home and reconstitute them in water. (In recent times, the authority of indigo dyers in

Figure 7. Dipping skeins of yarn in an indigo dye bath.

eastern Sumba has been usurped through the increased use of chemical dyes infusing commercial fabrics.)

Whereas skill, knowledge, and labor of women produces cloth, the large, blanket-sized *ikat* fabrics central in many ritual exchanges in East Sumba (and most familiar to foreigners) are worn by men. These *hinggi* are wrapped, cinched, and draped, resembling on the body something between a *sarung* and a kilt. They are also worn over the shoulder and often appear as sets displayed on the upper and lower body. Smaller shoulder cloths *(halenda)* are sometimes worn along with the head wraps *(tera)* that compose motif-rich male costumes.

Figure 8. A *hinggi* in its full length.

34

Reflecting dualistic principles of the Marapu belief system in their bifacial formats, these fabrics are vivid with motifs denoting cosmological symbolism, as well as local symbols of status regarding clan, gender, and rank (to be discussed below). Images typically repeat in mirror-image designs—both end-to-end and side-to-side—with a central mediating panel of usually more-abstract designs, separating two identical halves of a cloth.[12] *Hinggi* pieces are actually two separately woven, identically designed fabrics (of about one meter in width and three meters in length), which are finally hand sewn together to create a large mantle in which motifs are repeated four times.

Another type of cloth created in parts of East Sumba, *pahikung* (also called *pahudu*), is made through the patterned insertion of many narrow strips of wood *(lidi)* across a supplementary warp to produce a raised design in a finished fabric. Villages of the central coastal region of eastern Sumba (near the town of Melolo) make particularly fine *pahikung* textiles, often combining them with *ikat* warps (see plates 10 and 11). These two types of weaving long have been combined in women's tubular skirts *(lau),* which are sometimes decorated with shells or beads (see plate 12).

Aesthetic Standards

General aesthetic standards for eastern Sumba fabrics relate to intricacy, artisanship, and balance in designs. Methods employed in creating fabrics ensure a symmetry of design, and labor intensiveness produces quality. Painstaking work is evident in finished cloth, through rich colors and crisp, complex imagery. The deepest hues result from repeated immersions in dye baths, with periods of drying in between. Dyeing is a prolonged operation, often lasting weeks.

For instance, one indigo dyer submerged her yarns in a dye pot for three days before hanging them out to oxidize in the daylight. She repeated this ten times, to ultimately achieve a blue-black hue. Discerning of the quality of the colors in a fabric, Sumbanese prize those attained by a succession of dye immersions. Natural dyes are always preferred to chemical ones available in markets. The latter are largely an expediency related to the commercial trade, although some fabrics worn in the past by eastern Sumbanese were colored with imported aniline dyes, perhaps as a novelty. Chemical dyes, however, did not persist in the better fabrics from the region.

In creating *ikat* fabrics, the greater part of skill involves binding the warps to resist the dye. Warps are usually folded end-to-end from the center and then bound double as one pictorial field (the threads will ultimately unfold into a bifacial design). Thus, effectively binding the bulky bundles of threads encasing eventual motifs requires great care. Tight,

35

accurate binding yields clear images, with minimal bleeding of one color region into another.[13] People in eastern Sumba value patterns that are challenging to render (such as curves) using the *ikat* method. The number and clarity of finished hues add to this complexity, as exhaustive and exacting binding and unbinding is involved in creating a multicolored cloth. Masterful dyeing of one color over another creates a third tone. For example, red over blue sections of a warp will yield a wine color or a reddish brown. Muddy colors (referred to as *nda nabara kati lakua,* 'not cleanly made') are disparaged, and dyers try to achieve warm, rich secondary tones.

Although people in all regions of eastern Sumba use the plants noted above to obtain dye pigments, preferred colors of fabrics vary from area to area. Some regions, such as the central (Rende-Melolo) and southern coastal (Mangili) regions, produce cloth with high contrasts between deep, blue-black indigo grounds and undyed white motifs. The southern coastal area of Kaliuda employs a strikingly bright red, achieved through long immersions in kombu dye, using a mordant called *loba* (candlenut; L. *Aleuritas moluccana*) to intensify the color. Areas around Waingapu (extending to the Kanatang and Kapunduk regions to the north) tend to produce fabrics with warm browns and ochre tones, which lend them a more muted appearance.

Pahikung cloths, which require meticulous weaving between selected yarns, demand greater skill on the loom than do *ikat* pieces. Aesthetic standards for these fabrics relate to pattern complexity and tight weave, revealing no loose or misplaced yarns in either the warp or weft of a completed cloth. Intricate, raised motifs created by *pahikung* weaving reflect the time and craft involved in their rendering. Many highly valued Sumbanese fabrics combine *ikat* and *pahikung* techniques within one cloth, uniting two differently treated warps seamlessly by the same weft threads.

Marie Jeanne Adams (1969, 1980) describes Sumbanese fabrics as reflective of numerical preferences in Sumbanese cosmology[14]—that is, their design layouts conform to the numbers 2, 4, 8, and 2 × 8. In this way, the favored numbers become apparent in the mirrored designs within a typical *hinggi*. Each half of a *hinggi* is divided into four bands in Adams' description: the lower border *(talaba wawa),* the comb or crest *(hei),* the body *(tau),* and the upper border *(talaba dita).* The central section of a cloth is referred to as the center *(la padua,* also referred to as *wunang,* a name applying to human mediators between people or realms of existence). Adams describes this last panel as mediating between identical designs in the fields of the two ends of a cloth.

Many fabrics still repeat this basic organization, but many others in regions where there has been extensive innovation now depart from these design conventions. Thus, while all-over cloth patterns persistently mirror themselves side-to-side, variance is often permitted between the fields of each end of a piece. Although many are also divided into band-like regions, they currently do not necessarily follow the design scheme described above. Such optional layouts reflect a loosening or challenging of former design restrictions based in historical social hierarchies. In recent *hinggi,* the body *(tau)* section dominates the cloth with large, pictorial scenes. Once defined by banded sections with established margins, design fields of *hinggi* now often defy all boundaries, save the actual limits of the fabrics themselves. Indeed, current designs often push against their spatial limits, threatening to escape the cloth altogether. In this respect they might mirror the lives of some of their creators (whose adventures will unfold), revealing their altering notions of place and space.

As Adams contends (1980), aesthetic principles in Sumbanese fabric designs reflect values in social life, and these relate to cosmology, rank, region, and gender, which combine in the artistry of creating cloth. Concerns with alliance, fertility, balance, and power surface in vibrant pictures in fabrics. What also emerges is an inventive flexibility, a certain dramatic "spirit" *(hamangat)* in eastern Sumbanese social life. Thus aesthetic fields are inherently regions of dynamism. In current times (as in times past), Sumba's textiles register opened arenas of play involved in their conception and creation, stimulating demonstrations of value and identity. These conceptually multilayered fabrics frame relationships to the environing world that reflect the complexity of the worlds in which their design takes place (cf. Goffman 1974:248).

37

Webb Keane tells of a feud in western Sumba, instigated by a gift of a torn cloth from one man to another. The intention behind this tear was ambiguous. As both gift and insult, the fabric suggests the ways in which the values and interpretations of objects are "necessarily caught up in the uncertainty of social action" (Keane 1997:32). The vulnerabilities of cloth—changing shape, color, or size unexpectedly—parallel ambiguities of social life, where much is hidden between the folds.

Some Motifs

Infinite complications enter any discussion of motifs used in Sumba and inevitably involve the elusive nature of meanings attributed to pictures. While imagery in Sumbanese fabrics reflects historical circumstances involving regional and global influences, designs also arise from instances of individual choice and creativity that are impossible to isolate. As Robyn Maxwell concludes of many textile patterns throughout Southeast Asia, their original meanings have also changed, and nowadays weavers often look to their immediate world to explain the meanings of motifs and are no longer aware of what they may have meant to their ancestors (1990a:26). This uncertainty, however, leaves room for maneuver.

Motifs of eastern Sumba repeat and vary considerably between village regions. I cannot describe here all of the numerous images employed in the region but will introduce a few in terms of their importance in communities I worked in. Some of these motifs reappear in connection to people in later chapters and are discussed in more detail in social contexts.

The *andung* or skull tree is perhaps the most striking Sumbanese motif, having its origins in headhunting practices. In former times, villages of East Sumba featured central "trees," which were often actually large, transplanted branches secured by piles of rocks. Spikes were imbedded into the reconstructed trees, and heads of slain enemies were displayed on the spikes to demonstrate victory and reassert visibly the power of ruling nobles.[15] Some *maramba* families stylized the skull tree into an iconography resembling family crests, and the motifs are prominent in textiles from the central coastal region.

Skulls remain in the possession and memories of villagers. Some still insist that captured heads, buried under posts in times past, sustain the stability of structures. The captivity of souls of slain enemies is reproduced in fabric designs, as skulls stare out from their "trees," disembodied and in emblematic service to their "possessors" *(mangu da nyuda).* There is an ultimate, symbolic conquest in configuring severed heads of enemies into images in fabrics to be draped on the body—a pictorial reveling in the destruction of foes. Skull trees are an iconographic outcome of agonistic relations—metaphors not only of terror, but of a spiteful display of victory over others. One old man from a central coastal village in eastern Sumba

38

Figure 9. *Andung* or skull trees.

explained: "People were afraid to approach us in the past, when we wore the *andung* motifs on our *hinggi*s. They were reminded of our fierceness. They would take care to walk well around our village in the past. Our *andung* always scared them to look at."

Trees also denote life and fertility. *"Pingi"* is the word for "tree" in East Sumba, but it also can mean "origin" or "source." Numerous renditions of what locals and foreigners often refer to as a "tree of life" appear as symmetrically stylized plant forms in fabrics and in some instances resemble skull trees in their configurations. The tree in similar manifestations is seen throughout Southeast Asia in cloth,[16] suggesting fertility and renewal emanating from a potent source.

Other forms derivative of plants and creatures (but not necessarily recognizable as such to non-Sumbanese, being more abstract in design) often appear in the central sections of *hinggi*s; people in eastern Sumba say they are of much older origin than the more representational motifs. These patterns often resemble simplified abstractions of flowers (*habaku*) or butterflies (*karihu*) defined by lines and dots. Many people refer to such forms —which often appear in the central sections of *hinggi,* perhaps as counterbalances or mediations to newer designs within the cloths—as the most ancient symbols of local powers.

An ancient image in Sumbanese fabrics involves a front-facing human figure (*tau*). Similar figures appear in cloth across Indonesia, and some researchers have considered these as descending from the

39

Figure 10. Tree *(pingi).*

Figure 11. Flowers *(habaku)*.

Figure 12. Butterfly *(karihu)*.

40

Dongson cultural migrations one to three thousand years ago.[17] In Timor, Flores, Kalimantan (Borneo), and other islands, such figures are made up of geometric diamonds, triangles, and meanders and are abstractly recognizable as human forms. In eastern Sumba, however, the forms convey more personality. Although formulaic in design, they are generally more expressive or suggestive in postures and details, often showing internal organs and facial expressions. If such figures evolved from shared ancient sources, then the eastern Sumbanese versions have become considerably more animated and realistic than those of other Indonesian regions.[18] This expressiveness and realism carries through many more recently invented motifs.

Animals in Sumba are deeply connected with status, wealth, and the passing of time. Hoskins (1993a) tells of measuring time in West Sumba through the lifespans of certain livestock. The magnitude of public festivals in East Sumba is always reckoned by how many tails *(kiku)* were involved—that is, how many animals were slaughtered to feed guests. This count makes public the bravado of men and marks the worth *(wili)* of women and the relative status of each clan involved in a marriage exchange. Animals link people, viscerally, with higher powers and with each other, and demonstrate social standing.

Horses *(njara)* and chickens *(manu)* are prominent motifs in the southeast region of Mangili, an area known for the deep saturation of its dyes. Chickens in Sumba often symbolize protective, ancestral power. As

Figure 13. Eastern Sumbanese figures.

in much of Southeast Asia, they are important in augury, as people seek information through their entrails from the higher powers of Marapu ancestors. Cocks wield vigilant power, poised atop homes, graves, or looming in upper design fields of fabrics, heralding arrivals of that yet unseen by humans. Horses evoke wealth, mobility, and male bravado, and many of the *maramba* rank continue to prosper through their breeding and trade.[19] Horses are sacrificed at funerals of the well-to-do to accompany a departed soul. Just as they stimulated breeding, the Dutch likely influenced realistic images of horses in local fabrics (M. Adams 1972:16).

Aquatic and amphibious creatures such as shrimp *(kura mbiu),* crayfish *(kurangu),* turtles *(kara),* snakes *(kataru),* and crocodiles *(wuya)* relate to noble ranks, denoting qualities such as cunning, bravery, dualistic powers, and transformation to the next world *(awangu).* Adams notes the powers of their dual nature: "On another level of meaning, the textiles may serve as symbols of passage to the other world, which is essentially the under world of water, and of the upper world of the firmament. In this connection, *creatures that participate in both environments,* such as crocodiles, snakes, or winged snake-dragons, may be meaningful symbols of the way" (1969:167; italics added).

Many in eastern Sumba regard the crocodile in fabrics as a symbol of the rank of the prince, maintaining a certain status through its double nature. With the amphibious ability to live in two worlds—that of land *(tana)* and that of water *(wai)*—the creature is masterful *(talu)* in more than one realm or mode of being.

Like crocodiles, young noblemen have often functioned in multiple worlds, seeking prestige and identity by their ability to move between

Figure 14. Images from various realms: horses, chickens, crayfish, and stars in a cloth from Mangili.

42

realms. Although often employing intermediary speakers to address others or serve as initial proxies, noblemen nonetheless have claimed the credit and prestige that comes with outside alliances. Many times people in villages boasted to me of how their grandfathers or great-uncles had secured important treaties or contracts with Dutch or other foreign agents, and people often kept mementos of such alliances in their homes, in the forms of coins, bibles, or photographs.

In recent times, passages to not only the metaphysical world but also the physical world away from Sumba have become ingrained in Sumbanese imaginations regarding prestigious transformations. This perception suggests a modern, secularized analog to the long and arduous journeys taken after death. And as Marapu beliefs shift or break down under modern pressures (such as public schooling and religious conversion), such worldly ventures will likely gain in value. The numerous sojourns that facilitate the flow of fabrics to distant places are evidence of this new importance.

Throughout the past, the nobility of East Sumba adopted foreign motifs into its own royal regalia as emblems of alliances with outsiders. In this way, regal symbols such as the heraldic lion from the Dutch coat of arms, the schematic *patola* designs from Indian trade cloths, and

Figure 15. Aquatic and amphibious creatures from Rende.

sinewy dragons from Chinese porcelain entered Sumbanese design fields.

A family may cherish a cloth because it contains a motif associated with an ancestor or contains borrowed motifs from a prestigious article, such as an Indian *patola* trade cloth *(hundarangga)* acquired in times past.[20] The appreciation of specific images over others varies between regions. For example, people in the southern coastal areas prefer animal motifs in bands, while those living nearer Waingapu render all sorts of representational human activities into their cloth.

Figure 16. Heraldic lions of Dutch origin.

Figure 17. Pattern inspired by Indian *patola* cloth.

Shifting Historical Circumstances, Designs, and Practices

Given the vivid history of borrowing and losses of designs in East Sumba's cloth, there is much talk in and away from Sumba of a decline in the quality of the island's textiles. However, such decline does not seem an objective "fact." Aside from whatever compromises may occur over time in methods and materials, the fabrics seem to consistently reflect the times and conditions in which they were produced and the scope of influences these include.

In the early part of the twentieth century, Dutch missionaries and colonists began collecting fabrics from East Sumba (M. Adams 1969). Coincidentally, the natural hues of the island's textiles paralleled a particularly Flemish palette (evident in much of the painting of earlier periods) of warm ochres and red-browns, rich blues, and high contrasts with white.[21] The pleasing tones and practicality of the novel fabrics suited a Dutch domesticity characterized by cozy *(gezellig)* interiors that favored decorative cloth as curtains, table covers, and blankets.[22] Following colonial tastes, designs within certain textiles were rendered as more naturally representational.[23] To appeal to the Dutch market, motifs became increasingly figurative, a trait that grew to become a distinguishing feature of some regional fabrics. As had ancient *tau* figures in earlier textiles, these newer human forms took on a variety of expressive and idiosyncratic traits.

Dutch chroniclers of Indonesian life[24] wrote illustrated accounts of Sumbanese fabrics in journals published in the Netherlands, featuring photographs of lively figurative motifs in complex designs. The missionary D. K. Wielenga began collecting textiles in Sumba around 1905 and

45

Figure 18. Chinese dragon from porcelain ware.

contributed the initial collection of such fabrics to the Museum voor
Volkenkunde in Rotterdam in 1912. Thus, textiles and descriptions of
culture in Sumba were accessible to the European public through museum
displays and publications in the early twentieth century, and they aroused
interest.[25]

While museum collections of fabrics from Sumba were impressing the
Dutch public, the phenomenon of this collecting was affecting the eastern
Sumbanese and stimulating changes in cloth designs. This seems to be
when large, multiple human figures began to appear in fabrics from the

region, often rendered in manners suggesting realism.[26] Such forms also implied economy—large figures could be produced more quickly. By the 1920s, Dutch observers (such as Kruyt [1922] and Nieuwenkamp [1920]) critically noted changes in East Sumba's textile patterns and quality, and a European discourse regarding the degeneration of traditional forms began. It would continue through the century.

Figure 19. Figurative design in 1994.

The growing commercialism of the years since about 1980 has stimulated a greatly elaborated market for local designers, dyers, weavers, and traders—along with an increased diversity in fabric designs and quality. Many pieces have become rapidly designed and finished—a kind of village mass production in which aesthetics, quality of materials, meaning, and artisanship play minor roles. Such designs are favored for the simplicity of their reproduction, and the expedient use of chemical dyes has often replaced the more time-consuming processes involved in the production and application of local plant dyes. What is more, many commercial *ikat* pieces are now bound with the easier to come by (but far more permeable) plastic strips available in local markets; the result is extensive bleeding of dyes and reduced clarity of motifs.

There is extensive talk of "loss" *(ilangu)* among Sumbanese villagers, of "cloth like that in the past" *(hemba hama la mandai)*. As various trajectories have developed in a market for village cloth, so have local claims of authenticity and value, along with accusations of forgery and theft. Often I heard laments such as one offered by a middle-aged village woman:

> There is no one living now who can make cloth like we had in the past. That is lost now. Even the old women are nearly gone. The ones who could do that. We don't see that kind of cloth in Sumba now. Some might be in the ground, some might be with foreigners far from here, but we can't see it now. Now people copy from photographs in books from Western people.

Laments of loss often attach to social rank and to the attenuated political control of current *"rajas"* of village regions. What is more, villagers' complicity with Chinese or Arab merchants in the textile trade is blamed for the loss of designs and profits for village Sumbanese. One elderly village woman complained:

> Even the noblemen in our village—the highest!—sell cloth
> that belongs to the Chinese in Waingapu! Imagine! A king in
> Sumba takes some cloth from a Chinese hotel shop and then
> brings it back to his house and hangs it out front for tourists!
> And he tells them the cloth is old and from his family!
> Imagine!

These complaints surrounding eastern Sumba's cloth reflect conditions of multiple appropriation, involving indigenous Sumbanese, Chinese, Arabs, people from other Indonesian islands, and Europeans. Moreover, as people in Sumba refer to international publications on textiles and arts, they produce ethnically generic images. Thus fabric designs from the region now sometimes more closely resemble those from other Indonesian islands, or even those from regions of Oceania or Africa, than they do local creations (which include a variety of designs borrowed from foreign sources; see plate 13).

But all is not a matter of copying introduced forms and selling to outsiders. Some recent additions to eastern Sumba's tableau of textile designs and iconography reflect deeply personal choices in aesthetics and lives, revealing something of biographies. Accounts in the following chapters will portray the specific social, geographical, and imaginative places people occupy in the contemporary world as they create, use, and transport cloth, and in the process reflect upon themselves in the faces of numerous others.

47

PART TWO: BETWEEN THE FOLDS

"Wandi," "Hawewa," and "Parai Mutu" maintain individual commercial connections to the main town of Waingapu, and historical alliances and grievances carry on among the villages through numerous family ties. The regions are remarkable in the contrasts between them. Tensions between old and new forms appear in the peculiar qualities of the textiles produced in each village,

Waingapu is a centralizing hub for the fabric trade. The major commercial and administrative town, it contains about 30,000 people and is the most ethnically diverse place on the island. Government workers (*pegawai*, I.) in numerous bureaucracies migrate to the town from around Sumba as well as from other Indonesian islands (predominantly Java, Bali, Timor, Savu, and Flores). A section of town (called *Kampung Arab* in Indonesian, meaning "Arab Village") is almost exclusively Muslim; many of those who live there descended from initial settlers near the end of the nineteenth century. Although Muslims carry on as traders of various sorts, Waingapu's hotels and numerous shops are now largely owned by ethnic Chinese, who have migrated to Sumba from other Indonesian islands over the past couple of generations.

In 1994, the small Waingapu harbor was visited weekly by ferries, cargo ships, and tourist launches. Domestic flights arrived daily at the airport, five kilometers from the town. Waingapu had one main commercial avenue, with two banks, roughly fifty shops, and seven hotels—from a four-story, 27-unit accommodation that regularly lodged international tour groups to a couple of small, family-run places. The town also boasted two domestic airline offices, two hospitals, five beauty parlors, two gas stations, four schools, two mosques, and five churches.

Waingapu, made up largely of blandly modern or decaying older buildings, has the ambience of a generic eastern Indonesian provincial town. With no distinct center of social life in its layout, the town appears to have been constructed around makeshift commerce.[1] Indeed, largely settled in this century by foreigners, and containing a number of imposed institutions such as government offices and commercial shops, Waingapu contrasts starkly with the village-centered environments historically situating Sumbanese social life.

A relatively bustling area is the bus terminal and public market, active most of the day and night with the comings and goings of people from around the island. Another lively area of commerce is at the port, the region from which a monetary economy was first introduced to Sumba via the Dutch in the nineteenth century (monetization did not pervade the region until after Sumba's incorporation into an Indonesian state system). Although in village regions people often still trade goods and livestock in place of money, in Waingapu the necessary currency is the Indonesian rupiah.

The villagers coming to town to sell or buy goods in markets look markedly different from those who live and work in Waingapu. Following Indonesian national models of contemporary style (as many are government-employed civil service workers), townspeople wear tailored, "modern" clothing; usually live in framed, stuccoed homes of either Dutch colonial or 1960s-era tract-type construction; and possess television sets, motorbikes, and an occasional automobile. This situation reflects certain lifestyle ideals expressed by the Indonesian term "*kemajuan*" (progress), which is part of a widely promoted state ideology conjunctive with modern economic development (*pembangunan*).

In contrast to the residents of Waingapu, villagers in for a day of marketing are often shoeless and in hand-loomed dress, the women wearing *sarung*-like *lau*, their mouths stained black from betel nut, the men in *ikat* headpieces and wrapped in *hinggi*, often with a machete-like *kabela* tucked at their sides. Some villagers, however, (especially young men and women) will dress in their finest imported garb to come to Waingapu, anticipating being seen by friends and relatives or wanting to flirt and socialize at the public market. These villagers stand out in another way from the local residents; in their fancy satin-like blouses or new blue jeans and running shoes, they are dressed for a special event.

As the main entry point for tourists, and basically the site of almost all the hotels and shops of East Sumba, Waingapu is a centralizing locale for the textile trade of the greater region. Currently, there are a number of "art shops" in the town, including those in the three major hotels, selling village fabrics and handcrafts. Some men from villages, carrying large satchels of goods, walk the streets near hotels, displaying fabrics or crafts and hoping to sell directly to tourists. For them, this is the most lucrative way of selling their wares, avoiding middlemen and commanding high prices from unwitting foreigners. Areas at the entrances to hotels are regular congregating places for village peddlers, who migrate to them in the evenings, lay out their goods on the ground, and wait for customers.

The number of annual tourists to East Sumba was estimated (as of 1994) by the government tourism office in Waingapu to be upward of 12,000. Most tourists to the island came in organized groups; Dutch tours were the most numerous, followed by mixed groups of Europeans, Australians, and Americans, with occasional Japanese groups coming through.[2] After arriving in Waingapu, most tourists usually hiked, hired hotel cars, or took public transport to villages in the area.

CHAPTER 4
WANDI

In the dusty and chaotic square of the Waingapu bus terminal, the wait is never long for a *bemo* (a minibus that serves as public transport in much of Indonesia) to the village of Wandi. Although a number of *bemo*s go to the village, I usually boarded the one with the name of an American rock star (Cindi Lauper) inscribed on its side, as the driver tended to be a bit more cautious than some of the others.

The Bemo Ride

Boarding a *bemo* in Sumba is like entering a garish capsule of eclectic, popular culture—a cacaphonic and mobile warp of the imagination. Flashing, multicolored neon announces the vehicle number on the top of each van, interior walls are plastered with posters of Western rock groups or winsome Indonesian film stars, and the booming melodies of popular music usually prevent passengers from hearing the driver or each other during journeys. The cab of each *bemo* encases a distinctive decor, a montage of photos, dangling toys, and written phrases. The dashboard of Cindi Lauper proclaims, in metallic tape, *Cium nakal tapi asik* (I.; Naughty but pleasurable kiss). A large cutout of a long-haired blond male dressed in leather and playing an electric guitar is glued to the back of the driver's seat.

Although there is something absurdly anachronistic about emerging from a twenty-minute, unnervingly high-speed ride (to the sounds of deafening music and the constant honking of a horn) into the cock-crowing ambience of a thatched village, this is the reality of travel between many villages in East Sumba. Raucous and glaring, *bemo*s travel across the country, brash and pulsing with sounds and imagery of (largely male) youth, freedom, and mobility. Within their metal walls, beyond the constraints and protocol of village time and place, young men often behave wildly. The older villagers who ride the *bemo*s often appear dazed by it all. The *bemo* driver—who is likely to be of Savunese or commoner caste Sumbanese descent[1]—enjoys a despotic control over the speed and inner ambience of his vehicle. A money taker hangs out of the side door, shouting out the vehicle's destination. The *bemo* moves on, never stopping in one place too long. Some travelers, reveling in impunity through motion, dare to call out provocative remarks and *main gila* (I.; act crazy)—enjoying a mobile liberation in being continuously displaced from any specific location.

Of all "locations" people find themselves in in the region, the *bemo* provides the greatest contrast to village life. The sheer *velocity*[2] and sensory stimulation of a *bemo* ride facilitates the carnival environment many people experience in moving from one geographical place to another across the Sumbanese landscape. While it is tempting to consider the *bemo* as a truly "liminal" zone—a betwixt and between area in the Turnerian sense—in Sumba it constitutes a carnivalesque analog to village life, an analog both fleetingly ephemeral and extant. As part of a distinct, constant reality of traveling about the region, *bemos* embody imaginatively constructed social environments that are simultaneously utilitarian and flamboyant.

When Marie Jeanne Adams carried out her research in the 1960s, she had to ride horses from one village region to the other because there was no public transportation system on Sumba. By 1993, the interiors and routes of the hundreds of *bemos* on the island had developed into a sort of ancillary culture—one that asserted its place in the general social life of the region while imbuing this life with a boisterous, adolescent popularity gleaned from a motley mixture of outside influences.

Lavie, Narayan, and Rosaldo (1993), following ideas of Victor Turner, have noted the creativity that emerges within the grounds of "interstitial" zones. A *bemo* could be considered as such a zone; as it moves through space, it also embodies a type of "carnival consciousness" (following Bakhtin 1968) the above authors elaborate upon. Such a consciousness restructures "the world of earnest necessity into imaginative blueprints and perhaps later human potentialities" (Lavie, Narayan, and Rosaldo 1993:7). Like the pedicab drivers I described in central Java (1999), *bemo* drivers and assistants in Sumba live lives that are underscored by earnest necessity, while their very movement and "liminality" give rise to considerable serendipity and imaginative play—creating new social arenas in the process. These arenas, however, are not really "interstitial," but are distinctly occupied places. While shuttling between regions, they contain lives of their own. Similar conditions charac-

54

Figure 20. Sumba bus.

terize some of the stories of people in the following pages. Mixtures of influences inflect the travels and routes of these people, who live in particular places but who sometimes experience or imagine very different locations.

Kampung Raja

A *bemo* stops many times a day in the center of the plateau village of Wandi, and passengers emerge near the large stone graves and high-peaked traditional houses that mark Sumbanese settlements. Those exiting the *bemo*s usually do so to an audience. Several village verandahs face out onto the main lane, and the comings and goings of people are often the major events of the day, especially among groups engaged in cloth work, who spend long hours on their verandahs working and musing.

Older villagers tell tales, now considered naive and humorous, of their terror as children at seeing any white person (*tau kanuhu*) entering the lanes of Wandi. Their mothers used to tell them that the shoulder satchels typically carried by Westerners (in those days usually Dutch colonial officials or missionaries) were filled with the heads of local children. These heads were buried beneath new buildings or bridges, to ensure their structural endurance.[3] Head-taking myths explained why foreigners were so sophisticated and successful at construction. Such tales (which persist in some outlying villages of Sumba) were told to keep children within family areas and also as a folkloristic resistance on the part of Wandi's animists to outside influences.

Nonetheless, fabric motifs and designs that have emerged from Wandi in this century reveal substantial outside influence and local innovation. Situated near the port and market town of Waingapu, the village has been influenced by colonialism, Christianity, Japanese wartime occupation, Indonesian government control, and tourism more directly and consistently than villages farther afield.

A few kilometers from Waingapu, Wandi sits on a bluff. About four hundred inhabitants reside along a narrow, paved street running through the village, upon which *bemo*s from Waingapu frequently enter and leave. Bordering the street are a number of high-peaked, clan houses and several grave areas with elaborate stone markers—from ancient, table-like dolmens to eccentric poured and painted concrete sculptures. There are two main noble houses in Wandi, one of the current *raja* and one of his aunt, the wife of the late former king. Each house is distinguished by its size and nearby graves.

The current *raja* of Wandi (a recognized authority among numerous villages within several kilometers of the village) is in his forties, enjoys

55

welcoming outsiders to his household, spends much of his time riding his motorcycle to various villages on formal or informal business, and is the father of nine. He entertains visitors daily at his home in an atmosphere of relative informality.

The village of Wandi is commonly referred to as *Kampung Raja* (I.; Royal Village), distinguished by the homes and graves of nobility. People of varying social means and levels, however, live in the settlement, in what could be described as a hodgepodge collection of residences along the little road described above. In addition, a number of households skirt the village plateau on narrow streets about half a kilometer in each direction.[4] These houses are occupied either by people from Wandi's extended lineage or by a number of families originally from the island of Savu. Residents of the area generally refer to the main, hilltop village as *di atas* (I.; above) and to the proximal environs around it as *di bawah* (I.; below).

Other houses facing Wandi's small central road range from traditional high-peaked constructions to more modest homes made of sections of woven palm frond or simple thatch dwellings. There are also two "modern" houses of green stucco, with louvred glass windows and corrugated metal roofs. Most of Wandi's homes have electricity, and colorful bougainvillea grows over small seating areas in front of many of them. At the top of the village, overlooking a scenic vista (with vast open views of the arid landscape and barren, table-like mesas in the distance), stands the local Gereja Kristen Sumba.[5] Beyond the church, at the uppermost region of the hill, lie the broken graves of the original village of Wandi, before it was destroyed by a Japanese bombardment during World War Two (the region came under Japanese occupation for two years during the war). From these graves, one can watch soccer games or horse races, which regularly take place upon a field that borders the village on one side.

Because of its proximity to Waingapu's tourist hotels, foreigners frequently visit Wandi, wandering in on their own, led by local tourist guides, or descending from tour buses in organized groups. Passing through the gates of the village from the main road from Waingapu, one immediately sees textiles hanging from clotheslines, on looms standing against houses, or draped across the arms and bodies of any number of approaching people. Moreover, in walking the half-kilometer length of the village street, one gets the impression that every house along the way produces and sells *ikat* fabrics. Competing with the bougainvillea, the fabrics vibrantly color a village landscape cast in the neutral hues of dried palm leaf and thatch upon a ground of barren dust. These textiles delimit households, beckon foreign visitors, and mediate interactions between worlds.

Wandi is a lively place. Children run along the street, radios and tape players blare music, and people shout and chatter from their houses to one another and to passersby. Throughout the day, the village bustles as *bemo*s routinely deposit passengers in the center of the village and pick up others on their way back to Waingapu. Since the road is in view of most households, there is constant public interest and commentary concerning all who come and go.

Like those in most eastern Sumbanese villages, people of Wandi earn some livelihood from agricultural crops (mostly rice and maize) as well as from livestock (chickens, pigs, horses, water buffalo, and Bengal cattle). Yet, situated near the heavily settled Waingapu region, the land around Wandi has become populated and does not support extensive farming or grazing. Noble households have rights to land at distances from the village, where most grow crops and raise animals. Most people in Wandi, however, either work in some capacity with textiles or else hold jobs in the schools, shops, and offices of Waingapu.

When the original, inward-facing village was severely damaged by a Japanese bomb during the war, Wandi was reconstructed following a settlement pattern that departed radically from its former organization. Citizens of Wandi followed Dutch and then modern Javanese development concepts and rebuilt their village in a linear pattern, along a newly constructed public street. In fundamental ways, this reconstruction was a leveling transition for local society. By providing an uninterrupted route from one end of the village to the other over which all could pass, the street democratized the movement of people in ways the inhabitants had not foreseen. Although the residences of nobles remained central and obvious along this street, new options proceeded through village reorganization, and households sprang up in multiple forms and arrangements, relatively unbound by traditional village spatial constraints. Reconstructed, Wandi extended along a radically different orientation: facing a paved, linear stretch situating the village in a postcolonial world.[6]

57

A more diverse community began to develop, and the village gained in reputation for eccentric characters and textiles. Much of this peculiarity followed the ongoing influences of foreigners and the responses of local people. Not only had Wandi's inhabitants interacted for decades with Dutch colonial agents and missionaries, but they were more directly affected by the Japanese occupation (for two years Wandi was forced to supply food and labor to the invaders) than were villages at greater distance from the Waingapu harbor.

What is more, the reigning king of Wandi in the two decades after the war was an unusual man surrounded by tales that further advanced notions of the village's oddity in East Sumba. He lived with his wife in a childless household, and it was rumored that the marriage had never been consummated. The *raja*, as villagers told me, preferred to consort with women who lived under the sea and would periodically travel with his entourage to a coastal area some distance away for aquatic trysts. People report that he could stay underwater for days.

Because the *raja* left no heir, the leadership of the village was indeterminate for some time after his death. During that period Wandi became more haphazard in its organization. Eventually, a nephew replaced the departed *raja*, and he proved to be an amiable and relaxed man. Following his ascendancy, Wandi continued along a path of relative social openness, setting it apart from many noble villages in Sumba.

Presently, Wandi receives frequent international visitors. Fabrics fluttering from porches, clotheslines, and trees attract the eyes of foreigners. A variety of people in the village produce and trade these fabrics, and we will meet a few of them below.

The Rise of Biba

> Local tales are not merely about the local; they remap the relation of near and far, unsettling their hierarchies.
>
> —Anna Tsing, *In the Realm of the Diamond Queen*

When I first met "Biba" and her husband "Hasan," they ran a small shop in a shed-like construction near the entrance of Wandi, from which they sold sundries (sugar, coffee, soap, and cigarettes) and a few fabrics made by Biba. In those days, their textile business was in a nascent stage, and the pieces they offered were stored in a small covered basket at the rear of their store. Biba worked frequently on *ikat hinggi*s, binding and unbinding warps while tending to her shop and overseeing her youngest children. Hasan carried on intermittent business as an agent in livestock sales. They both often sat as proprietors in the shop, however, and their attitude to visiting foreigners was polite but confused in the face of not being able to communicate. Neither Biba nor Hasan knew any English, and most tourists spoke little if any Indonesian.

First entering their shop in 1991, I viewed the cloth the couple stored in their basket. One fabric caught my eye as unique. Its motifs were dominated by winged angels, something I had not seen before in Sumbanese fabric imagery. Twin angels with large noses and long red hair stared out from the cloth. Biba explained that her inspiration for the design had come from an old children's Bible that contained many illustrations of Europeans (the book itself was likely a legacy of the Dutch Reformed Church). The central motif of the *hinggi* posed the angels gracing a seated Sumbanese ruler.

Figure 21. Biba's angel cloth.

59

Speaking to Biba at that time about the piece, I sensed no humor or irony in her ideas or intentions in designing the motifs. A professed Protestant, she explained that she was using pictures representative of "present times" (*waktu sekarang*, I.) in Sumba. The angels in Biba's cloth traced a story of changing social and cosmological perspective and new means for expressing it. They also expressed Biba's sense of a self-determined morality in her life course and choices:

I made this design myself in 1985. I put the angels with a *maramba* ruler because I wanted them to be in agreement [*persesuaian*, I.]. I wanted to show that God can help the Sumbanese. I wanted to express my Christian beliefs [*per-

cayaan Kristen, I.] in a cloth too. I became Christian when I was in secondary school. Then we had to choose a religion [*agama*, I.] to stay in school. It was a government law. My parents had to accept this, but they didn't understand. But I started to believe in Jesus and in God, like in the Christian Bible. And then I went to church by myself every Sunday and sang the Christian songs. Then I went home to my parents, who were still Marapu people. This cloth is how I put two kinds of worlds together. Since I was a girl, I have traveled between different worlds [*jalan antara dunia-dunia yang berbeda*, I.]. And I had to try to get along in each one. That's how my life is. It's like that now too. It's just like that.

As the angel *hinggi* was among those for sale, I decided to buy it and asked the price. Although Biba had done all of the work in creating the fabric, a months-long process that included the actual production of plant dyes, Hasan was designated to negotiate its sale with me. This was comical at times, as he would literally repeat both to Biba and me what the other had just said (we all stood within five feet of each other) regarding the fabric for sale. Finally we agreed upon a price, I paid it, and we amiably said our good-byes. I left the shop not to see the couple again for almost two years.

When I returned to Sumba in 1993, Biba and Hasan still maintained their shop, but the sugar, cigarettes, and other items they sold were hidden from view behind the fabrics displayed against every wall. *Ikat* and *pahikung* pieces from around the region were exhibited for sale, and I recognized familiar patterns of specific villages as well as some elaborate new motifs. The shop had been transformed into a kind of tourist gallery for the village and region, reflecting an increase in outside demand for local textiles.[7]

The small shop had been my entry point into the lives of Hasan and Biba, and my relationship with them developed to the extent that I was eventually invited to their home, a short distance away, at the bottom of the Wandi plateau. Over the months our friendship grew, and I spent many hours at their house. In the beginning, however, although we could communicate in Indonesian, there were barriers between us, discernible in the couple's perplexity in not knowing exactly what to make of me (as a Western researcher I was considered to be of very high status) and what their appropriate behavior should be in our relationship.

Hasan is a Muslim. His mother is of Sumbanese commoner lineage, and his father is a descendant of immigrants from Bima, Sumbawa, an island to the northwest of Sumba. His paternal lineage (which is how he

60

reckons his descent) has lived in the Wandi region for three generations, working as traders, with the women often producing fabrics. Biba is from an inland village, from a family of little means. Some in Wandi rumor that her family is of the lowest, *ata* caste, although Biba claims to be of a commoner lineage.

As a girl, Biba excelled scholastically and completed high school—an unusual accomplishment for a female from a poor family in the hinterlands. She went on to get a civil service job as a clerk in a government office in Waingapu. Although some people say that Hasan "bought" Biba from her impoverished family for money[8]—and that is how she came to live in the Wandi village area, according to the couple—Biba first met Hasan while walking home one day (she lived with relatives near Wandi) from her office job in Waingapu.

After marrying (with the approval of Hasan's family, but to the dismay of Biba's) the couple settled in Wandi. As the family grew, Biba stopped working in Waingapu and instead began to sell small goods from a kiosk (which she constructed herself from woven palm leaves) on the main road near her home. Her profits, although modest, were enough to justify renting the larger shop at the entrance to the village, where she could stock more items. She began to include her own textiles in her inventory.

Biba came late to the fabric arts, migrating from an inland village region where weaving has not been practiced historically.[9] Most of her current skills she learned from her husband's mother (an accomplished weaver and dyer). Biba's *ikat* pieces are distinctive in their departure from commonly seen designs and in the often expressive, idiosyncratic character of her motifs. Her inventiveness and resourcefulness have propelled her along paths far afield of her natal village and her current household.

By 1992 Biba and Hasan had become accustomed to welcoming foreign tourists into their small shop and had secured several commercial connections with outsiders. They had shipped textiles to Holland and Germany and had received a catalog from a museum exhibit in Europe of older Sumbanese textiles in foreign collections. This impressed the couple as an irrefutable source of archaic Sumbanese textile designs. Although unable to read the booklet (which was printed in German), Biba studied the photographs of cloth pieces it contained and copied some of the motifs, incorporating them into her own fabrics.[10]

Later the same year, Biba resolved to venture away from Sumba, to explore the tourist market on the island of Bali she had heard so many local people refer to. A number of men from Wandi were regularly leaving for Bali at this point, transporting boxes of fabrics and selling them to

61

tourist boutiques or to foreigners at hotels. Biba had heard that the profits the Sumbanese trading in Bali were receiving were several times over what was paid for fabrics at home. She decided to explore the market for herself and expand her commercial options. She was also intrigued by the idea of seeing a place far from her home. In December of 1992, she boarded an airplane for the first time in her life and took off for the fabled island to the west.

Leaving her husband and five children behind, Biba entered an environment she had only been able to imagine and that would expand her life in ways yet to be determined. She spent her first night in Bali in a small, inexpensive hotel in the heart of the tourist enclave, Kuta Beach, in the midst of restaurants, pubs, and souvenir shops. Months later she would tell stories and laugh at her innocence, but at the time she felt complete amazement at the number of foreigners, their dress and demeanor, and their obvious wealth.

Since that time, Biba has made numerous trips to Bali and Java. Eventually in 1994, Hasan (who up to that point had been timid about traveling away from Sumba) agreed to join her, and they both went to Jakarta accompanied by another Wandi villager, Luka. Leaving their children with relatives, they stayed abroad for six weeks. (Some aspects of their voyage will be described in chapter 9.)

Through their rising fortunes of 1994, the couple were making ever more elaborate plans to attract tour groups to their home and make business trips away from the island. Not only had the two secured a number of connections with well-to-do tourists visiting Sumba and foreigners living in Jakarta, but they also had made the acquaintance of Javanese and Balinese entrepreneurs and elites involved in textile collecting.

The relationship of this particular couple differed from most other marriages I knew in East Sumba. Biba was the initiator, traveler, and astute businessperson of the two, as well as the artist and textile worker, and her husband openly acknowledged this. Their livelihood and improved economic conditions were largely the result of her initiative and organization. As such, she received the respect and attracted the envy of others in Wandi.[11]

Born to an undistinguished family in a small, inland hamlet, Biba had overcome many odds in becoming a prosperous and traveled resident of Wandi. Reactions of villagers varied. Although there was a certain amount of deferential behavior from Biba toward the wife of the local *raja*, the two often spent hours gossiping and laughing together and seemed to have formed a genuine friendship. Others in Wandi, including relatives of Hasan, were openly resentful of Biba's success. For some of the village men who had squandered their earnings from the textile trade, her recent affluence was a particularly bitter pill. Neighbors began to circulate derisive stories about the couple, alleging dishonesties in business dealings and marital infidelities while abroad. There were also whispers of sorcery regarding Biba.

In the eastern Sumbanese communities I spent time in, an undercurrent creeps through social life—within villages, families, and households. Borne through emotions of jealousy and suspicion between people, such feeling is referred to as *katiu eti*. Conspicuous displays of prestige symbols are common, but they arouse correspondingly fierce rivalries and feuds. *Katiu eti* is considered by many in eastern Sumba as inevitable and ubiquitous—where there is prosperity there is also resentment, a basic tension in community life.[12]

To avoid the anguish it causes, one might refrain altogether from demonstrating material gain (a restraint that is rare in Sumba) or redistribute one's recent wealth. Aside from contributing to public rituals or hosting feasts, a prosperous person or family will be asked in no uncertain terms by relatives or neighbors for a portion of whatever profits they have received from lucrative ventures. To avoid ill feelings and possible dangers, something will usually be conceded to those asking.

This grew to be the case with Biba and Hasan. Biba often expressed frustration at the nature of the community and its ever-present jealousies, while describing herself as a virtuous person, who gave her fair share to relatives and community events. An example of her generosity that she often related involved a succession of pigs she kept:

> Let me tell you what I do and this is the truth. Even though my husband is a Muslim, I keep a pig at a house up the hill, away from our house. And I give my child food to give it every day, and order her to go up there. This is at my expense! And then if there's a funeral, I always have a pig to offer. After I give one pig, I get another. I've always done that. Even though Hasan is Muslim[13] and forbidden to keep a pig, I do it myself, away from our house, to try to keep peace for us in this village. I'll tell you, it's always like this with the Sumbanese. If someone prospers, then someone must immediately become their enemy. It's always like that in Sumba! [*Selau begitu di Sumba!*, I.]

The tensions emerging within the community caused the couple to begin to redefine their places within it, and Biba often made statements to me such as the one above. Conflicts between the two, however, seemed few and concerned, if anything, Hasan's lack of astuteness in dealing with

63

foreigners. The couple's older children had also become involved in the production and trade of textiles, the teenaged son collecting his own fabrics for future sale to tourists. Pre-teenaged daughters were already developing skill in weaving.

By 1994 Biba was commissioning work from other village women in Wandi. Simultaneously, she always had five to ten fabrics in various stages of completion in the workshop she carried on behind her house. With a keen design sense and an inventive approach to her motifs, Biba's animals and people bore an expressiveness of face and gesture that delighted foreigners. Although she continued to produce her own designs, these were often mingled with motifs she copied from catalogs or photographs of older Sumbanese fabrics.[14] Her textiles became complex mixtures of her own inventions and images from distant sources.

Biba's *hinggi*s teased certain limits, juxtaposing angels with *maramba* rulers or placing ancient floral or faunal symbols with her own interpretations of forms. Once I saw her watch a horse and rider prance past her house, then quickly rush to draw the gestures she had seen. These she later copied onto tautly starched warp threads and still later rendered these images into a bound warp, concentrating intensely on her work. Eventually the horse and rider resurfaced in a finished cloth, and there was a liveliness to their postures at either end of a *hinggi*, separated by a central band of ancient butterfly motifs. Biba was pleased with the design and quality of the cloth, and proudly showed it to me. As to any intended meaning of the fabric, she expressed that she had used her own design with another from antiquity to "balance" (*kasi timbang,* I.) the cloth, to allow the new to coexist with the old, to combine her own creation with that from the past. Weeks later she would sell it to a passing tourist.

Behind the couple's home sat a separate kitchen structure (*kaba au*) filled with barks, leaves, and paraphernalia for dyeing, and a number of clotheslines and bamboo racks stood in the yard to hold yarns or woven cloth. An area specifically for indigo dyeing sat in a remote corner of the yard, away from other work sites. Although a Muslim, Hasan maintained a fear like others in Sumba regarding the liquids of the indigo plant. Whenever I watched Biba dipping skeins of cotton yarn into the fetid, blue dye baths, Hasan kept his distance, apologizing for conversing from ten or more feet away, but saying that he was "still afraid of getting too near the dye place" (*masih takut mendekati tempat warna,* I.).

As discussed in chapter 3, indigo is a perilous substance, and anxieties surrounding it determine its place in households and who will approach it. Menstrual blood, urine, and indigo are among liquids employed in witchery in the region, and people can be unwittingly victimized by a woman who puts even minute quantities of these into food or directly onto the skin of others. Aside from falling victims to the pigment's supernatural dangers, men can disrupt the chemistry and efficacy of indigo by their proximity to the dye bath.

Alfred Gell regards magic as the negative contour of work, haunting technical activity like a shadow. The value of women's work in Sumba is sometimes founded in and protected by magical beliefs, which take technical skill out of the realm of the ordinary. It thus becomes "magical technology," which "consists of representing the technical domain in enchanted technology form" (1994:59). In eastern Sumba, this "enchantment" persists in the realm of textile production—particularly where it involves the use of indigo dye—maintaining a distinct contour to women's work.[15]

Biba told of how Hasan's brother had been *wingu katiku* (dizzy) for weeks after walking over some spilled indigo dye in his bare feet. She also speculated that handling some damp blue yarns may have caused her own miscarriage years before. One late evening in 1993, Biba assisted in the delivery of a child; it emerged from its young mother pale and lifeless. Some women surrounding the stillbirth suggested that it may have been caused by the mother sitting too near an indigo dye bath days before.

Despite some adherence to ancient taboos, Hasan and Biba's home life had taken on some distinctly modern trappings by 1994. After a lucrative venture to Java and Bali, they installed an electronic entertainment center in the front sitting room of their modest house. A shelved, Formica console displayed a new color television set, a cassette player and two stereo speakers, and numerous gifts given to the couple during their travels away from Sumba. Hasan and Biba also modernized their kitchen, paving the dirt floor with concrete and replacing the wood-fire pit with a propane burner.

65

In composing a distinctive way of life for herself and her family, Biba had excelled within and ventured beyond a strictly domestic sphere. Her exploits had expanded local notions and controversies regarding what women might do in the world, especially regarding mobility. Biba's relative freedom of movement was partly predicated upon her (ascribed) lower caste status and the fact that she had formerly gone far beyond her family social boundaries by first converting to Christianity and later marrying a Muslim. She was less bound by strict kinship networks than many women of the region. A certain social marginality for Biba provided a threshold for creativity and action (see Turner 1967, 1969). Such enterprise emerged from a keen intelligence and a venturesome individuality. Moreover, her husband did not impede her activities or imagination, and seems to enjoy the experiences and profits they have provided.

Biba's fabrics have refigured through imagery her historical world
while creating links to a broader one. As her social connections have
increased and diversified, so have her interpretations, plans, and activities. From a commerce that formerly issued from a small basket, Biba's
textile trade now includes other women of her village and eclectic design
concepts. While still producing her own designs, she has also acquired an
extended knowledge of "traditional" ones—ironically through the catalogs
and brochures of foreign institutions.

Marilyn Strathern notes that, given the way work is oriented to social
others, power lies in the effective definition of the scope of relations that
such work can create (1990:156). Biba has been skillful in not only her
work (which, involving cloth and dyes, possesses a certain historical
power locally), but especially in its orientation to social others. Her endeavors have proceeded in a manner that has defined effectively a scope
of relations while tremendously stretching the possibilities of that scope.
In this way, she has claimed a power of maneuvering for herself in a certain elusiveness to local terms, acquiring a broadened self-definition, re-
formulated through her connections away from her island.

Stigma, however, has followed her successes. Local jealousies have
increasingly generated tales of sorcery (*marungu*) and infidelity (*njuraku*)
connected with Biba. While resentments follow most personal gains in
East Sumba, in Biba's case they are aggravated by her low-caste standing and gender. Many of her male denouncers resent what they see as
Biba's illicit appropriation of Sumbanese "culture"[16]—the politics and
play of which they consider within the purview of men. Biba's endeavors
and connections have unsettled local hierarchies.[17] I will return to her
later.

66

Luka's Perspective

> *Things sold still have a soul. They are still followed around by their
> former owner, and they follow him also.*
>
> —Marcel Mauss, *The Gift*

In the early 1980s, *hinggi* cloths that departed from the generally
bifacial format typical of Sumbanese design began to appear in Wandi.
The new designs followed a sequential order with a sense of "top" and
"bottom."[18] These fabrics also situated "scenes" in a field simulating
three-dimensional space—that is, they altered the usual perspective in
eastern Sumba's textiles. This new perspective[19] construed space and
organized motifs in a way that invited display of the cloths in their entire
lengths. From the top of a cloth to the bottom, a narrative unfolded pictorially—typically with a nobleman leaving his home on horseback, meet-

Figure 22. A tale told through the length of a cloth.

67

ing up with attendants and horsemen, and moving toward a battle with
numerous other figures. The formerly mediative central panels of *hinggi*s,
with their *patola* motifs or abstract Sumbanese symbols, were now absent
from these radically altered pictorial fields. Still bound by considerations
of dualism—in that they were constructed (as conventional *hinggi*) of two
identical, long, narrow cloths that were then sewn together in the center
to form one—these new fabric designs repeated exactly side-to-side but
differed dramatically end-to-end, forming a diptych of woven forms. The
design and production of these fabrics, according to many local people,
were initiated by a Wandi man by the name of "Luka," a local maverick in
textile artistry.

Luka was born of a *maramba* father and an *ata* caste mother, and his siblings (including half-siblings) numbered more than twenty. As a boy, he was largely unacknowledged by his father and the noble half of his family, so his mother's caste determined his own status to a large degree. Speaking of his more ancient lineage, Luka claims to have descended from Indian ancestors, whom he has interpreted as being the first settlers to Sumba, following what he has read of history in Indonesian school textbooks. Always considered clever and energetic by his family and neighbors, Luka excelled in school. After high school (with the financial support of an uncle) he went to the city of Kupang on the island of Timor, to a teacher training college. He left, however, within a year and returned to Sumba.

Luka said that besides feeling restless with the routines of his studies at college, he missed his family too much when abroad and also wanted to return to what he felt was the relative freedom of schedule involved in village life. He also commented that "in Kupang I felt without a name [*nda pangara*]. Every night I only thought about home, about my mother and my younger sister. It didn't suit me there."

To be "nameless" and unrecognized is an alienating condition for people in Sumba at all levels, and one that Luka's loneliness on another island exacerbated. Indeed, the importance of making a name for oneself has been recognized in numerous studies of Sumbanese life.[20] Upon his return, he created a scheme to design textiles for the then budding tourist market of the early 1980s and to perhaps embellish his "name" (*ngara*) in a novel way at home. According to many, he had always been highly imaginative and skilled at drawing, and he felt that designing and selling fabrics could be enjoyable and lucrative for him. Luka had studied English through high school and in Kupang, enjoyed meeting foreigners, and was intrigued and excited by the idea of a steady business with them.

When I first met Luka, in 1991, he was thirty years old and not yet married, an unusual status in Sumba for someone his age. Intelligent and outgoing, he was one of a number of men who frequented Waingapu hotels, displaying their wares for tourists to see. Yet Luka was somewhat ahead of the game in his dealings with foreigners. His adequate English skills afforded him access to tourists. His congenial disposition and wit served him well in interacting with them. In fact, Luka was especially gifted with "social grace"—having mastered a certain timing, coordination, and knack for responding to contingencies that Renato Rosaldo (in his characterization of Ilongot sociability) considers as part of the mastery of social unpredictability (1993:256).

In the year I met him, Luka had designed a number of innovative *hinggi*s for sale to outsiders. He had ascertained what aspects of Sumbanese culture were most intriguing to foreigners and had created motifs and designs emphasizing those aspects. Bringing in elements of cultural forms from around the island, he supplemented the (already eclectic) local tableau of motifs within the recent genre of diptych design fields. One style of cloth originating with Luka became extremely popular; it featured complex scenes of an annual horse jousting festival, an event called the *pasola,* carried out in West Sumba. Although most people in Wandi knew about the *pasola* only through stories and few had ever journeyed to the west to see it, cloth-bound vistas of the equestrian battles began to flourish in the village's *ikat* textiles.

In addition to the *pasola* scenes, Luka's fabrics sometimes incorporated narratives of the historical battles of local kings, mythical stories of animals such as the cockatoo (*kakatua*) or the crocodile (*wuya*), and even characters from the ancient Indian epic, the *Mahabarata,* which he had studied in school. His textiles consistently employed a sense of space and time—a sequentiality and a teeming flamboyance of interactive beings that was revolutionary to local design fields.[21] Moreover, Luka had experimented with dyes, using saltwater or mud to enhance or alter some colors and ingeniously combining natural and chemical pigments to great effect (although always claiming to foreigners that his dyes were completely natural). He gained in reputation locally through a rapid success in his fabric business and employed his mother and four sisters in the production of cloth.

69

By age thirty, Luka had attempted on several occasions to ask for young women in marriage but had been refused repeatedly by their families. Despite his promising success as a textile entrepreneur, the noble and commoner families he had approached did not want a person with a slave-caste mother to marry into their kinship circles. And a woman's household rarely, if ever, agreed to marriage with a man of lower caste standing. In eastern Sumba, people sometimes refer to the superior or inferior quality of a person's "blood" (*wai ria*), a belief of inherent biological difference between individuals based in historical notions of social caste. It was upon such a basis that Luka's proposals were denied.

From the time I first met him, I witnessed many locals teasing Luka about being unmarried and about the possibility of finding a wife from among the foreign female tourists visiting the island. Such jesting was taken half in earnest by the artist/entrepreneur, who often spoke of how he would like to marry a "white person" (*tau kanuhu*) and enter into a nuptial and business partnership. And imaginably, such a marriage might also elevate his dubious social status within a local context.

In those days, Luka was beginning to prosper. By the late 1980s, using profits from his trade in textiles, Luka had ventured for the first time to Bali, where he stayed for a few months examining and copying some

Balinese motifs from paintings and temple reliefs.[22] At the same time, he noticed the self-styled personas of some of the Balinese artists, especially in interaction with an international market. For the first time perhaps, Luka recognized the distinctive value to foreigners of "primitivism" as "art," a style that had been enthusiastically taken up by many Balinese, following an awareness of global tastes.

He returned to Sumba with a new kind of self-consciousness—as someone with an individualistic, artistic persona—and set out to create a unique market as a designer. He had also become increasingly mindful of the exotic value to foreigners of his Sumbanese cultural heritage. At this point, Luka embarked upon a creative course of action—informed and stimulated by his experience in the wider world, his sense of position in his home environment, and an imaginative recreation of himself through it all.

Here, I temporarily shift to the other side of the world to reframe Luka's endeavors in a broadened context. Late in the year of 1991, I attended a symposium at the Asian Art Museum in San Francisco dedicated to Indonesian arts and cultures and concurrent with the museum's exhibit Beyond the Java Sea. Following several scholarly papers, a textile expert and tour leader from New York began to speak on the society and fabrics of Sumba, a place she had visited a few years before. As she presented her slides in synchrony with her lecture, I recognized most of the locations and some of the people on the screen. I was suddenly startled at a slide featuring a man in full Sumbanese regalia. The vivid and greatly enlarged image (projected before an audience of about two hundred, many of them local society women) was of a man bedecked in every imaginable sort of Sumbanese finery. Wrapped in yards of *ikat* fabrics and wearing gold, ivory, and carnelian jewelry, Luka glared defiantly from the screen as the lecturer informed the audience that this man was one of the prominent princes of Sumba, one day to be a regional king. I realized that while marginalized by the elites in his own society, Luka had achieved nobility (with certain elites) in that of another. In the imaginations of those seeing him as a projection in San Francisco, he was uncontestably a royal.

This irony stayed with me when I returned to Sumba again in 1993, and all the more when I realized that Luka's profits and initiative had diminished during the time of my absence. Since his earlier days of enterprise, Luka's fortunes had declined, along with his entrepreneurial zeal. Rampant copying of his designs throughout the region had left him discouraged, as he experienced loss of control and profits resulting from his own initiative. Indeed, numerous woven *pasola* scenes were hanging from porches in a number of local villages, for sale to incoming tourists.

Luka's designs had escaped from him, and there was nothing he could do to retrieve them. Appropriated and reinterpreted by a variety of opportunists, his inventions were reproduced by Chinese merchants and villagers from all social castes.

Moreover, Luka complained that he could not, in any case, earn enough from his efforts in textile work:

> It's like this: Most tourists buy the cheaper pieces. The ones with the chemical dyes and the dirty colors. Many people in the villages make cloths very rapidly. They use big motifs on their cloths because they can make those quickly. Like the ones you see with big men on them.[23] Those ones are easy to make. And those are what the tourists want. Even when they see good cloths, they often choose the cheap cloths to buy, and pay high prices for them.

Disgruntled, Luka abandoned textiles altogether and tried for a time to be a tourist guide. However, he was not organized or assertive in charging fees from his clients, and profited little, aside from small gifts and monetary tips. He had improved, however, upon his English skills and had also gained further insights into foreigners. And although he did not prosper economically from his cross-cultural endeavors, Luka did amass a certain body of knowledge, along with eclectic wardrobe items given to him by tourists. These distinguished him from most men of the region.[24] In fact, distinction continued to be one of his main concerns.

71

One time, during an all-day festival (*pamangu*) that involved a gathering of clans in Wandi, ritual speakers (*da wunang*) from each group were demonstrating their oratory skills. A number of men had been verbally sparring with one another, and by the end of the day the occasion had taken on an informal, bantering tone. It was then that Luka injected a novel twist into the event. As the volleys of artful speeches subsided, Luka claimed a staging point in a yard between households. He then spoke in English for more than an hour. Through his speech, he listed people he knew from foreign places ("from America, Don and Ann; from Germany, Hans and Dieter," and so on) and told of their visits and the gifts they had given him ("Miss Elena give me black pants from France . . . James sleep in my house for three nights and eat with my family . . . ").

This generated more bewilderment than admiration from the audience. Rather than taking offense, most of the remaining ritual speakers witnessing Luka's performance appeared amused, injecting (somewhat mocking) punctuating "responses"—such as "*O!*" (Yes!) and "*Nu!*" (There!)—in the pauses within his English oratory. Luka's attempt at a prestigious speech act (*pulungu hamu* 'beautiful speech') had left the community largely confounded, but had also provided entertainment.

Despite his flare for performance and talent at design, Luka was not, ultimately, a consistently able manager of the business aspects of textile trade. As is the case with many Sumbanese village men, he was unable to manage money in a way that would perpetuate prosperity in monetary terms. He would spend his profits on pastimes like gambling or in making contributions to public events, such as buying pigs for funeral rites. This failure at "capital accumulation" is typical of many Sumbanese, descending from village societies historically not based upon monetary exchange, but instead upon reciprocity of goods and services, as well as on spending what one has on sumptuous display.

Largely for such reasons, Chinese and Arab merchants of Waingapu have prospered as agents in the textile trade. Nonetheless, Sumbanese men engaged in this trade also express their goals as gaining affluence through making large sums of money and are aware that others (such as Arabs and Chinese) routinely reinvest profits into business enterprises. In reality, however, it is difficult for them to follow such tactics, given pressures from relatives to redistribute wealth and a prestige system long based upon costly public displays of prosperity.

Many eastern Sumbanese combine or straddle the worlds of commodities and gift exchange in terms of their ideas and practices, some more adroitly than others. Marilyn Strathern notes that in a commodity-oriented economy people thus experience their interest in commodities as a desire to appropriate goods; in a gift-oriented economy, the desire is to expand social relations (1990:143). In East Sumba, both conditions maintain and overlap, although sometimes with unbalancing results.

East Sumba's textile traders in some ways resemble the economic innovators of Java described by Clifford Geertz (1963), operating on both sides of the line between traditional and modern economies, yet not always effectively in terms of both worlds. The line between such economies, however, has become less defined across Indonesia since the time of Geertz's writing. Although certain boundaries persist between economic arenas, at least in eastern Sumba they are sometimes quite permeable.

This permeability follows the shifting nature of commodities and the ways in which their flows follow forms of social play. Arjun Appadurai has considered commodities as things with a particular type of social potential (1988:6). As such they might map out existent and emergent social realities observable in the dynamics of exchange, rather than only in the conditions or relations of production. In the intersection between local producers and foreign consumers of eastern Sumbanese fabrics lie tremendous tensions and new opportunities—which reveal concerns for both goods and expansions of social relations.

In 1992, Luka began to sell some of his pieces through Hasan and Biba's small shop at the entrance of the village. For some months Luka and the enterprising couple had a good business relationship. Luka would often drop by their shop or home, and as the numbers of visiting tourists increased, he would employ his knowledge of English to translate between the parties and was often given a commission if a sale of fabrics transpired. Later Luka would join the couple on their six-week excursion through Bali and Java (described in chapter 9); this trip would change their relationships.

Luka is perhaps the most inventive of the fabric workers I knew, in terms of his concepts, aesthetic sensibilities, and persona, and his story is one of the most volatile. Given to sudden shifts in location and direction, Luka is nevertheless entrenched in local social life, and many of its conventions impinge upon him. This fact will become evident later on. The importance of Luka's inventions lies in the traces they have left of his awareness and actions,[25] which are visible records of creative processes. Intimated in his narrative cloths is a desire to go beyond established norms, in the construction of a new conceptual frame—an altered reckoning of time and place. Although Luka's designs employ many historical motifs, they re-situate them within a revised, contemporary frame filled with personified characters moving through spaces and times with distinct beginnings and endings.

73

Kata's Forum

Although women produce these necessary and symbolic vessels, men have traditionally controlled their distribution and marketing, along with other forms of communication with the outside world.
—Barbara A. Babcock, "At Home, No Women Are Storytellers"

Uphill from the home of Biba and Hasan, on the central street of Wandi, in a high-peaked house set back from the road, live "Kata" and her husband, "Umbu[26] Taniku" (a nobleman), with two small children. Kata, her mother-in-law, and other female relatives produce *ikat* fabrics in bordering makeshift structures. Umbu Taniku prides himself as a bold and prolific designer of textiles, and the pieces from his household teem with scenes of regal processions and riotous battles and tend to be quite large.

Umbu produces unidirectional depictions of heroic events, derivative of Luka's initial design concepts. In recent years, he has become increasingly ambitious, producing more and periodically taking boxes of

Figure 23. Large *hinggi* containing regal characters.

74

textiles to trade in Bali. To facilitate a more rapid process, the women use many chemical dyes. Although the designs Kata ties and weaves are usually complex, imaginative, and crisply rendered, the final colors are often garish when compared to the soft-hued fabrics colored with plant pigments. Umbu Taniku's mother, who also lives in the compound, disapproves of the use of the market dyes and resents her own displacement as the master indigo dyer of the household. She scoffs at the too-bright blues of the family's fabrics and scolds Kata in private for using the artificial pigment.

At twenty-four, Kata is fifteen years younger than her husband and has been married to him for four years. She comes from a nearby village, from a *maramba* family, and her marriage to Umbu Taniku came at the "promise" (*njanji*) of several water buffalo and an amount of gold items, a bride price (*wili tau*) of which only a small part has been paid off to her family. This "extended credit" is common in eastern Sumba, where the debt for obtaining a wife may be paid off over years by a husband or his kin.

His marriage to Kata is Umbu Taniku's fifth; the four others ended in divorce. Umbu, a convert to Protestantism, speaks of himself as "*moderen*" (I.), as someone who follows the times. Divorce, rare in former times (men would often simply take another wife, with the previous wife remaining as part of the household, despite tensions), is not uncommon among Sumba's Protestant converts.

Kata spent most of her days in her compound, in the company of female kin or neighbors, producing fabrics to be sold to tourists or agents. Like a number of noblemen, Umbu Taniku was often away on his motor-cycle; he left the island to sell textiles in Bali about three times a year. On one such trip in 1994, he stayed two months.

Gregarious and bright, before her marriage Kata had received a cer-tificate from a teacher training school in Waingapu to become an ele-mentary school instructor. She had begun to teach before she was married; but after her marriage, Umbu Taniku forced her to quit. All Wandi women created cloth, he said, and she ought to devote herself to producing textiles for the commercial market. In fact, textile skill has long been a prerequisite for women marrying into the village.

Kata learned textile processes from her mother. She had been espe-cially skilled at the patterned binding (*pahondu*) of warp yarns funda-mental to *ikat* fabrics. This dexterity, she says, had been an essential factor in Umbu's decision to marry her. She had not fully realized, how-ever, that she would not be able to continue with her teaching career, which she greatly enjoyed, after her marriage and that in many ways her daily social world, in spite of being widened by the extended family she acquired through marriage, would become limited to her husband's family and her immediate neighbors in the new village.

But her social imagination expanded through the foreigners who fre-quently visited Wandi and her husband's tales of his ventures to Bali. Moreover, Kata had studied English in high school, and Umbu Taniku had not. This gave her some entrance into the conversations and bargaining that went along with the tourist and textile trade.

Yet despite her capabilities, much of Kata's energy appeared to be spent in trying to maintain her marriage in the face of her husband's wanderings. She sometimes spoke to me of the problems between them, saying she felt abandoned by Umbu's frequent absence. He would often go off and return the following day. What is more, Kata would be left in the household with her mother-in-law, who she complained always regarded her with a critical eye.

When not sitting at her loom or binding sections of a warp for dyeing, Kata sometimes gravitated to the porches of neighbors or received friends in her own compound, where she shared in local gossip and commentary. Her closest friend was a woman of the same age who had grown up in Wandi, but married into a family in Kata's natal village. According to this young woman, her husband drank frequently and had repeatedly beaten her. Finally, she decided to *palai kabeli la uma* (run back home) to Wandi, to the house of her parents, and had been there for several months in 1993. She and Kata often commiserated on the plight of women, although Kata always emphasized that her husband did not beat her. Nonetheless, she felt neglected and feared that if she ceased to create fabrics, Umbu might divorce her.

Ever more valiant in theme as years went by, Umbu Taniku's designs evolved into a baroque succession of pieces. At the same time, his fabrics continued to incorporate a number of "traditional" designs, such as *patola* motifs inspired by Indian trade cloths, local plant forms, and animals such as crocodiles and birds. While becoming more worldly through his off-island travels, Umbu has consistently reasserted the traditional position of his wife, as one who stays at home and produces cloth. Like a number of men, he revels within the mobility and freedom provided by this particular dialectic, following (and preserving) a status system based in a paradox of men's and women's places in the world. And in villages, this discrepancy in mobility and actions often created tensions.

In response to her position, Kata often expressed regret that she had given up a teaching career:

> I studied at school but now I only cook and work on cloth.
> I'm not permitted to travel to far-off places like Biba and some
> others. No. Instead I'm left to be a stupid village woman with
> no other experiences of the world.

Her sense of position was ambivalent. Although she struggled to maintain her marriage through dutiful obligations (which include continuing to weave with care the textiles that enable her husband to travel to Bali), she at the same time protested her situation, speaking openly about the inequities in her life.

When Umbu was away, Kata's work area was the site of frequent visits with women friends. During days spent sitting in her compound, I heard tales from a variety of women. A theme running through many of the stories concerned failed expectations in marriages and disappointment in the "character" (*hara*) of husbands. In addition to philandering or lazy husbands, there were also detested in-laws of one sort or another, and some women suspected such relatives of sorcery against them and their children. These suspicions led to further devious actions. One woman told me of purposely dumping the contents of an indigo pot, which she was convinced had been intentionally poisoned by her sister-in-law:

76

I believe she put some of her own urine in the indigo dye!
She tried to work magic against me. I knew this because I saw
her pour a little yellow water into the pot. Later I maybe
would be sick from this entering my skin. In the early morning I turned the pot over behind the weeds, in the back of our
yard. I put the pot back empty. People in my house were fearful that a spirit emptied the pot, but I kept quiet so that my
sister-in-law would not know what I did.

Women would position themselves within such contentious environments by asserting their own virtues in the face of things. Disaffected
wives would recount their relentless efforts at maintaining marriages and
the textile enterprises that usually went with them in Wandi. Besides the
allegedly beaten woman above, who had returned to her parents' home
in the village, there were others who openly voiced their dissatisfaction
with domestic life. One woman often complained of her feckless husband's inability to succeed in business and of how he wasted his time and
their money playing cards and wagering. She mentioned that before she
had come to Wandi as his wife, she had believed they would have a prosperous life because he had told her that he was successful in the commercial textile trade. Now she barely had enough to live on and felt angry all
the time. Conversely, her husband (a cousin of Kata's husband) would
often visit Umbu Taniku when he was at home and complain of his wife's
lack of affection and her constant nagging.

Although Kata shared in the griping with her cohort, she persisted in
maintaining the home and the textile production. She never appeared
completely engaged with her dyes or yarns, however, and often paused
and conversed while she worked. There were no motifs of her creation
in the fabrics, as Umbu insisted upon being the sole designer of textiles
from his compound. In producing the cloths, Kata fulfilled a duty and
carried out specific designs of her husband while often musing upon other
matters.

Within Wandi, her female neighbors spoke of Kata as a persevering
and moral woman. She reflected certain local ideals in her self-presentation and in the manner she carried on her family life. Her realm was
firmly bounded by the domestic sphere, however, and Kata had not
enjoyed travel opportunities (despite her expressed desire to travel) or
the extended public prestige conjunctive with a nationally and internationally recognized art form and the culture it emerges from.

Kata worked with cloth in a situation similar to many women in East
Sumba. Her pieces were produced in anonymity; it was her husband who

claimed credit for them publicly, as if they came solely out of his own enterprise. Kata's contribution was taken for granted, as part of her inherent domestic duties. Her personal desires and interpretations of her life, unlike Biba's, were not visible within the fabrics she produced, but instead were audible in her immediate environment, in a shared social forum with other village women.

However, according to Kata, she herself instigated one important change in her husband's household fabrics:

> My husband's mother is a skilled indigo dyer, and I believe that she wanted to work magic against me. After I first came to Umbu's house I was sick. I lost our first baby before it was born. I was thin and weak. When we began to make many cloths to sell to tourists, I agreed with Umbu to use some chemical dyes. Not all, but some colors. The big change that we made was to buy blue dye in the market and stop using indigo from Sumba. We told my mother-in-law that this was because the new dye was faster to use and we could make more *hinggi*s and then prosper. This was true. But she was angry and still is. She told us that we are pushing her out of the family work and also going against custom. She says our *hinggi*s are ugly.

78

This was an instance in which Kata had asserted control, although it was toward the betterment of the textile trade that was in some ways at the center of her woes. Her mother-in-law, preempted from a position of potency in producing indigo dye baths, now sullenly assisted in other aspects of fabrics production or attended to cooking at the back of the house. Once I heard her wail out that the fabrics hanging in front of the home were *njala wora* (false blue) and for *turis nduba* (stupid tourists)—a disparagement overheard by neighboring households.

While the fabrics Kata bound, dyed, and wove enframed fields peopled with heroic male figures waging wars and smiting enemies, her weaving compound contained the stories of women in uncelebrated, domestic battles. The narrative cloths she produced, and the female narratives surrounding her production, accentuated the discrepancy between the activities of men and women. In many cases, such discrepancy created an intractable situation of perpetual conflict, giving rise to both empathy and antipathy between village women.

Kathleen Stewart has discussed gendered social "places" as interpretive spaces established through encounters with the Other; that which is "just outside the boundary of the established domain" (1990:46) charges the borders between conventional spaces of men and women. From such

Figure 24. Gendered dualism: gold *mamuli* given as part of the bride price.

borders emerges an ongoing discourse, a continual negotiation and telling of the condition of things. Thus "traditional" gender ideologies, while on the surface often rigidly asserted, are simultaneously contested through everyday talk and interpretations.

While women in East Sumba often appeared both marginalized and stationary in their family compounds (producing the very fabrics of mobility, independence, and social prestige of their men), they controlled much local commentary on tensions in their communities.[27] As interpreting subjects or backtalking sideliners, women orchestrated the emotional tenor and family politics of village life through their narratives, gossip, and jokes.

Wide gaps in mobility and experience between men and women fuse tensions. Yet the frequent absences of men from their homes provide "interpretive spaces"—forums for women to voice the concerns of their lives, with whatever humor, sorrows, ironies, or rages these might involve. Such voices also provide points of entry into the relationships that make up households and communities.

Rambu Hamu's Connections

*The contest lay not between love and duty. Perhaps there never is such
a contest. It lay between the real and the pretended.*

—E. M. Forster, *Howards End*

Married to a high-ranking nobleman in her late teens, "Rambu Hamu"
(now in her forties) had come from the west of the island after her marriage was arranged by her family. Together the couple have nine children.
Rambu Hamu spends most of her time at home, assisted by numerous
servants. Although four of her oldest children have been converts to
Protestantism since high school,[28] as of 1998, Rambu and her husband
still resisted conversion and followed Marapu practices.

In fact, much of their time was spent attending various Marapu ceremonies (mostly funerals), which might occur several times a week in the
region. "Umbu Ama" wielded social clout and enjoyed wide deference
throughout the area. Clad in a leather jacket and jeans and often surveying his domain on his motorcycle, he prided himself as a modern man
who also maintained a good degree of influence within his realm.

The large porch of the family compound was often the gathering site
for various visitors, either relatives, local people, or officials consulting
Umbu Ama on matters from livestock exchange to dispute settlement.
Although not holding any legal office under the Indonesian state system,
Umbu Ama (like others of the *maramba* rank) maintained customary
controls in his village region, while abiding by national laws.

Although congenial to outsiders, including tourists, the couple spoke
no English and frequently relied on their neighbor, Luka, to assist them in
communicating with foreigners. Rambu Hamu recalled the time when she
and her husband lived in an inland agricultural region as boring compared
to her current life. As a noblewoman, she had few domestic responsibilities; she spent most of her time overseeing the duties of servants and
nursing her children. In those days, she did not know weaving; she took
up the art when she moved in the late 1970s to the village of Wandi,
where every woman was expected to know how to create cloth.

Although not an industrious or inventive weaver, Rambu produced a
continuous supply of relatively small pieces, most of which were not sold
but were worn by the men in her family or given as gifts to relatives. Her
husband was often away from home, traveling about for any number of
reasons, and Rambu especially enjoyed visitors when she was otherwise
alone weaving on her porch. During such visits she engaged freely in
conversation, saying that having company to share tales with enlivened
her work.

Rambu wove on the porch in the center of her family compound, largely secluded from the public area of Wandi, although one end of the compound was open to a clear view of the main lane. On the walls surrounding the porch were photos, plaques, and calendars—all memorabilia of family, friends, and events, including a portrait of Umbu Ama's father (wearing traditional garb) rendered in pastels, which a street artist in Yogyakarta, Java created from a photograph. Side by side on one wall were two posters, one advertising a match between two American boxers (Spinks and Tyson) and showing both men in fighting modes, the other a cross-section of gynecological anatomy—a medical illustration showing the positioning of an intrauterine device.[29] Together, the two posters graphically asserted a kind of gendered modernity, whether intentional or not on the part of the people who displayed them.

By 1994, Rambu Hamu had ventured several times to Yogyakarta and Jakarta (Java) on missions relevant to textiles. Her most exciting journey (in 1993) was connected with a sizable exhibit of Sumbanese material culture sponsored by a major corporation in Jakarta and held at a large and prestigious gallery.[30] At that time, Rambu was feted as the sole representative of Sumbanese royalty involved in weaving. She also functioned as part of the gallery display for a few days, sitting on a woven mat on the floor in traditional costume and weaving for all to see. During the two weeks she spent in Jakarta, she was accommodated for part of her stay at the Hilton Hotel. A scrapbook in a locked cabinet in Rambu's house preserved photographs of the Jakarta events. In the photos, Rambu poses with numerous officials and collectors, and even one Javanese film star. Several Western collectors also appear in the snapshots, smiling, arm-in-arm with the Indonesians. Rambu also appears in photographs taken at a restaurant, at the zoo, and at Jakarta's immense theme park Taman Mini Indonesia Indah (Mini Park Beautiful Indonesia)—a major tourist attraction and one that displays numerous reconstructed environments representing ethnic groups across the archipelago, including the Sumbanese.[31]

Although Rambu Hamu is well traveled when compared to the vast majority of women in Sumba, her journeys away from her island largely followed a prescribed Sumbanese decorum concerning female mobility. Rambu spent several nights at a posh, Western hotel in Jakarta, yet she did so with other family members and was at no time completely on her own, that is, beyond a network of kin. The rest of her stay in Java was spent at the homes of relatives, themselves civil service employees living in Jakarta.

Through her Javanese ventures, Rambu Hamu built upon her personal prestige in Sumba as well as the renown of her family and village. She became locally regarded as a person who had seen other places and could talk about them. At the same time, because she stayed with Sumbanese relatives in Java, she operated within a certain *uma kabihu* (traditional family household) framework, albeit one far afield. In this way, Rambu Hamu was able to expand upon yet stay within a historically gendered "field" of behavior—that of women not traveling beyond family household networks unescorted. Her social position and mode of travel contrasted with those of Biba.

Because of its proximity to Waingapu, Wandi is a more socially bustling and interactive village than most others in the region, and its social atmosphere allowed Rambu Hamu access to outsiders, in contrast to the more insular lives many women led in other villages. In recent years, a few foreigners have at various times lived in her home while studying weaving in Wandi, and among them were some who had studied and become conversant in Indonesian. Rambu was able to speak at length with the Western women and ask them numerous questions about themselves and their home countries.

Maintaining a reserve befitting her social position, Rambu Hamu was at the same time inquisitive and visibly engaged by new kinds of experiences. Although other villagers were hesitant to gossip openly about Rambu, many of her age peers considered her conservative in dress and manner and generally unapproachable because of her status. Yet this same status afforded her opportunities to travel or to welcome outsiders into her home. And this freedom, in turn, fostered resentments within local social spheres. For although travel and powerful social connections bring prestige, this is inevitably followed by jealousies, as in the case of Biba and Hasan.

Not a physically energetic woman, Rambu Hamu usually avoided situations where she might have to walk even short distances. When visiting metropolitan areas of Java, she also limited her sightseeing and shopping considerably (when compared to other locals abroad), complaining that the activities were too tiring. However, Rambu had abundant energy and imaginative resources when it came to conversation and storytelling, and she seemed to remember events and descriptions from the past in minute detail.

It was on Rambu Hamu's porch that I learned of many of the social connections in the village (sanctioned and illicit) and of her own moral view of her life and her village. Rambu also commented upon her idea of the ideal male-female relationship:

> Here's what I believe, and I think that it's the same situation
> around the world. It's the nature of men to travel about and to
> have girlfriends in those travels. It's like that. So, a marriage

can only be lasting and have happiness if the man loves the woman a little more than she loves him. This is the only way the woman can keep any control over the home situation. It's like that.

This, in her mind, set right the structural inequality in mobility and behavior between a husband and a wife seen in most households in East Sumba.

Historically, noblemen in East Sumba have taken more than one wife, and this convention, although in decline, continues in some villages. In fact, local people regard the practice as a main reason villagers resist conversion to Christianity, which forbids polygamy. In 1994, rumors circulated in the region that Umbu Ama was on the look-out for a second wife. In his travels throughout the area, Umbu made no secret of his interest in young women and often joked that a second marriage was imminent. However, in private conversations with me he maintained that he and Rambu Hamu had a spoken agreement that he would not take another wife, and that if he did so, Rambu would return to her family's home in the west of the island. Apparently not willing to risk such a loss, Umbu expressed resignation to his wife's wishes.

Rambu Hamu's social connections and demeanor have been assets in her travels to Java, as a kind of ambassador of traditional Sumbanese culture. Stately and gracious, she exemplified ideals of Sumbanese nobility. As the wife of a high-ranking nobleman, she enjoyed contact with various local government officials, who facilitated her participation in prestigious cultural events in Jakarta, such as the exhibit mentioned above. In recent times, she had become much more traveled than her husband, who did not particularly enjoy venturing abroad, but preferred the comforts and deferences of his home village.

Rambu Hamu vocally asserted certain historical, local values and seemed to carefully maintain a particularly conscious noble presentation of self. While her skill at weaving was relatively recent, as was her position in the village, she adeptly presented herself as a traditional, local noblewoman to outsiders. Although somewhat indifferent to the artistry and meanings involved in textiles, she secured a number of influential connections with Javanese elites and government officials involved in the promotion of Sumbanese fabrics. And while evidently enjoying these connections and the prestige they brought, Rambu Hamu was at the same time uncomfortable away from her island, preferring the familiarity of home and family.

Others in the region, however, expressed resentment at Rambu's mobility and connections. *Maramba* women in other villages sometimes

spoke bitterly of how the Wandi woman had (with apparent ease) established herself as the sole representative of Sumbanese culture at the event
in Java. What is more, they were critical of the fact that Rambu Hamu
was a relative novice to the fabric arts and to the coastal region of East
Sumba. Numerous tensions arose with other noble families active in the
textile trade, yet throughout it all Rambu Hamu maintained her poise.
Her position was paradoxical: of one maintaining an ideal presentation of
self based in historical cultural models (a kind of local "society women"
in a national context), yet at the same time comparatively detached
from certain elements of the "culture" (such as cloth production) she
represented.

Rambu has distinguished her home within a broadened, Indonesian
context, reinforcing her husband's preeminence in the process. In 1993, a
video crew from Jakarta taped Rambu Hamu and Umbu Ama in a piece
on Sumbanese traditional village life. The couple dressed in their royal
finery and posed on the porch of their traditional home and amid stone
megaliths. Some time later, the videotape appeared on national television,
and the couple watched themselves in the home of an affluent relative
in Waingapu. As a celebrity and cultural asset, Rambu attained certain
power and control—which she was most concerned with applying to her
immediate household. Seeing herself with her husband on national television also reified the images of an ideal self and life in a new way. She
and Umbu Ama were indisputably aligned—publicly and visibly—to
greater political powers in Jakarta.

84

CHAPTER 5
PARAI MUTU

"Parai Mutu" is the source of some of the finest textiles in Sumba. The village is referred to by many Sumbanese as *na paraing huri mahari* (the village of strong custom) or *yang paling tradisi* (I.; the most traditional). The two hundred inhabitants of the village are reputed to tenaciously adhere to concerns of social caste. Situated between a bend in the river and a twist in the road, Parai Mutu sits atop a bluff overlooking a long cultivated valley bordered by barren hills. Gardens and livestock support most of the people of the region. The peaks (*tualaku uma*) of Parai Mutu's clan homes are visible from a distance, and in 1994 the village had recently rebuilt a large ceremonial house (*uma bokulu*), the most impressive structure in the area. More than sixty kilometers from Waingapu, Parai Mutu is connected to the town by several public buses that pass each day.

Parai Mutu

Unlike Wandi, Parai Mutu is not dissected by a thoroughfare, although the road that runs along the coast of East Sumba runs near its village entrance. On sunny days, it is difficult to focus one's eyes in the village, so intensely white is the limestone earth it sits upon. Highlighted by a bleached ground, the houses and large megaliths of Parai Mutu are stark and impressive. Like a Sumbanese *hinggi*,[1] homes appear in a bifacial manner along two opposing rows, with the central yard (*talora*) of the village dominated by huge, elaborately carved gravestones.

Despite the commoners (*tau kabihu*) who also inhabit Parai Mutu, the elevated settlement is widely considered a noble village (*parai maramba*). The home of the highest-ranking nobles of the region is a mammoth two-story affair (something seldom seen in village architecture in Sumba), with a wide verandah running most of the way around it. Flaunting exterior panelling of yellow-hued water-buffalo hide, the household is flanked by an immense satellite dish a few meters from its outer walls—an apparatus that was installed in the summer of 1994, shortly after Parai Mutu was first wired for electricity.

People's activities are not apparent from the fronts of homes, as in Wandi; one must go behind them to enter family compounds. Consequently, most people in Parai Mutu do not immediately see the arrival of guests, but speculate from within their compounds as to whose approach might be indicated by the sound of a motor vehicle. Moreover, the impression of social life in the village is one of confinement to these compounds.

There is little of the bustle and meandering conviviality of Wandi, but, rather, a guardedness to Parai Mutu life.

In Parai Mutu the contentions between households can be felt. There is a secrecy (*kamandi*) and jealousy (*katiu eti*) between homes (not infrequently expressed by residents), and people from other village areas who visit Parai Mutu comment upon how difficult it is to call at more than one home because of the risk of offending people, so intense are the resentments between families.[2]

In the fertile riverine areas beneath the *maramba* village plateau lie several small hamlets occupied by commoner and slave-caste families; these are included within the Parai Mutu domain. Although containing some high-peaked *uma*, these villages are "lower" in their architecture, with gravestones of lesser size and splendor than those in the upper village. In these small villages, people also produce cloth, and most households rely on incoming merchants from Waingapu or people living in the plateau village to sell their textiles to outsiders. *Maramba* families from Parai Mutu also commission piecework from families in the lower villages and sometimes have them finish off a *hinggi* woven in a noble family compound. Depending upon the relationship to the family, such work may or may not be paid for, as some families live in hereditary servitude to the households of royals.

86

Although the absence of activity in public view in Parai Mutu suggests desolation, upon approaching most households one immediately hears the banging of the shuttles of looms. Within cloistered family compounds, women produce textiles, with as many as ten engaged at one time in binding, weaving, and dyeing.

Parai Mutu sells some of the most expensive fabrics on the island, and these textiles often travel to the trading centers of Bali and Java. Toward such ends, there is relentless competition between households for the outside market, as people copy or invent their own renditions on local motifs. Not only are women of Parai Mutu among the most skilled and industrious of cloth makers, but certain men of the village are some of the most ambitious and wide-ranging traders of Sumba's textiles.

Pingi *and* Kapuka

The distinction between the terms *"pingi"* (a trunk of a tree, a center, or point of origin) and *"kapuka"* (a tip of a branch, a limit, or the far reaches) is an ideological polarity in Parai Mutu thought.[3] This polarity was suggested by Forth (1981) in relation to marriage exchange and the accompanying property transfers, but the concepts are also evident in recently expressed notions and practices involving a broadened social world. The trunk–branch tip relationship (see also Fox 1980a, 1997), moreover, corresponds with the binary concept of "center and periphery," which has been widely noted in Southeast Asian polities.[4] Historically it appears that people of Parai Mutu have perceived of themselves as at a certain center (at least in terms of social hierarchy) while regarding the peripheries of their domain in terms of valuable opportunities and alliances.

Parai Mutu villagers are expressly concerned with issues of social caste and affiliation with central ancestral clan houses. The caste levels of nobility, commoners, and slaves are evinced in village life.[5] Villagers adhere to rules of prescriptive marriage alliance, following a kind of circulating connubium described by Needham (1980) and more specifically by Forth (1981). The marriage of sons, however, occurs along far more flexible lines than that of daughters, for whom (if of *maramba* rank) marriage is frequently problematic, as requirements of caste and economic standing of a prospective mate become especially restrictive.

The eight noble households and four households of commoners in Parai Mutu each shelter a number of servants, referred to as "children of the house" (*anakeda kuru uma*), a euphemism of sorts for the classification of slaves. Social divisions and caste stratification manifest starkly between the highest and lowest members of the hierarchy, and contrasts in dress, demeanor, and even physical size are evident. Members of the nobility are often tall and fair-skinned (they purposely avoid the sun whenever possible); and although often dressed simply when in family compounds, they always wear the carnelian and gold jewelry that mark the royal caste.

87

The central village contains about two hundred full-time residents. Perhaps as many claim the village as their home but reside in other areas (most in the main town of Waingapu, a few as far off as Java) because of employment.[6] Yet such people return to their family homes, and some spend weekends and holidays in the village. While similar to "center" and "periphery," the concepts *"pingi"* and *"kapuka"* also parallel notions of time depth for villagers—that which is old (*mandai*) and established (with corresponding alliances and bases in the past for social identities) and that which is new (*bidi*) and innovated (with recently formed relationships and positionings of individuals in broadened social contexts). Such historical senses of self and place (based in clan, caste, and gender) sometimes are challenged as people create and transport cloth for an international market and experience whatever personal successes or frustrations that might follow.

The following sections glimpse at how identities are maintained or re-created by a few villagers, identities often involving intricate social and commercial networks. These networks become articulated when people push their social options to the edges of their worlds.

Travels of Ana Humba

> *. . . in keeping with the principle that we can construct reality in the image of our desires.*
>
> —Isabel Allende, *Eva Luna*

For several months from 1993 to 1994, I rented a small house near Waingapu, in order to have a place to retreat to and write, as well as store the various things I needed to own while on the island. Rare was the day, however, that I was able to experience solitude or uninterrupted reflection (everyday conditions considered aberrant in East Sumba), as I usually had at least one visitor by noon.

On numerous occasions, one guest in particular came to stay for a period of a few days, and I would sometimes accompany her by bus when she returned to her native village of Parai Mutu. "Ana Humba" and I had become friends on my first visit to Sumba in 1991, when I studied the *ikat* technique with her mother and lived in her family home. For several weeks this household was my center in the village (and indeed on the island), as I studied with the older noblewoman who was one of the most

88

Figure 25. Ana Humba's collection of cloths from around Sumba.

accomplished creators of cloth in the region. During this time, I began to know something of the lives of the rest of the family.[7]

Ana Humba would descend from a bus in front of my house about twice a month during the periods I was there and usually stay for at least two nights. She would bring vegetables or fish from her village, and she would take over the kitchen for the period of her visit. As I had spent a good deal of time with her family, I was expected to open my home to her as well, which I always did. Eventually her stays became a regular routine, and I usually welcomed her company and cooking. I also came to realize that my home was one element within a network of social options Ana Humba consciously explored in constructing a wider social universe for herself.

Early on in her regular visits Ana Humba happily informed me that she was able to come to my place so freely because the house I rented belonged to an elderly member of her extended family (someone she referred to as a "grandfather" [*ama boku*] but who was actually more distantly related) and thus could be considered a kind of clan house. Because of this, she could stay the night without fear of reprobation from her kin.[8]

As Forth noted in Sumba in the 1970s, "for a woman habitually to stray too far from the house is considered unseemly behavior" (1981:41), and this attitude is still pervasive in Ana Humba's village. The unescorted travels of women are often conflated with earthly and metaphysical dangers, and to travel to undetermined points outside of kin networks is not a usual practice for Sumbanese women. Ana Humba, however, had managed to ostensibly stay within yet elude conventional boundaries on her mobility and social world.

Of all the women I knew on the island, Ana Humba had a knack for getting around Sumba. She regularly went to Waingapu on missions related to fabrics, carrying them to sell to merchants or picking up various items needed in her family's compound, such as cotton yarn imported from Java, available in Waingapu's public markets. She also enjoyed shopping for herself, frequently buying cosmetics or clothing or going to a town beauty parlor to have her hair styled. Although usually clad in a plain cotton blouse and a simple, tubular *lau* while in her family compound, the itinerant Ana Humba would carry out business in Waingapu dressed in her finest satin and lace clothing imported from Java, her face transformed by makeup.

At age twenty-eight, Ana Humba had not yet married (in eastern Sumba women generally marry between eighteen and twenty-three). The reason for this prolonged status, as she and her family explained, was that a man of the proper rank and means had not materialized.[9] Her two unmarried sisters (one thirty and one twenty-four) also still lived with their parents. Yet, as long as I had known her, Ana Humba had spoken of being at the brink of entering into a nuptial partnership of her own choosing, often without the knowledge of her family. She seemed to enjoy the intrigue of her "secret" beaus and occasional liaisons in Waingapu, and her travels pushed the margins of her social and moral existence.

In addition to her frequent movements about the island, Ana Humba had also extended beyond her family and cosmological boundaries and beliefs, becoming a Protestant convert, the only one in her household. She explained:

> Most young people don't know what Marapu is about now. We can't understand it. And the priests don't explain it. They speak in a secret language at rituals and this has no meaning to my generation. We go along because we don't want to act against our parents and traditions, but we don't know what is being said.

There was an assertion of individuality in her explanation:

> Prayers from the priests to the Marapu ancestors are on behalf of the whole community. One cannot pray directly for oneself. As a Christian I can pray directly for myself. I'm connected straight to God on my own.[10] Marapu worked well in the past, for the way things were, but it doesn't relate to modern times. Now things are more complicated because we're involved with the rest of the world through business. And we know more now. We've received educations.

Ana Humba frequently asserted herself as *"moderen"* and subscribed to some of the notions of progress put forth by the Indonesian national government and the Christian churches in Sumba. Moreover, she used such notions as means to criticize other women (such as the noble Rambu Hamu of Wandi) for being too "traditional" (*tradisi*, I.) and "narrow-minded" (*pikiran sempit*, I.), while positioning herself as more with the times. Although Ana Humba lived under the roof of her ancestral home (in a village considered throughout eastern Sumba as restrictively traditional), she had ingeniously devised ways to create social possibilities and alternate identities[11] for herself beyond the constraints of her village life. Fabrics provided the avenue to other places and experiences.

Whereas her mother and one sister in particular had come to be regarded as among the most formidable designers and cloth makers in the region, Ana Humba had been a desultory textile worker, although she knew the processes well. Sitting and working on fabrics had always been boring to her, she claimed. She was much more suited to commerce and the meetings with people and travels involved. Ana Humba described herself as an *orang bisnis* (I.; businessperson).

Beginning in her late teens, she enjoyed journeying about the region on the paths of textile production and trade. When the women of her family needed prepared indigo pigment from villages at some distance, she would go by bus (accompanied by a servant) to get it. If textile work was commissioned out to people in the lower villages (such as a kind of woven border on the edges of *hinggi* cloths called *kabakil*), Ana Humba expedited it. By the 1990s, Ana Humba enjoyed a broad network of mercantile relationships, including textile workers from around the region, Chinese merchants in Waingapu, and several foreigners she had encountered in Sumba.

When she was twenty-three, Ana Humba had been permitted to go with her oldest brother (a civil service employee) to Jakarta and then to Bali, leaving Waingapu by plane. This, her first venture away from the island, lasted four months. She often spoke to me of how much she enjoyed this trip and how it changed her ideas of the kind of life she might have and of "what there was in the outside world" (*apa ada di dunia luar*, I.). Of her stay in Jakarta she related the following:

> I'm telling you this, the first few days in Jakarta I was just scared and ashamed of myself too. Because my clothes weren't modern like the people in that city and also because of my hair, which was kinky [*keriting*, I.]. I knew the people would know from my hair that I was from NTT [Nusa Tenggara Timur] and not from Java. But then I bought some new clothes at a department store, tied my hair back, put makeup on my face, and just went out one night with my brother and some of his friends. After that, I went out constantly. Yes, I even went shopping alone. I did that. That's the kind of life that suits me! I want to live in Jakarta one day.

91

Ana Humba realized that she had been allowed to make this extended excursion because her brother was her escort. Often she spoke of wanting to travel again away from Sumba but hinted that she would likely do so only by being taken by a Western friend (such as me) or by marrying a man who lived off of the island (which she repeatedly hinted at doing). In the time that I had known her, Ana Humba had engineered liaisons of sorts with several men staying in Waingapu. All of these were native Sumbanese of high rank and held civil service jobs in metropolitan centers such as Jakarta (Java), Kupang (Timor), or Denpasar (Bali). The men periodically returned to Sumba for family business or government duties.

Instrumental in these liaisons were two main factors: the travels legit-imized by a textile business that facilitated Ana Humba's mobility, and the Waingapu hotel owned by the most successful Chinese family involved in the textile trade to tourists. Ana Humba regularly supplied the Chinese family with pieces she collected from various villagers[12] and sometimes afterward carried out clandestine meetings at the hotel with prospective mates. But there was yet another element in this textile-trade-and-tryst schematics. During my stay on the island, I unwittingly became a kind of relay point, as Ana Humba's trips to market from my house often involved stops at the Chinese hotel. Often such market tours would last much of the evening.

During 1994, Ana Humba frequently spoke of an elopement plan she had devised with her current suitor; the plan would involve surreptitiously leaving the island to meet him in Jakarta at the end of the year. She would wait, however, for the funeral of her father, who had been sit-ting in state in the family home for many months, wrapped in more than a hundred *ikat* fabrics. Later in the year, this plan evaporated (for reasons Ana Humba would not initially clarify, other than to say that she had lost interest), but yet another was soon formulated regarding a new prospect living in Kupang, on the island of Timor to the east.

Over time, it became evident to me that Ana Humba's imagination, creativity, and actions largely took form along her travel routes and stays. Her paths had twists and detours too numerous to follow and often mapped out contradictory yearnings. Her movement was motivated by her (sometimes capricious) desires and advanced by the fabric trade, which allowed her alternative milieus and experiences that would be im-possible in her village context. In the subterfuge of her itinerant "space," Ana Humba was able to constantly manipulate (and be affected by) an expanded social world; this expanded world enabled emotional and con-ceptual processes that continually reshaped her own sense of self. Her identity was as fluid as her movements, and comparably elusive. She had adeptly moved through a historically male domain—which involved travel, trade, and external alliances—while simultaneously remaining within the gendered protocol (however loosely interpreted) of Sumba villagers.

After one of her visits, I would accompany Ana Humba back to her village. This developed into a kind of routine, and I became another legit-imizing personage within the routes of her travels. We usually boarded a large bus called Lambada (after the sexually provocative Brazilian dance, which had become part of the local transport-cultural lexicon), and to the tunes of Indonesian popular music, we rode for two hours to the village of Parai Mutu. My traveling companion would carry a large bag of skeins of yarn or some other items needed for the family workshop, as well as newly purchased clothing or toiletries for herself.

The Artistry of Madai

> To be sure, the work of art draws its content from reality; but from visions of reality it builds a sovereign realm.
>
> —Georg Simmel, "The Handle"

Dual, multicolored crayfish against a dark woven background hung from a clothesline across a section of verandah, shading the area behind them. In this alcove, a small, briskly moving woman passed a shuttle beneath raised warp yarns. As she repeated her weaving, a *kombu*-red crocodile surfaced in the border of the fabric. The woman continued this process for hours, until a chicken interrupted her labors by landing on the upper beam of her loom. Waving the bird away from her fabric, "Madai" turned and looked out on the courtyard.

In dramatic contrast to her younger sister, Madai is a reclusive woman. Two years older than Ana Humba, she is the eldest daughter of the family. Slight, shy, and hard-of-hearing, Madai is exceedingly energetic and alert. Of all the women in the *maramba* household, she worked the most diligently on fabrics, meticulously binding her own designs on unwoven yarns or sitting in the courtyard weaving. By age thirty (in 1994), Madai had attained notoriety in eastern Sumba as an upcoming doyenne in design and weaving, recently eclipsing her mother who, because of age and failing eyesight, had ceased to design and

93

Figure 26. Crayfish and other creatures.

create the textiles that had earned her house a reputation for fine fabrics.

Madai worked incessantly on cloth. She would remain intensely focussed on a piece for several hours, leave it to eat or nap, and then return to her work for the remainder of the day. Her designs featured assorted historical motifs of the village region, which she reinterpreted idiosyncratically. Her pictorial sense was as polished as her practical skills, and she exquisitely combined motifs and techniques to create novel pieces. The days of Madai's life, from what I observed, were largely caught up in the poetics and production of beautiful cloth. Indeed, her absorption and artistry approached the sublime.

Others in her family regarded Madai almost as someone of another world. Her mother and sisters would speak of how she had never had any interest in anything besides creating fabrics. Quitting school at age twelve (the only one among her siblings not to finish secondary school), Madai emphatically told her mother that she had no need for further knowledge, that she only wanted to work with cloth. And having expressed an absolute aversion to marriage and leaving her family home, she remained in the household to become a superlative textile designer and artisan.

Although she seldom conversed verbally, Madai enjoyed discreetly watching the comings and goings beyond her loom and engaging in her own eccentric forms of commentary. While able to speak and doing so on occasion, she preferred communicating by means of exaggerated facial expressions and hand and arm motions. Quick to see humor, usually at the expense of others, she had a knack for mimicry and parody. Under her scrutiny, most foreigners appeared comical in their physical features, dress, and movements, and a group of tourists sometimes caused her to be overcome with laughter, whereby she ran inside of the house. After their departure, she gave vivid impressions of one or two of the foreigners she had found especially ludicrous. Her pantomimes drew riotous laughter from all who watched.

Madai's keen powers of observation, her imagination, and her wit found a steady outlet in her fabrics. In fact, it seems to be through cloth that she articulated and directed her "speech" (*batangu*). She especially enjoyed reinterpreting certain animal motifs to create striking images, distinctively recognizable as her own. One motif that she recreated in various forms is that of a crayfish (*kurangu*), said by many people in eastern Sumba to symbolize transformation to the next world (*awangu*) and to generally befit an older nobleman. Madai sat for hours painstakingly binding the sections of yarns that formed the creature, wrapping minute areas to form distinct geometric patterns within the crayfish, elaborating upon its anatomy in one way or another. She visibly made the motif something of her own, innovating upon a former design, reconfiguring a number of crayfish within the design field of a *hinggi*, perfecting a form and attempting to (subtly) alter the ways it had been seen in the past.

Madai also produced *hinggi* that, influenced by those initiated in Wandi, were unidirectional in design layout. Parai Mutu fabrics of this sort, however, do not depict events in time from one end to the other as do Wandi narrative cloths, but continue a type of representational field made up of floating, archetypal forms. Anchored at the bottom are often twin crayfish or skull trees; numerous animal and human forms are suspended in the long space above. People in Parai Mutu persist in their affinity with specific motifs, as well as the high tonal contrasts in which they render them. Figures are often white, against a background of deep indigo or dark reddish brown. Moreover, the social caste of a household relates to the degree of color saturation within the fabrics it produces, with nobles creating the richest colors and the crispest, most complex motifs.

One device that achieves depth of field (and in this way, a spatial perspective) is peculiar to Parai Mutu. This consists of figures within cloth colored a lighter blue than the characteristic dark indigo of the background. Combined with other motifs in red or white, these paler forms recede to another plane as shadows (*mau*), and people say that they represent beings in the parallel world of the Marapu ancestors,[13] although no one seems to know who originated such designs in fabrics. Madai delights in giving such otherworldly forms sprightly body gestures and intensely arresting facial expressions; her shadowy, evanescent creatures glare at the observer from pale blue faces, revealing bared fangs and glowing yellow eyes.

95

Rendering her images with complete authority, Madai often appeared smugly self-satisfied with her creations as she sat in her sheltered work area in a corner of the family compound. Her pieces consistently

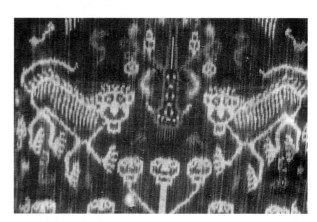

Figure 27. Creatures in cloth.

commanded the highest prices of any in her region, and she would not part with her fabrics for any less than her asking price. Her repertoire included all of the weaving techniques carried out in East Sumba, and her work is elegantly detailed, deeply colored, and finely crafted, in contrast to much of the commercial cloth of the area. Moreover, she was also skilled at hand spinning cotton (*pahuduru*) and weaving it into tight, distinct designs—a difficult craft with handspun yarns greatly admired by others in Sumba. Handspun pieces are increasingly rare, as for decades now village weavers have mostly used the imported, factory-made yarns from Java and elsewhere.[14]

In the interior of her household, Madai's mother kept locked away a few pieces that she herself had woven as a teenager and brought to Parai Mutu as part of her marriage presentation. These pieces also featured intricately rendered animals upon grounds of the deepest blue-black indigo. The older woman, "Rambu Ina Matua," had shown superb skill in textile design early on and could achieve technically precise and elegant images employing the *ikat* and *pahikung* techniques. For years she had also kept under lock and key particular pattern guides (called *pahudu*)[15] for *pahikung* motifs she created long ago and that continue to grace the compound's fabrics.

In 1993, the aged father of the household died, and his widow over-saw his enfoldment in numerous fabrics she had produced and saved for this occasion, as well as many pieces made by Madai. As of 1994, the patriarch still formed a large, swaddled mound in the center of the house, which had been structured as an altar. An offering stand sat before the corpse, and an old photograph of the deceased as a young man hung on a post behind it. Following custom, food and water were offered on the stand at the foot of the departed patriarch when others ate, and some members of the family slept around the deceased upon woven mats on the floor.

Madai slept in the room with her father every night and took naps there during the day. She seldom left her family compound and had not been outside of her village, by all accounts, for several years. Indeed, she seemed to keep a kind of vigil over the life of the household in general. The perimeters of her social universe, unlike those of her sister, Ana Humba, were closely circumscribed, extending from the center of her house to the kitchen building and latrine behind it. Yet, like her sister's, her borders were largely of her choosing. Within this small, familiar enclave, she held warrant to the type of life and activities that suited her, by all indications. What is more, there was a kind of wry self-satisfaction to Madai's demeanor unlike any I had ever known. Perhaps through real-izing the inherent power in constructing images, Madai consistently refused to be photographed, maintaining a control over pictures of herself as she did with her own rendered forms in fabric. Sitting in the aeries of her weaving compound, she worked incessantly and passionately on her bound and woven creations, fixing the rest of the world within her own peculiar gaze.

Adventures of Umbu Pari

> With no challenges, the social world would be without events.
> —Shelly Errington, *Meaning and Power in a Southeast Asian Realm*

In another family compound, I witnessed the end of an argument as it loudly culminated with chickens and pigeons flapping away from the household in terror. Some birds took refuge under the house and others looked down from eaves as "Umbu Pari" ran across the yard to escape the screams of his mother and the pan of water she had hurled into the air. Tensions had been constant between Rambu Ina and her son for a decade. Years before, Rambu Ina told me, Umbu Pari had sold to a European collector some of the family's gold pieces along with a cloth she had brought to her marriage. She no longer kept articles she valued in the high rafters of the family home, but stored them in a locked cabinet next to her bed.

A new motif of remarkable origins had recently appeared in the compound. Pasted on doors to the rooms of a recently constructed hotel in Waingapu were decals with pictures of kangaroos below the name of the door manufacturer. According to the hotel staff, tourists would frequently comment on the stickers, asking jokingly whether they were left on the doors to appeal to Australians. One morning, most of the decals were gone. Shortly after this time, the kangaroos appeared on walls of the inner courtyard of a home in Parai Mutu.

97

Umbu Pari had for some years been an active trader (and occasional designer) of the textiles that emerged from his family's courtyard. Now in his mid-thirties and married with two children, Umbu Pari had attended

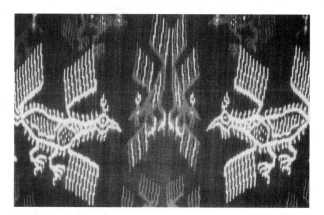

Figure 28. Cocks in active mode.

university in Timor years before and obtained a degree in business. His fortunes, however, rose and fell over the years, as he strived to maintain a steady fabric enterprise for himself.

Umbu Pari always seemed to have a strategic plan involving textiles, and he often spoke of potential exhibits in other lands as his ultimate goal. He was resentful when Rambu Hamu of Wandi had been the representative of things Sumbanese in the Jakarta exhibit of 1993 (chapter 4), as she had neglected to take fabrics from his household for display and had not promoted his village. His angry words to her caused a falling out between him and the Wandi nobles. After that, Umbu Pari accelerated his talk and schemes for controlling an exhibition abroad. In 1994, he designed a kangaroo motif in *ikat* based upon the picture in the decal described above, which he claimed as the emblem for his upcoming textile exhibit in Australia.

Through his many extended trips to Bali, Umbu Pari acquired something of an international cachet and an ethnographic self-consciousness of himself and his village. Although usually residing near Waingapu, where his wife held an office job, he frequently returned to Parai Mutu for prolonged stays. As Umbu Pari developed the flair of a global entrepreneur, he also functioned as a self-appointed arbiter of culture and tradition in representing his household and village to foreign visitors. As the only one in the family compound who spoke and understood English to any extent, he was able to arbitrarily explicate the scene in his household and the meanings in its textiles to outsiders without fear of objections from other family members.

Thus Umbu Pari adeptly conversed in English, peppering his vocabulary with numerous American and Australian slang expressions. Markers of foreign alliances had become integral elements in the manner he conducted himself in local Sumbanese contexts. With a reputation for "talking big" (*bokulungaru*), Umbu Pari frequently boasted to other Sumbanese about recent textile sales to affluent foreigners or upcoming travel plans away from the island. His chicanery earned him a reputation among the network of nobles in East Sumba as a braggart and a rogue.

In the early 1980s Umbu Pari began to make jaunts to Bali. He stored a photo album in his parent's home, documenting the evolution of his adult life: his trips abroad, stylistic shifts in dress, and foreign associations. Early photos show the young nobleman at a small Balinese hotel in the company of several European tourists. In the snapshot, he wears his hair long, dangles a cigarette from his lip, and strikes a wide-legged pose in flaring, floral bell-bottoms. Numerous photos chronicle Umbu Pari's persona through the decade, with notable changes in fashion, but always with himself centrally framed, often in the company of foreign companions.

Since the mid-1980s, Umbu Pari had attracted several paying European guests to his ancestral home as students of the *ikat* textile process. Years ago in Bali, he realized the potential interest his traditional village might hold for foreigners and began to actively promote a "homestay" and weaving-study program involving his family compound. Several people came to the household to study for extended periods. One Swedish woman had returned every summer to stay for several weeks, becoming friends with Umbu Pari's gregarious cousin, Ana Humba. This periodic hosting of foreigners lent his family some prestige locally, as well as causing inevitable resentments.

In 1990 Umbu Pari became a parent and took up part-time residence with his new wife. As he and others tell of the marriage, his Sumbanese girlfriend had become pregnant, and a hasty marriage was negotiated between the two families—a connubial arrangement that took the formerly footloose prince by storm. Since that time, by many accounts, the couple lived together in a tempestuous relationship, characterized by Umbu Pari's frequent absences.

After his marriage, Umbu Pari continued to trade along the routes of Sumba's textiles, although he was now somewhat constricted by family responsibilities. He initially attempted to persuade his wife to produce cloth, claiming that such an enterprise could become a lucrative one for the family. She, however, preferred her clerical job in Waingapu and resisted being incorporated into a fabric-production scheme. Moreover, Umbu Pari's wife, "Tali," resented his travels after their marriage and stated that she did not want to produce textiles because that would encourage his leaving the island to sell them. The couple often argued about this, and Pari would then return to his *uma* in Parai Mutu for extended visits.

At the time of his marriage to Tali, Umbu Pari was carrying on a long-distance romance with a Swiss woman he had met in Bali a year earlier. The two had been communicating through letters, and the European knew nothing of Umbu Pari's wife or child. In fact, what she knew of her Sumbanese beau's life was what he had constructed for her, which had emphasized his *maramba* rank and traditionality. Umbu Pari told me that what he had imagined coming out of this relationship was a profitable business partnership in textile trade (the woman was said to own art galleries in Bali and in Switzerland) and perhaps an ongoing, although intermittent, romantic affair.

The unannounced arrival of the woman in Sumba, however, abruptly preempted his designs for the future, as the gallery owner soon realized the domestic reality of Umbu Pari's life. Embittered, the woman created a public scene in the lobby of a Chinese-run hotel[16] in Waingapu, telling Pari off in an emotional mixture of English and Indonesian. She left the island the following day. Umbu Pari's reaction was to blame both the foreign woman and his wife for his malaise:

> I can't believe that she [the European] would be angry with me because she found out I have a wife and a baby. What does that concern her? So what? *Just take it easy, I say!* [This was the only sentence of the diatribe articulated in English. The rest was voiced in Indonesian]. What matters is that we could do a good business and I could still see her in Bali sometimes. But it's my wife too. She doesn't want me to go anywhere. She's jealous all the time of me. She has been pestering me to take her to Bali with me [his wife had never been away from Sumba], but I said no. I want to enjoy myself, and she would ruin my trip.

After the hotel lobby scene, there was a revival in the nobleman's reliance upon augury (*uratu*). Before undertaking a trip away from the island or pursuing a new alliance, he would sacrifice a chicken and, with the help of a *ratu*, examine its entrails for signs of the potentialities of an upcoming meeting or event. Augury has been long common practice for people in Sumba about to begin a new undertaking (such as marriage, trade, or warfare) and persists relevant to present concerns. Umbu Pari, however, would often want to keep his plans "secret" (which he expressed as *unu eti* 'within the liver') from the people of his family and village and would seek out accomplices in divination from villages some distance away. Multiple, wide-ranging chicken sacrifices (*uramanu*) became part of his circuit of connections and intrigues.

During 1994, Umbu Pari spoke often of his upcoming exhibit of Parai Mutu textiles in Australia and flaunted his kangaroo motif as visible proof of the new project. He and his older brother were to transport fabrics and participate in the event, the date and exact location of which were unclear. The two had never been outside of Indonesia, nor had anyone else in their family. Although Umbu Pari had spoken widely about a foreign gallery connection or event such as this many times over the years, thus far an exhibition had not materialized.

I recall one instance in particular, regarding an ill-fated transnational contract. Umbu Pari had received a sizable commission from a Dutch artist to execute several designs in large *ikat* pieces. The man had given Umbu Pari a catalog featuring some of his former work; it included several photographs of large metal and cloth sculptures that appeared to be sit-

100

ting in European corporate lobbies. The project he requested from Umbu Pari included an order for six large textiles, all with abstract designs created by the artist. Motifs consisted of bold, zig-zagging, triangular forms, which were to be colored in red, blue, and white. They bore no resemblance to anything that had ever been made in an eastern Sumbanese village.

Umbu Pari made much publicly of receiving this order from a European artist, one obviously successful in his own land. He spoke of little else for weeks (according to villagers) and, in the evenings, was often seen in the restaurant of the Hotel Orchid in Waingapu, imbibing bottles of beer and boasting to other patrons (tourists and locals) of the scope of his successes.[17]

Nonetheless, although Umbu Pari had purchased some of the necessary materials to create the commissioned fabrics with the first monetary installment received from the Dutch artist, he had not anticipated other costs and did not carefully organize or supervise the actual production. Eventually, several months after his first payment to Umbu Pari, the Hollander returned to Sumba, expecting to collect at least two finished cloths. He was presented with one uncolored warp that had been incompletely bound with strips of palm frond to roughly reveal the design he had specified. Outraged, the Dutchman cut his losses, transferring his project to the village of Wandi. He hired another man, who had a reputation for producing fabrics in a timely manner and who was also skilled at the binding of warps. After several months the man (with the help of other family members) finished the pieces for the foreigner and was paid what was considered a handsome sum for his efforts. Since that time, Umbu Pari has felt rancor toward the man who eventually received his commission.

Resentments between villagers (particularly between male entrepreneurs) arising from competitions in the textile trade agitate many in eastern Sumba. Such jealousies result in accelerated efforts on the part of the disgruntled to go beyond what their rivals have created. Although these contests may involve mere bravado, occasionally original and influential innovations occur, such as the narrative-based fabric designs invented by Luka and described in the previous chapter.

It remains to be seen whether Umbu Pari's kangaroo will join the pantheon of prestigious motifs to be seen in future textiles of East Sumba. Although he has for years enjoyed a certain kind of access to knowledge of the outside world that his female kin do not share, he often misinterprets the expectations of his foreign connections, as happened in the cases of the Dutch artist and the Swiss gallery owner.

Yet cosmopolitan knowledge has enabled Pari to compose for himself a certain personal style, as an embodied iconography of prestige. Barefoot and clad in a *hinggi* by day as he presented himself to tourists in Parai Mutu, he might don Nike running shoes, jeans, and a University of Illinois T-shirt—topped off with a jauntily tied headcloth[18]—and ride his motor-bike to Waingapu in the evening to socialize. His public postures were largely unrelated to the actual quality or meaning of the cloth he promoted, but turned upon the prestigious displays related to social connections the textiles afforded him. Through his "performance" of such connections, he pushed limits, even when such displays were based upon delusions—or perhaps because they were.

Umbu Pari's preoccupation with fashion evokes what Stuart Ewen has noted about the power of style, its emergence as an increasingly important feature in people's lives, and how this cannot be separated from the revolution and sensibility of modern life. Style, in this sense, is a visible reference point for life in *progress* (1988:23). While the styles of Sumbanese traditional dress were always integrally linked to prestige and power, knowledge of foreign fashion trends and of "newness" in an expanded, volatile world often matter in recent status contests. Umbu Pari's dress and behavior suggest a shift toward a "modernist, subjectively focused personhood," which Deborah Gewertz and Frederick Errington (1996: 486) consider to be in contrast to former identities based in local kinship and community links. Jane Schneider and Annette Weiner (1989) make a similar point involving the role of cloth in shifts to modern fashion. Yet subjectivity or personhood have likely manifested everywhere in ways we cannot know, long before "modernism."

Unlike Luka of Wandi, Pari was not possessed of exceptional artistic or conceptual talent regarding fabrics, but he succeeded in reinforcing certain modern status symbols with antecedents in the past—relentlessly aspiring to and sometimes reveling in a system of prestige based on alliances with outside powers and the visible symbols of them. Such alliances and symbols will emerge as we meet him in later chapters.

102

Mia's Boundaries

> *Ina Manu, Ama Rendi, ana wuya rara ana kara wunang.*
> *(Mother Chicken, Father Duck, the red crocodile children and the turtle children are safely between them.)*
>
> —Kambera proverb

This proverb, which villagers told me, characterizes the centrality of hierarchical power relations in Sumba. It articulates (through a type of paired, gendered animal imagery employed in most Sumbanese expressive culture) the beneficial, protective value of rulers to their subjects. Mia's behavior often exemplified those relations and values.

Every evening "Mia" descended to the river that skirts Parai Mutu to the east, accompanying other women on their way to bathe. As Mia squatted in knee-deep water and splashed herself, her black *lau* floated to the surface, encircling her. Eventually, she carried a bucket of water on her head, uphill to the household as the path became invisible in the last light of day.

Mia, in her early twenties, from birth had been one of the "children of the house" of the clan home in which Ana Humba and Madai lived. An

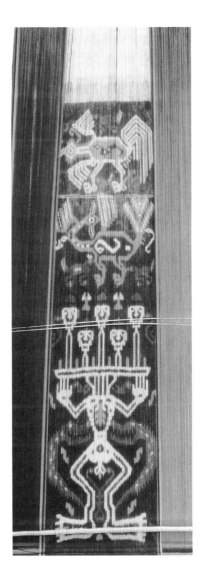

Figure 29. Designed by Madai, woven by Mia.

103

accomplished weaver, she usually sat in the family courtyard creating cloth. A short, energetic, cheerful woman, despite her poor dress (she wore old clothing handed down from her mistresses),[19] Mia appeared to be in good health.

Mia's parents live in a small hamlet below the Parai Mutu plateau and subsist by farming a variety of crops, part of which is given to their over-lords, as is the cotton yarn Mia's mother often spins or dyes in her home. Mia lived with her parents until she was nine years old, then went to the upper village to serve in the household of Madai and Ana Humba's family. Her parents were also born into positions of servitude to the same *uma*. This situation was not based in debt bondage, but rather (from what I was told by Mia, her mother, and people of the family they served) went back a number of generations to times of local warfare. No one seemed to recall the forebear of Mia who had been taken as a captive, but it was generally said that several generations back such an incident had occurred.

In the days of warfare between villages in Sumba, it was common practice for captured people to become the chattel of their captors. As *tau ata* (slave people), such people lost connection to their ancestral lineages. Without a link to the ancestors, the Marapu, a captive was not considered a full human being.[20] *Tau ata* became utterly reliant upon people of the house they found themselves belonging to, as they no longer had ancestral protection of their own.

In the past, the *maramba* caste in eastern Sumba appears to have been generally despotic and capricious in its administration of domains.[21] Villagers told me of some cruelly abusive rulers of past times, who would kill slaves for mere sport. Into the twentieth century, specific slaves (*dangangu*) were sacrificed at funerals to accompany their deceased owners to the next world. This was not regarded as cruelty, but rather as a means of transformation, and thus there was a certain honor in such deaths. Nonetheless, the noble caste wielded the authority to determine life or death among its lower-ranking dependents. In current times, such practices are illegal under Indonesian law, as is slavery in general.

Although it might seem that there would be a local movement to abolish the practice of hereditary servitude within the democratic con-text of modern Indonesian statehood, there has been no massive rush to "freedom" in Sumba. Although Christianity theoretically discourages such bondage relationships, many Sumbanese converts retain *anakeda kuru uma* as their servants. These Christians parallel a current tendency in Balinese society noted by Fredrik Barth, in that they "participate in a modern sector [which in Sumba includes religious conversion] driven by concerns of upward social mobility, material wealth, and security [all of which conflate neatly with Protestantism], and not by a coherent world theory affirming science or democracy" (1993:341). "Inequality" inheres in eastern Sumbanese notions of humanity and has not been supplanted by world religion or national ideology.[22]

Captivity of people is against state law and church doctrine, and coercion did not appear to be involved in cases involving servants I knew of. Many of the people currently in such servitude exhibited no inclination to alter their social positions. With little if any formal education or personal resources, such people were without means to navigate their way through an alternative world. In fact, many "children of the house" I spoke to expressed confusion and fear at the prospect of ever having to leave the environments they had always lived in.

Mia had never been beyond the Parai Mutu domain in her life. Some of the other servants frequently accompanied members of the noble family (such as Ana Humba) to other villages or to Waingapu, as guardians and assistants, but Mia had always remained behind as someone needed in the household. Her aptitude in weaving further reinforced her home-bound position. She carried out the designs of the household, wielding her shuttle with skill and evident pleasure, and was the only servant permitted to weave Madai's designs, a task she was proud of.

In addition to producing fabrics, Mia carried out domestic chores and every evening massaged one of the noblewomen she depended upon. Yet she always appeared ungrudging, often to the point of felicity. Working near women of the *maramba* household in the weaving compound, she enjoyed listening to gossip and often laughed with abandon at Madai's pantomimes. Although definitely beneath and beholden to the family, she did in some ways appear to be a part of it.

105

Mia would sometimes accompany me to the river (*luku*) to bathe in the evenings, as it was improper for women to go alone. At these times I would ask her questions about her life, taking care not to intimidate her. From what I could gather, Mia considered herself fortunate enough, in that she enjoyed weaving and she said the family she served was not too "harsh" (*jangga eti*) with her. She also enjoyed the liveliness (*remi*) of the family compound with the visitors it frequently hosted. Indeed, Mia was more content with her life than many others of her caste. I do not intend, however, to gloss a system of social inequality (which can be quite severe) in relating something of her life.[23]

Once, after Mia told me that she had never been beyond the Parai Mutu area, I asked her if she was curious about the rest of Sumba or other far-off parts of the world. She answered that she would be afraid to go to distant places (*tana maliru*). She added, laughing, that she was even afraid to go down to the river by herself, fearful of spirits of the dead (*da ndewa mameti*) near the water at night. Once, a spirit had pulled her away from the sheltered cove where women bathed, drawing her toward the center of the stream and trying to drown her. Mia reckoned that the unseen culprit was female, because she discerned the smell of indigo (*wau wora*) around her as she was in its grasp. I asked her where she thought the spirit might be from and why it had tried to harm her. She answered:

> I think that it was the soul [*ndewa*] of a woman who died years ago, when I still lived with my parents. This woman didn't have any children. She died. People say that she was angry before she died and that she wasn't given the right kind of burial. Her family wasn't careful about the funeral and so her spirit grew bitter [*njadi paita*] and it stays around this area. There are some dead who do that. We never go out alone at night.

I asked Mia why the spirit had chosen her to accost, and she replied:

> My mother thought it was because she didn't have any children on earth, and she was trying to take me. But maybe the spirit saw I was alone, with nobody to protect me. Another girl from the big house [the household she served in] was with me, but she remained on the bank of the river. We need protection at night. Especially women. We need someone to guard us from dangers [*akatu*].

Mia had told Madai of this mishap the night it happened. Madai listened intently to the story and was inspired to use ghost-like creatures in her fabrics for the first time. Thus, Mia's tale of peril in the river prompted a series of haunting creatures from the family compound in which she lived. Although Mia did not herself create the images, her description of her experience in the grasp of a supernatural being stimulated Madai to try to render such beings in fabric. Whereas Madai delighted in the weird imagery, Mia expressed discomfort with it and did not weave any of the cloths containing the ghost-forms, saying that they disturbed her own spirit.

Aside from the supernatural, Mia was also fearful of earthly situations that were alien to her. She told me that if she went to a village where she was unknown, no one would receive her, and she didn't know what would happen to her then. People might think that she was a crazy person (*tau katoba*), someone wandering aimlessly, with no place to be. She added that she would feel ashamed (*makia*) if she were in the company of a member of the *maramba* household because she would not know how to behave in a strange place.

Along with numerous domestic chores, it fell to Mia to make sure that the oil lamps did not go out inside the house during the night. The people of this household (and region) express fears of the dark (*kapatang*), saying that it facilitates dangerous forces to draw near the sleeping inhabitants. Indeed, sleep (*katuda*) is a state of profound vulnerability, and one should repose in safe environments. Often I blew out the small oil lamp next to my sleeping area, only to awaken an hour or two later to find it relit. Through the night, the lamps cast a soft glow that rose into the lower rafters of the high-peaked roof, illuminating and accentuating recesses and passages.

At times, the family spoke to me of marriage prospects for Mia, from which they would receive a bride price after agreeing to a mate for her. Thus far, she had proved too useful in the household to part with, although the family she served would be able to negotiate for her husband to reside in their area. One young man had been caught sneaking into the kitchen where Mia slept, under the cover of night, a couple of years earlier. Also an *ata*-caste person from a nearby hamlet, the man had been beaten by the oldest son of the *maramba* family for his trespassing. This punishment involved a wooden leg stock kept on the rear family verandah. The youth's legs had been secured in the stock, and he had been lashed on the back several times. From what I could gather, his advances to Mia ceased after that. Whenever Mia heard the story told, she lowered her head and giggled.

107

Bounded by her spatial experience, Mia's world extended from the river in one direction to her parents' hamlet in the other—a distance of perhaps half a kilometer. She reckoned space and direction by the waterway and, despite its dangers, seemed more oriented to it than to the asphalt road beyond the village gate. The road represented another kind of flow, journeying away from comprehension. Although fearful of forces in the river, Mia became more communicative with me at the water's edge. This was at the border of her environs and out of earshot of the household she served. Mia's concept of that world beyond her village was defined by certain dangers and compelled by phenomena such as the density of light. Lightness or darkness conditioned activities and locations, defining beings, actions, and sites. In Mia's imagination (as she expressed it), regions beyond familiar illuminations, waterways, and structures were ominous, not options for increased mobility, prosperity, freedom, or anything she would consider desirable. In terms of a life course, her choices occurred within the confines of her known world. An environment infused by the sounds of banging shuttles, the smells of dye stuffs, and the movements of a nearby river defined the scope of Mia's life.

CHAPTER 6
HAWEWA

After an hour bus ride from Waingapu, I often traveled a narrow road running three kilometers inland from the sea, passing numerous households along the way, and ending at the village of "Hawewa." The village—composed of two distinct sections—includes about six hundred people and is bordered by dry, chalky hills on one side, a river circling around half of the village area, and a government-constructed irrigation canal at the eastern boundary.

The Road to Hawewa

The green landscape along this road is one of relative fertility in East Sumba, with continuous rice paddies fed by the canal and the river. The northern side of the village includes some eccentric megaliths (including likenesses of departed *maramba* in the company of crocodiles, pigs, and dogs) and several high-peaked *uma*. The large house of the reigning *maramba* is central in the village.

Packs of children greet foreign visitors at the main village entrance, chanting "Hello mister! *Kasi pena*" (I.; "Give me a pen"). Lone tourists and tour groups frequently enter Hawewa, and villagers appear ready to sell the visitors textiles, yet are often reticent and confused about how to relate to the tourists. Many village women choose to hide indoors from strangers, sending fabrics for sale out with their sons or young daughters. At the home of the *raja,* tourists sign a guest book and pay a fee (of about fifty cents) to be admitted to the village, where they can walk about and take photographs. The *raja* himself is usually not available, either sleeping, playing cards inside his house, or out surveying the region on his motor bike.

An amiable, phlegmatic man, the elderly *raja* has fallen under considerable criticism by relatives and people from other villages for being lax in the administration of his immediate domain. In recent years, Hawewa has come under pressure from the government for the litter strewn throughout the village and for the unkempt look of its children. A move to "clean up Hawewa" has resulted in a more tidy village, yet the atmosphere of the reigning monarch's home is less industrious than is the case in either Parai Mutu or Wandi. Nevertheless, global influences accent the household—the lone element of decor on the *raja*'s outer front wall asserts a masculine heroic prowess in the form of a poster of Sylvester Stallone from a *Rambo* film. The muscular American action hero strikes a bare-chested, defiant pose against a palm-thatch wall.

The other portion of the village domain sits across a road. High-peaked noble houses, along with the more modest houses of commoners, are arranged in two rows facing a central strip of dusty ground. At one end of this settlement lie large funeral megaliths. In the center is a small, wooden ancestral icon (*katoda*) supported by rocks. Most of the inhabitants of each section of Hawewa adhere to Marapu beliefs and practices.

People say that the bifurcation of the village occurred several decades ago, following a disagreement between two *maramba* brothers concerning a prospective marriage contract of one. After the brother took the controversial bride, he simply founded another village beside his original one. To the present, people are allied to one half or the other of the domain, although considerable interaction takes place between inhabitants.

In contrast to the residence area of the *raja,* there is a concern with tidiness in this portion of the village realm. Many people explain this as the influence of a more fastidious family group of noblewomen, who want to distinguish their households from the unkempt environs of the current *maramba* overlord. Huge banyan and mango trees shade sections of this part of Hawewa, and weavers at looms sit on the verandahs of most homes. The region of Hawewa is famous for a type of weaving known locally as *pahikung* or *pahudu*.[1]

Numerous cloth-producing households sit along the road that leads to the divided village. There are also two churches along this road: the Gereja Kristen Sumba (Sumbanese Christian Church, an outgrowth of the Dutch Reformed Church) and the Bethel Church (an evangelical Protestant denomination brought by American missionaries). People who live next to the road, as opposed to the more secluded villages set back from it, are predominantly Christians and attend one of the two churches nearby.

109

At the beginning of the Hawewa Road, a few kilometers east of the village, is the workshop of a local entrepreneur of mixed Chinese-Sumbanese parentage. About twenty-five women work for him in a concrete structure, producing fabrics of various sizes and styles, which are shipped directly to shops in Bali.

The range of textiles produced by this commercial textile workshop and the divided village of Hawewa reflects the scope of social worlds they emerge from. Although distinctive designs and techniques are particular to the area, the identities and behaviors of the people throughout the region of Hawewa defy unified description—presenting no typical village or villager, much less producer of cloth. The next stories tell of some of the motivations and necessities situating people in relation to threads, dyes, and looms, and subsequently, in interaction with others in the larger community.

Figure 30. Figurative *halenda.*

Rambu Nina's Household

In social relations, an important concept is expressed by the word papa
*("as one hand is to another", that is, "counterpart"). Depending on the
point of view taken, two hands can be seen as a like pair or as an
opposed pair.*

—Marie Jeanne Adams, "Structural Aspects of East Sumbanese Art"

"Rambu Nina" and her cousin "Tabi" created some of the finest supplementary warp, or *pahikung*, cloths in Sumba. Both in their late thirties and never married, the women spent most of their days working on
fabrics on the back verandah of their home, facing out upon a courtyard
of bright pink bougainvillea and wandering pigs.

The road dividing their settlement from that of the *raja* runs just past
the women's yard, and from their porch they observed people or vehicles
passing by. Approaching their home from this lane, I would usually come
upon them sitting on woven palm-frond mats, working on looms. A
maramba household, theirs appeared to be run by women. An aged,
invalid father was usually inside, but Rambu Nina's mother was keenly
observant of the goings on in her compound.

The home of this family neatly combines the new and old. Under a
high, thatched roof typical of traditional homes, the interior is divided
into neatly painted plywood rooms. Pictures of flowers and family photo-

graphs decorate the walls. Numerous female servants live in a kitchen structure behind the home, and one or two share in the work of fabric production.

Early in my fieldwork, as I approached the family compound one morning, Rambu Nina was in the throes of a heated argument with a driver of a hotel vehicle from Waingapu. A Sumbanese employee of Chinese hotel owners, the man had brought a tourist to Hawewa to look at *halenda* (long, narrow cloths worn draped over the shoulder) the village was noted for. The tourist was discerning, and the driver had brought him to the home where the best weaving was done. Speaking some English, the man had functioned as an interpreter between the seller (Rambu Nina) and the tourist. Apparently, after a price was agreed upon between the two parties, the driver demanded from Rambu a rather hefty commission from the sale. An argument ensued, and Rambu Nina finally snatched back the *halenda* (which the driver, as the intermediary, was holding), commanded the agent to leave, and stormed into her house. The driver sullenly returned to his vehicle and quickly drove away, with the hapless tourist in tow.

Following this altercation, Rambu Nina leveled a lengthy, impassioned diatribe against Chinese merchants in Sumba and their agents. She denounced the avarice of outsiders seeking to profit from the fabrics made by villagers. Then she displayed the densely patterned cloth she had nearly sold so that I could see its evident high quality. The price she had settled on with the tourist had been the absolute lowest she could agree to. She was furious at the driver's attempts to profit at her expense and said that he was likely already getting a good fare from his passenger, in addition to his wages from the hotel.

111

Rambu Nina had taken back into her house one of the intricately woven cloths that distinguished her household. The *pahikung* pieces she and her cousin produced were filled with complex motifs appearing in a raised, white succession on backgrounds of indigo blue or rust red. The cousins sometimes applied pale tints of indigo or yellow to some of the white motifs after the pieces are completed, thereby lending the cloth a richness of varied shades. Motifs incorporated into the fabrics were birds, water buffalo (which are not seen in many textiles from East Sumba), elephants, and human figures, in combination with intricate schematic patterns. Most were images historically employed in Hawewa fabrics, taken from pattern guides stored in their home.

Rambu Nina remained unmarried, she told me, by choice, preferring the peace and freedom of occupation she enjoyed in her parents' compound. This, she said, was preferable to being "tied,"[2] with no volition in her life. To illustrate examples of domestic situations she had knowingly avoided, Rambu related travails of other women she knew, especially her cousin "Paeti" (the daughter of a prominent *maramba* family in Hawewa), who had been married to a man ten years before in the village of Parai Mutu.

The story of Paeti's life, in various versions, was well known in the region. As a girl, by all accounts, she had excelled in school and had eventually gone to a university in a city on the island of Java—something no woman in her family had ever imagined doing. After one year, however, Paeti was brought back to Sumba by an uncle and given as a bride. According to Rambu Nina (and others), this was against her will, as she very much wanted to complete her university degree.

A tragic family event took place in Sumba while Paeti was carrying out her studies in Java. After many years of an allegedly abusive marriage, Paeti's mother took her own life. Found in the family home after drinking insecticide, the mother left behind only one child, her daughter in Java. Reasons for Paeti's permanent return to Sumba at that time vary. Rambu Nina claimed that her cousin was forced to marry as a way to bolster the family's alliances and bring in bride wealth and prestige for her widowed father, who had suffered humiliation and blame over his wife's suicide. Paeti herself conceded to others that her own grief caused her to resign herself to family duties and to carrying on customs as her family wanted.

Although not visibly unhappy or abused in her married life in Parai Mutu, Paeti was regarded by Rambu Nina as someone who (despite her intelligence and initiative) got something other than what she wanted in life. When Rambu narrated Paeti's tale, she recounted the historical mistreatment of women in her cousin's family, citing this as evidence that in many cases it was better to live without a husband altogether. Rambu frequently recounted tales of dispirited women as foils to the person she had consciously become. Moreover, she consistently emphasized her own choice in this.

Rambu Nina's cousin and partner in fabric work, Tabi, came to live at the family home some years ago, after a mishap that became one of the tales that has reinforced Rambu's self-sustained independence:

> When Tabi was in her twenties, she went to live with her older sister and her husband, to help with the children and the housework. She lived with them for about one year and then there was a problem. Tabi was pregnant. She finally admitted it was from her sister's husband! I tell you, what a problem that was!

At this point in the story, Rambu Nina paused for questions. My questions had been, "How did Tabi's sister react? Who was in the most trouble— your cousin Tabi or her brother-in-law? What happened then?" Rambu responded:

> With Tabi the older sister was not angry, because she saw her
> as innocent [*nda njala*].[3] But she was very angry with her
> husband, and for a while he had to leave the house and stay
> elsewhere. Later he returned to live with his wife again.
> During this time Tabi was fearful. Almost crazy at one point.
> She wanted to lose the baby before it was born and drank
> teas made of poisonous plants. At that time, I cried and
> begged with Tabi to give me the child to care for. Finally she
> agreed, and came to my family house to have the baby; she
> has lived here for twelve years now and is happy and so is her
> son. But her son is the closest to me.

Now Tabi and Rambu Nina worked as a close-knit family and weaving team, and the tall boy conceived through the infidelity described above often lounged sleepily about the verandah when not at school. The cousins concentrated intensely upon their work in a tightly coordinated camaraderie extending through their fabric production, interactions between themselves or involving others, and the daily routines of their lives. This partnership also structured the way the women related to outsiders in their home-based textile trade.

113

Rambu Nina and Tabi faced agents and merchants with premeditated resolve and were among the most astute sellers of fabrics. Like Madai in the previous chapter, the women would rather realize no sales at all than market their cloths for less than what they deemed them to be worth. Furthermore, they simply did not transact with someone they did not like. Among the ill-favored were a number of hotel drivers and local tourist guides, as well as almost all of the ethnic Chinese merchants on the island. A couple of these dealers, however, had managed to remain in the women's good graces and regularly called at their home for the fine pieces produced there. Through these middlemen, the cousins' fabrics eventually make their way to some of the more exclusive galleries in Bali's tourist centers.

A standing male figure frequently animated the fabrics that Rambu Nina and Tabi produced.[4] In addition to the scarf-like *halenda,* the cousins also created tubular skirts (*lau pahudu*) typical of their village. The bottom panels of the *lau* were graphically decorated (using the *pahikung* technique) with a repetition of this type of figure, in a posture with arms raised upward (in what Adams, 1969, refers to as the "orant" pose), knees slightly bent, and genitals evident. Below the figure was a crayfish or lizard of some sort, which appeared to be biting or licking the genitals.

Although many men in Sumba claimed that the animal in this relation to the human figure symbolized the bestowing of Marapu powers upon the man (and represented how ancestral power carried through male lineages by way of procreation), certain older women in the region told me that the motif had emerged in former times (most were uncertain exactly when) as a joke (*lucuan*, I.) upon men. I heard women from various households of the region whispering (humorously) of the motif's allusions to castration.[5] In fact, a few old women told me that the motif had been invented long ago by a woman in Hawewa to humble her husband.[6] Rambu Nina and Tabi said they did not know the origins or meaning of the motif but were well aware of a certain dual significance it carried.

Weaving for the cousins formed a purpose, a haven, an identity, and a reliable income. While the more sedentary Rambu Nina preferred her family compound, Tabi enjoyed journeying to Waingapu to trade their textiles. Her travels, however, were not marked by the sociability and intrigues of those of Ana Humba of Parai Mutu (although she enjoyed visiting relatives), but took form as resourceful marketing and intense back-room bargaining with selected merchants. Tabi was successful in securing regular commissions in advance from these merchants, who received exclusive rights over the textiles she and her cousin produced. In this way, the two women realized a steady income from their work as they created batches of designs for established clients.

While securing a livelihood from the fabrics they created, the cousins were disinclined to follow the expanded trade routes and social circles the textile trade might also facilitate. Rambu Nina claimed that before the Jakarta exhibit of Sumbanese textiles (mentioned in chapter 4) took place in 1993, she had first been asked (by a Javanese organizer) to appear at the exhibition gallery in the distant city and carry out weaving demonstrations. She had refused, however, because at that time the funeral of a relative was to take place. The cousins (and the entire family) adhered to Marapu customs, and it would be unthinkable for them not to attend funerary rites for departed kin.

Many people in eastern Sumba, including Christian converts, are loathe to abandon duties toward the dead. Concern for protocol regarding departed relatives not only maintains certain quality control of the textiles buried with the deceased, but also firmly anchors people to ancestral places. Such concerns bound Rambu Nina to her village.

After Rambu Nina declined participation in the Jakarta textile exhibition, which would have required travel to a distant place and an absence of several weeks from her village, Rambu Hamu of Wandi had agreed to attend the event. The Hawewa cousins were eventually highly critical, however, of the fact that Rambu Hamu of Wandi had been spokesperson and representative for eastern Sumbanese culture at large. Rambu Nina claimed that Rambu Hamu's statements on textiles and culture (which were printed in a widely circulated Jakarta newspaper and read by many in Sumba) was only marginally applicable to Wandi and also reflected what Javanese officials had wanted to hear.

The cousins complained that the Javanese sponsors of the exhibition had solicited simplistic representations of traditional village life, which ignored variations between regions. They resented having been collapsed into one homogenized "Culture of Sumba" by a single representative from their island. Moreover, Rambu Hamu did not descend from a family of textile producers, as did the Hawewa women, and in their views had no business representing the general region (by way of weaving) to outsiders. The cousins protested that their Wandi rival was not *langataka* (genuinely local with roots in the past), and they felt that they had been misrepresented in Jakarta.[7]

Both women felt that they might best distinguish their household by continuing to produce high-quality fabrics and by controlling the market for those they created. A self-consciousness of being "genuine" emerged from their comments and conversations, as a means of setting themselves apart from others. Rambu Nina and Tabi each commented that they were maintaining the integrity of local textiles in the face of commercialism. At the same time, they enjoyed specifically local and noble identities through their creations.

115

The cousins both stayed within and expanded upon historical and local notions of gendered roles and place. While neither aspired to the wider circles of Rambu Hamu, Biba, or Ana Humba depicted in earlier chapters, they did persist in a deliberate command of their lives and movements. Rambu Nina and Tabi also maintained, consciously, a conservatism in their enterprise and demeanor. This overlapped a steadfastness in business practices and life choices and an ongoing resistance to male authority. Indeed, Rambu Nina in particular had a reputation locally as a kind of contrarian. She, like Madai, Ana Humba, and numerous women in eastern Sumba, had not moved personally along the circles of exchange in marriage. Although their uncle, the village *raja*, generally receives the deferences typical toward someone of his rank from most people in the Hawewa domain, the cousins often poked fun at the elderly monarch, ridiculing what they considered the inept manner in which he administered the village. Within an overtly patriarchal system, the two women had composed and maintained a system of power and identity for themselves based in their own interpretations of their community and the world.

Figure 31. A *halenda* by Martha.

The Devout Martha

> *Each region has its own affective value. Under the influence of diverse sentiments, it is connected with special religious principles, and consequently it is endowed with virtues* sui generis *which distinguish it from all others.*
>
> —Emile Durkheim and Marcel Mauss, *Primitive Classification*

"Martha's" presence along the road to Hawewa was not to be ignored. As I walked by her modest house of plaited palm fronds one day, she shouted to me, insisting that I approach her verandah. As I did so, she rolled out a *topu* (a woven palm leaf mat that serves as furniture in Sumbanese homes) and invited me to "sit and share in a chew of betel nut" (*mandapu pahapa*). She then commenced without prompting to synopsize the story of her life.

Martha sat on her porch for most of the daylight hours, weaving largely uniform, market-quality *halenda*. Her house is surrounded by fruit trees, and the front verandah faces upon the road. People often stopped in if they saw her, or Martha called to pedestrians as they passed. Although uncertain of the exact year she was born, Martha estimated her age to be sixty-seven. This reckoning corresponded to the year a mango tree was planted outside her parents' home, in the past often a custom that followed the birth of a child. While her precise chronology was indefinite, Martha was something of a regional historian, and she gave many accounts of past relations and conditions in the Hawewa region. Active in numerous community endeavors, she also acted as caretaker to the Bethel Church, which sat next to her home.

Born into a commoner-caste household, Martha married at sixteen and over the years gave birth to ten children (six of whom survived infancy). She then began to fall ill, acquiring what she described as a kind of arthritis that caused paralysis of her right arm. Until she was in her forties, Martha followed Marapu beliefs and customs along with the people of her hamlet. When her health declined, someone from another village suggested to her that she try Christian prayer. Martha met with a local pastor, learned the method of praying on her own behalf, and then began

116

periodically attending the local Protestant church, the Gereja Kristen Sumba, on Sundays. After several months of prayer and churchgoing, she made a complete recovery from the pain and paralysis that had burdened her for years. She attributed this to the Christian god, and formally converted to Protestantism.

Her husband, however, stubbornly refused to accept the new faith, and continued with Marapu ways. After a few years of his resistance, as Martha tells it, a certain sickness entered the soil:

> I'll tell you that Satan [*Setan*, I.) was in our soil. It became
> white and all of the trees and crops began to sicken and die.
> We nearly starved. I prayed so hard then. All of the plants
> were yellow. Even the tree that was planted at my birth near-
> ly died. I told my husband, "You see, this is because you are
> still Marapu. This is because you believe like the village
> people and pray to a stone [*watu*—referring to a stone and
> wood ancestral altar, a *katoda*]. If you convert, maybe God
> will listen to my prayers and help us."

At that point, her husband countered that Marapu believers also revered a supreme being and that it was likely the same one that the Christians prayed to.[8] Martha argued that this was not the case: the Christian god had no connection with anything Marapu. If her husband wanted the benefits of this god, he would have to follow the faith completely, abandoning Marapu in the process. Finally her husband complied. Then, as Martha explained, things began to change:

117

> After my husband became a Protestant, things improved
> greatly around here for us. At that time, someone from the
> government also came to help us. He gave us something to
> put in the soil. Things got better and I know it was because
> God finally heard and helped us. I believe this one hundred
> percent! And I know that prayer and hard work are the ways
> to health and prosperity in this life. This is what many of the
> lazy village people have to learn.

The evangelical Protestant movement spread through eastern Sumba in the 1970s, and Martha became a follower after the small Bethel Church (one of a number on the island originally funded by American missionaries) was erected on a plot of land next to her house. She soon became instrumental in finding new converts and in organizing events involving the church. She also functioned as its caretaker.

In 1994, Martha was producing a steady supply of relatively small black-and-white *pahikung halenda,* which she sold to various agents from around the island. Although competently made, the pieces were far simpler in design and thus more quickly produced than those produced by the noblewomen of Hawewa. The yarns were purchased at the market, the black ones already chemically dyed. Martha's *halenda* sometimes ended up in articles of clothing, such as shoulder bags or vests, in tourist boutiques of Bali (see plate 20). While largely unaware of the sartorial outcome of the fabrics she created, Martha nonetheless produced them with an ideological fervor that suggested a Sumbanese rendition of the Protestant work ethic.

Because her elderly husband was in poor health and was unable to work (although she claimed that if it were not for her vigilant prayer, he would be dead), Martha largely supported the household through her weaving. Sitting on the front verandah of her home for much of the day, she wove continually and chatted to whoever was present. The designs decorating her pieces were mostly of a human figurative type seen in the Hawewa region—frontward facing, with upraised arms and bent knees.

The genitals and attendant lizards evident in the fabrics of Rambu Nina and Tabi, however, were absent from Martha's cloth. Affected by the sexual puritanism of the Bethel Church, Martha removed these elements from her designs. Her figures were thus neutered and the reptiles that stood beneath them abbreviated into diamond shapes or completely omitted.[9] Martha intentionally excluded the genitals of her human figures and referred to this change in distinguishing herself as a Christian convert:

> We Christians do things another way in our cloths. We feel shame at some of the designs of the past. We don't think in a *pagan* [*kafir,* I.][10] way any longer. I can still weave a picture of a man, but not like the Marapu people do it. I made those kind of pictures before, but not now.

Martha did not make a direct verbal reference to genitals or overt nakedness, but these were what she had avoided in reformulating her motifs. Each week she would carry a stack of cloths to the public market a few kilometers from her home and usually sell most of them. She enjoyed market day because it afforded lively conversation with friends and acquaintances, receiving and passing on information about events in the community.

Every Friday morning at the dusty, open-air market, among the scores of other people laying out goods, from factory-made clothing imported from Java to local garden produce, Martha sat on a stool and waited for people to approach her; these usually included a few Chinese agents from Waingapu. Someone who also came almost every week was

Ana Humba of Parai Mutu. She would buy four or five of Martha's pieces and then would attempt to resell them either in her village to incoming tourists or in Waingapu. Martha would speak about her travails and her prayers to Ana Humba (who she realized was a Christian) and nod approvingly as the Parai Mutu woman took her leave, carrying several *halenda*s with her. In Martha's estimation, Ana Humba exemplified one redeemed from the *kafir* ways of traditional village religion and was also a moral maverick as the only Christian convert in her family. Moreover, Martha viewed the younger woman's travels about the island as evidence of a kind of enterprise she admired. She was unaware, of course, of other aspects of Ana Humba's ventures.

After the weekly market day, Martha always boarded one of the numerous *bemo*s of the region. As a passenger, she would remark disapprovingly upon the loud pop music and the posters of half-naked rock stars in the small van that transported her back to the Hawewa road. She would also compete with the raucous tunes, delivering an impassioned commentary on the local state of things, a kind of mobile sermonizing she indulged in after a heady day of selling her cloth.

The Sing Ha Workshop

> *Economic innovators . . . are Janus-like: halfway between the past and the future, they face in both directions. It is their ability to operate at once in the traditional world of established custom and in the modern world of systematic economic rationality which is their chief resource.*
> —Clifford Geertz, *Peddlers and Princes*

119

At a crossroads of the main road from Waingapu and the road to the village region of Hawewa, behind a general store, sat the Sing Ha textile workshop. Inside a concrete complex constructed around a central courtyard, as many as twenty-five women worked on fabrics. The workshop was divided into eight rooms, containing workers and projects, with dye stuffs, pots, and wooden racks filling the courtyard.

Figure 32. Weaving in a factory environment.

The Sing Ha workshop was an example of perhaps ten enterprises of its sort in East Sumba in the mid-1990s. Functioning as small textile factories, these enterprises were mostly operated by ethnic Chinese entrepreneurs employing Sumbanese village women. In the case of the Sing Ha endeavor, the owner was half Chinese and half Sumbanese. From his mixed ethnicity, Sing Ha enjoyed business connections with Chinese relations in and away from Sumba, as well as family links to cloth makers in the Hawewa region.

Women employed at the workshop were among the poorest people in the area, yet all were skilled at textile processes, taught by their families or as servants in *maramba* households. Some of these women had fled from their villages to escape arranged marriages. Others were divorced and without other means of support. Reliant upon the workshop for their sustenance, the women slept on mats in the small rooms where they worked. Windowless to the outside world, most rooms opened in upon the central courtyard.

Textiles from this factory were medleys of all the motifs and techniques to come out of East Sumba. Like some of the more baroque pieces produced in Wandi, Sing Ha's fabrics contained myriad images and embellishments, in attempts to attract foreign consumers with an overwhelming montage of forms. Created through the *ikat* process and the *pahikung* techniques, some fabrics were made of multiple, alternating strips of the two types of weaving, resulting in a patchwork effect.

120

Dyes at Sing Ha's workshop were often a mixture of natural and chemical, although some high-priced cloths were produced using only plant dyes. Colors were the same as those used in most villages, and an indigo dye pot occupied a lone site beyond the concrete confines of the complex. Following custom, the blue-tinted earthenware vessel sat isolated in a special processing area at the edge of a yard, well behind the building.

Maramba families in the region ridiculed cloth from this workshop as haphazard in design, with no historical links to any particular village domain or household. Moreover, these same critics noted the scrambled mixture of women who produced the fabrics and their alienation from village environments. Women such as Rambu Nina and Tabi of Hawewa (as well as Madai of Parai Mutu) asked indignantly how the Sing Ha textiles could be sold to unaware tourists as creations coming out of traditional Sumbanese villages.[11] Yet Sing Ha was remarkably successful in marketing his fabrics to shops in Bali, where they were touted to foreigners—in their very flamboyance—as masterworks of Sumbanese weaving.

Weavers at Sing Ha's establishment worked three or more to a room, sitting on the floor on palm-frond mats. There was less of the relaxed sociability of weaving environments on village verandahs; in fact, some of the women appeared sullen in the dim light of their work quarters. If a Marxist example might be given of workers alienated from the means of production, the women at the Sing Ha enterprise could personify this. Moreover, most had also been alienated from their homes and villages, which in Sumba embody the means of production of most producers of cloth. In their isolated, cell-like work areas, the women occupied environments acutely removed from those enjoyed by weavers at village homes. The Sing Ha workers carried on a village craft, born of a type of sedentary sociality that typifies the days of many women in Sumba, within the dramatically different concrete confines of a factory environment.

When Sing Ha spoke to me of his enterprise, he used Indonesian terms of modernization such as *"produksi"* (production) and the all-encompassing concept of *"kemajuan"* (progress). He also said that he was aware that people in America and Europe no longer wove their own cloth by hand, that they were completely advanced and employed mechanization, like people in Hong Kong and Singapore. He reckoned himself as one of a generation of pioneering entrepreneurs—combining traditional production methods with modern ideology and organization in creating a Sumbanese textile factory.

121

The small factory had come to be a self-enclosed, female hamlet of sorts, with those within its boundaries looking downward toward looms or inward toward the courtyard. What is more, the women were easily surveyable in their workrooms from the central courtyard.[12] Sing Ha exercised power through a controlled environment—by structuring the possibilities of social interactions and spatial perspectives within it. While I never heard reports of the entrepreneur's behaving harshly to the weavers in his employment, his surveillant authority was central in the constricted confines of his factory, which bounded the worlds within it to a far greater degree than did most village environments.

For the women, living on their own and working at an enterprise outside of historical family or village circles was a distinctly recent phenomenon in Sumba. Like the Malay village women who worked in the much larger, Japanese-owned factories of Aiwa Ong's study (1987), the Sumbanese women were also the focus of community speculation and gossip regarding their displacement from normal family circumstances. Often villagers hinted that they were "immoral women" (*kawini kajari*), outside the bounds of local propriety. Unlike the Malaysian workers, however, the Hawewa Road workshop women did not dress in an outlandish way by local standards or venture out much in the community. The women who lived at the workshop spent most of their time within its confines. Yet curiosity and tales about who the women were and how they had come to be employed at Sing Ha's enterprise pervaded the surrounding community.

Along with a number of disenfranchised women from various villages, a few relatives of Sing Ha also created cloth, including a teen-aged niece who had been too unruly for her parents in Waingapu and was sent to work for her uncle. In the company of these women, although isolated within a small room of her own, was an apparently autistic adult daughter of Sing Ha, who would periodically peer out from the curtain that covered her window to the courtyard and shout emotionally toward whoever stood near.

Sing Ha (in his fifties) grew up in the region of Hawewa, but his father was from a family of Chinese storekeepers in Waingapu. His mother had been of commoner caste from Hawewa village, and the couple had married against the will of both families.[13] Nonetheless, merchant relatives assisted Sing Ha's father in setting up a small general store in the town of Melolo, behind which the family lived. Growing up, Sing Ha participated in both the village world of Hawewa and the shopkeeping world of his Chinese relations, without completely belonging to either. Sing Ha credits his dual marginality for instilling self-initiative while providing him with the benefits of both worlds:

> When I was a boy my father's family always said that it was a shame that I was so dark-skinned, like the Sumba people. I was the only child in my family who had dark skin. And when I visited Hawewa with my mother, they all made fun of my Chinese face. Then I got older and I turned everything to my advantage. I combined Chinese business ability with the textile skills and family connections of the Sumba villagers.

He eventually became a trader, married a Chinese woman from Waingapu, took over his father's store, and in the mid-1980s initiated the textile workshop behind it. Ana, Sing Ha's older sister, became a superb cloth-maker (through studying with her mother and aunts in Hawewa) and in the early days assisted in the workshop and the designs to come out of it. After a few years, she opened her own shop in Waingapu, prospered, and eventually moved to Bali, where she now has an "art shop" in the tourist region of Kuta Beach. Sing Ha regularly supplied her with fabrics from his small factory, and Ana also acted as an agent in selling his cloths to other shops in Bali. Sing Ha had been to Bali himself numerous times, and although he took on airs of cosmo-

122

politanism through his sojourns, he generally preferred life in his family compound.

The entrepreneur prided himself on being a progressive and virtuous man and spoke of his enterprise as not simply a business venture, but also a philanthropic undertaking:

> I produce many textiles from my factory and I also give
> employment to some very poor village women. Many have no
> place to go, and if they are good at making cloth, I take them
> in. And many of them have been referred to me by the local
> pastor [from the Bethel Church], after they have had some
> serious problems in their villages. Then they come to stay
> here and they have work and food and a place to sleep.

Sing Ha was influenced some years ago by his sister, Ana, to join the evangelical church and was among a growing number of Chinese followers. Bethel sermons emphasize enterprise and abundance, and ministers often preach parables that conflate prosperity with virtue. Moreover, the church provides a certain affiliation with Americanism,[14] a modern vision of abundance many Chinese in Sumba choose to identify with, rather than with village cultures of the region. The church also facilitates a number of business connections among its members involving followers in other areas of Indonesia.

Although many indigenous Sumbanese (such as Martha) also belonged to the Bethel Church, they were less inclined to create wide-ranging business links through it than were Chinese members.[15] Whereas the Dutch-influenced Gereja Kristen Sumba had, in my observation, permitted considerable syncretism between Christianity and animism, the Bethel Church generally regards traditional Sumbanese beliefs and practices with censure. Hence, followers of this church (whether ethnic Chinese or converts such as Martha) often distinguished themselves more emphatically from indigenous village people.

Sing Ha identified with the Chinese merchant class and drew sharp divisions between himself and local villagers. In the late 1980s, he fell out with his Hawewa relatives (the result of a textile business agreement gone sour), and the village guarded their fabrics from him after that. Some villagers, such as Rambu Nina and Tabi, regarded Sing Ha with consternation and bitterly resented his copying of clan motifs. With the constant reinvention of designs by women in his workshop, however, the entrepreneur was not at a loss for ideas and images. His productions continued, elaborating upon previous designs. Sing Ha's concrete compound, a kind of haven for some of its weavers, also spatially situated them worlds apart from much of their former lives.

Worlds Apart

The lives of the Sing Ha textile workers could fill a volume in themselves. As might be expected, there was a degree of turnover in the workshop, as women were reconciled with parents or mates or left to become servants in other households. As such, there is no neat collection of "just-so stories" to describe the factory community, but a couple of glimpses of women within it should prove illuminating.

One young woman I came to know, Lina, had fled her village in the west of the island, in resistance to a family-arranged marriage. Lina wove cloth in the compound and helped with the cooking for the rest of the women. Highly energetic, she welcomed the opportunity to talk, and on a few Sunday afternoons, she walked with me along the road to Hawewa. Lina told, dramatically, of how she had stealthily escaped her family village one night, riding a bus across Sumba and arriving in Waingapu at three o'clock in the morning with two thousand rupiah in her pocket (then about one American dollar). She proceeded to find employment as a laundress in a Chinese-run hotel. After several months, Lina left the hotel when a situation was arranged for her at Sing Ha's small factory.

Lina had been working at the workshop for almost a year in early 1993; she spoke of saving money and eventually going to Timor or Bali, the two distant locations she had heard local people speak about. When she had lived in Waingapu, Lina had been impressed by the demand for things Sumbanese by the tourists staying at hotels. Lina imagined that she might be able to improve her own condition through this market. She had come to Sing Ha's, she said, to develop her fabric skills and to learn some of the textile techniques specific to eastern Sumba. Such skills would enable her to find work in a metropolitan center or, she imagined, perhaps start her own textile business one day. Lina had noticed the clothing some of the tourists wore, fashioned from a variety of fabrics produced in Indonesia, including Sumba. Inspired by tales of Bali and Timor she had overheard local men telling at the Waingapu hotel where she had worked, Lina envisioned a metamorphosis for herself on the islands. She regarded her employment at the workshop as an apprenticeship while imagining a quite different future for herself.

A more sullen weaver at the workshop was called The Quiet One (Tau Kamandi) by her co-workers. From a distant village, this woman had worked at Sing Ha's small factory for several years. Some said that she was divorced, but the facts of her life history were mysterious, although a few workshop women told me that she had been driven from her village because of witchery. She was an excellent weaver and sat for long hours at her loom.

The silent woman was somber, and although she tolerated others around her, preferred to work in solitude. She was especially good at *pahikung* weaving and concentrated intensely on her work, which was always the most complex of any to emerge from the workshop. She had established something of a space for herself in the complex, and wove in the one room that had ample light. Others at the workshop (including Sing Ha and his wife) reported that Tau Kamandi had not left the compound since she had arrived sometime in the late 1980s. Sing Ha said that she would probably spend the rest of her life in his employment.

Although the Sing Ha weavers were allowed to take Sundays off, Tau Kamandi spent her Sundays as any other day and continued to weave in her workroom. Everyone in the compound would attend the Bethel Church in the morning (a kind of requisite for the resident women), while the quiet woman would remain behind. In the largely deserted quarters, the sounds of the lone weaver's shuttle would join those of the rants of Sing Ha's daughter as the two cloistered women went about their day.

125

PART THREE: SHUTTLING BETWEEN WORLDS

Anyone can own anything from anywhere.
—Sally Price, *Primitive Art in Civilized Places*

The previous chapters have described episodes in the lives of specific people of eastern Sumba as they are connected in some way with fabrics. The next two chapters enter environments where the lives and creations of some of these people converge with those from the outside world. These meetings follow the intersecting routes of textile trade and international tourism and take place on and away from the island. As we have seen, connections with foreigners long have been markers of status for people in Sumba. Examples of recent connections follow—in their numerous manifestations.

Sally Price's statement on a current global condition characterizes something of the relationship in which, at least in East Sumba, the local and the foreign meet. With a growing awareness that image is reality in their presentations of themselves to outsiders, many Sumbanese exploit the yearnings that draw foreign seekers into their villages. The tension between outsiders and insiders—between knowledge and ignorance—is the currency with which various Sumbanese pursue and sometimes realize profit. Gaps in information and forms of desire are interpreted and exploited in constructing images for a global consumer culture, images that often reflect the nature and variety of the links between a "first world" discourse and a "third world" response.

The kinds of knowledge arising from encounters with outsiders differs greatly among people involved in textile production and trade in Sumba, yet each person devises schemes toward empowerment in local settings. Although the previous recounting of Umbu Pari's kangaroo motifs, Martha's neutered figures, and Ana Humba's adventurous travel itineraries may seem like isolated tales of eccentricity, they are examples (among many) of individual acts toward reformulating identities in an ever-changing world. Inasmuch as such acts are facilitated or thwarted by the commerce and lore in which people participate, the conceptual and political worlds of East Sumba's social mix becomes articulated in a variety of gestures and episodes that enlist (or resist) new forces in local life.

Plate 1. Flaunting fabrics for sale to outsiders from a village verandah, Prailiu.

Plate 2. Musicians and dancers in local cloth (and imported shirts) at a village festival.

Plate 3. A weekly market during the dry season in eastern Sumba.

Plate 4. An *ikat hinggi* (seen in half its length) draped over a line. Motifs include crocodiles, birds, and skull trees. Design on the other side is identical.

Plate 5. An *ikat*-clad statue of Christ beckoning in front of a church in Waingapu.

Plate 6. A *maramba* couple poses at a family grave. The husband wears a *hinggi* set (across his shoulder and on his lower body) and a headcloth *(tera)* in combination with a "Sumba" T-shirt. His wife wears a *lau* with a blouse imported from Jakarta. On her head sits a tortoiseshell comb.

Plate 7. A fabric-draped coffin holds the body of a woman wrapped in fifty *ikat hinggi*. The body is removed from the box at the grave, then buried in all of the fabrics that wrap it.

Plate 8. A *patola* trade cloth (from the Gujarat area of India) owned by a noble family in East Sumba. Although the age of this cloth is uncertain, similar fabrics were trading through the Indonesian archipelago since at least the fifteenth century. They are especially prized as prestige goods in Sumba. Note the undyed warp in the background with some motifs that have been bound in palm frond strips, showing images similar to those of the *patola* cloth.

Plate 9. *Ikat* method: binding sections of the cotton warp with strips of dried palm leaf.

Plate 10. *Pahikung* (supplementary warp) method on side panels bordering a central panel of *ikat* cloth.

Plate 11. Weaving *pahikung* side panels using sticks *(lidi)* to raise the extra warp threads. The same weft thread will weave through the central *ikat* panel, joining all sections as a seamless cloth.

Plate 12. Two village girls wearing *lau* created through *ikat* and *pahikung* techniques and also featuring beadwork.

Plate 13. Design inspired by a European museum catalogue of "tribal" art. These figures likely originated from pictures of Dayak textiles from Kalimantan (Borneo).

Plate 14. *Hinggi*s on display near village graves in anticipation of a European tour group's arrival.

Plate 15. Biba's angel cloth, combining Christian and Marapu imagery in modern recombination of religious sentiments.

Plate 16. Pieces inspired by pictures of old Sumba textiles in European museum catalogues.

Plate 17. A tale told through the length of a cloth, proceeding from the top to the bottom. Here a narrative unfolds, beginning with consultation with the ancestors at a clan house (here in four-fold), followed by a nobleman with attendants setting out on horse-back to go to war (note skull trees), culminating with a riotous battle in the lower section. Such cloths began to appear in Sumba in the 1980s.

Plate 18. Dancers at a *pameran* (I., exhibition), a fabric and culture fair for tourists visiting Sumba.

Plate 19. A yellow-tinted "primitive" textile for sale to tourists hangs from a tree.

Plate 20. *Pahikung* cloth from East Sumba transformed into handbags in a boutique in Bali. Cloth from the island of Timor, to the east of Sumba, is folded on the shelf below.

CHAPTER 7
WORLDS CONVERGE

Communities are to be distinguished, not by their falsity/genuineness,
but by the style in which they are imagined.
                    —Benedict Anderson, *Imagined Communities*

Authenticity, too, is something sought, fought over, and reinvented.
              —Edward M. Bruner, "Epilogue, Creative Persona
                            and the Problem of Authenticity"

A convergence of worlds occurred every other week in eastern Sumba in the mid-1990s, in organized cultural displays (*pameran,* I.; exhibition) for foreign tour groups. Rife with intense competition between local people, these events took shape over a couple of hours as impromptu settlements. *Pameran* spaces became international carnivals where people claimed regions of ground for themselves in makeshift mercantile settings. Moreover, *pameran*s proceeded as stages: carefully calculated personas were displayed along with fabrics as visions and desires of locals and tourists became entwined. As Toby Volkman concludes regarding the nature of tourist events in Toraja, Sulawesi, "Tourism implies a distinctive sort of gaze. That gaze may become a model for local gazes too, put to work along with other kinds of cultural visions and revisions" (1990:91).[1] This chapter focuses on a field that incorporates many gazes.

The Pameran

In August of 1993, a large bus with "Party Doll" written on its side parked at the entrance of the village of Lambanapu, and twenty-five foreigners hesitantly disembarked. After months of drought, the ground sent up clouds of dust as the squinting tourists descended to an explosion of rhythmic music and frenzied dance. A group of fabric-draped men and women wielding swords and daggers with mock ferocity beckoned the startled visitors into the village center, to the sounds of accompanying drums and gongs. Clad in shorts and summer hats, the tourists held cameras of various sorts. This particular group had come with the *Spice Islands* cruise ship, which circled the Lesser Sunda Islands once a month. Sunburnt Europeans, Americans, and Australians exited the tour bus, most of middle or retirement age.

The rosy cluster of tourists followed the dancers to benches circling an arena near the center of the village.[2] Two local guides gave welcoming speeches in English. Several lively dances proceeded, culminating with a

Figure 33. Locals and tourists meeting in a place contoured by cloth.

line of fetching young women, clad in elaborate fabrics, swaying slowly to the rhythm of drums while carrying baskets of betel nut toward the uneasy visitors. The guide then explained the social significance of offering betel and laboriously instructed the increasingly worried tourists in how to use it. Most refused the stimulant as it was offered to them, but a few tentatively tried it, soon spitting it onto the ground. The tourists expressed squeamish distaste and also humor among themselves. They were closely scrutinized by chuckling villagers.

Typically consisting of regional music, dances, and mock rituals such as weddings, a *pameran* is staged in the center of a village by people

dressed in traditional finery.[3] The tourist group (which arrives by chartered bus) watches the performances, listens to commentary by (usually)
Dutch- or English-speaking tour leaders, then wanders about the village to
view hundreds of textiles displayed for sale. The number of tourists might
vary from as few as fifteen to as many as a hundred. One of three competing Waingapu hotels coordinated the events with villagers and a foreign
tour company. Tour groups attending *pamerans* were often from cruise
ships and represented the wealthiest foreigners to visit Sumba.

Village homes sat outside the center cordoned off for performances.
Visitors participated in a "cultural center" constructed for them, with
local centers, the clan homes, viewed from a distance. In turn, most
villagers observed the tourist groups from afar, forming a larger circle
around a smaller one and enjoying another performance altogether.

In the disparity of worlds of villagers and visitors, a play of stark
differences emerged. In the grass-fringed recesses of their verandahs, local
people chewed betel nut and peered out under thatched eaves—at the
framed tourist space fleetingly manifested in the village plaza. There they
also viewed the regional "movers and shakers" of the textile and tourism
trades—touts, guides, hoteliers, entrepreneurs—presenting and selling the
"culture" of Sumba to the foreigners. A *pameran* was a play of worlds in
tenuous overlap, with the vendors and villagers watching the tourists
watch re-creations of Sumbanese village culture—a kind of nested puzzle
of reflexivity.[4]

A Labyrinthine Bazaar

Early in the day of a *pameran*, a dozen or more *bemos* would enter a
village, filling the air with dust and a clash of discordant music. Numerous
vendors arrived in the vehicles, carrying their cloth and artifacts in bags
or with a colorful assortment of rolled fabrics stacked and tied to the top
of the vans. Sellers attending a *pameran* ran the social gamut of textile
traders in East Sumba, from small vendors who frequented hotels to more
affluent shopkeepers and entrepreneurs.

Hopeful traders would descend from the *bemos* and quickly claim
areas of ground on which to set up displays. Hanging numerous clotheslines over which they draped their cloths, some suspended *hinggis* in
their full lengths from trees. By midmorning, a multitude of fluttering
cloths created a labyrinth of colorfully pictorial backdrops and territorial
zones for the vendors as they awaited the arrival of potential buyers.
Flurry and excitement animated the spaces between the hundreds of
banner-like fabrics as rumors circulated concerning the number, nation-
alities, and affluence of foreigners due to arrive.

Family groups usually displayed their goods in the same area, creating

133

Figure 34. Villagers behind the scenes watching tourists watching villagers.

134

temporary communities bounded by walls of cloth. A compelling curiosity spread among the sellers regarding who exactly was selling what to whom and which vendors were profiting the most. Younger men of each vending group eventually meandered throughout the labyrinthine bazaar, spying on rivals and attempting to lure tourists toward their own merchandise. Space, discourse, and intentions all interplayed within an architectural domain of cloth to create a lively mix of interrelationships.

When the group from the *Spice Islands* cruise ship entered Lambanapu, about a hundred hopeful vendors (perhaps three-quarters of them from other villages) awaited them within the multihued maze of cloth. Normally a small, quiet village with no major road running through it, Lambanapu had been transformed into an international bazaar. After the dances and music ceased, the tourists entered the textile labyrinth; for local people, this was when the real excitement began.

History according to Luka

An unusually long and graphic *hinggi* hung from the branches of a banyan tree and waved slowly in the breeze. The swaying motion enlivened images of people and animals along five woven meters, and several tourists stood gazing up at the elaborate cloth. An elderly Dutchman was sternly appraising the piece in a low voice to his wife, who admired the design in its length. Other tourists paused to look at the *hinggi*, then passed on to view some of the other suspended fabrics facing in every direction.

After observing the onlookers, Luka stepped from behind his woven panorama and greeted a small group of viewers with a broad smile and the statement (in English), "I design this *hinggi*." Two Australian women readily engaged with the Wandi artist, asking a series of questions about the motifs in the cloth and the techniques in its production. Luka augmented his answers with the assertion that he was the son of a king and knew firsthand the history and meanings behind local fabrics. The women's interest waned, however, after Luka told them his price for the *hinggi*, which was, according to the tourists, three times what they had been told by their guide was a fair price for a "Sumba cloth." The Dutch couple lingered, however, and the man suddenly offered Luka one-third of his asking price.

Luka did not balk at this paltry offer, as low bids were often part of the bargaining process involving fabrics and foreigners. To further promote the *hinggi*, he claimed this was a "special piece" among the hundreds at the *pameran*. Besides being the longest and most visually complex *hinggi*, Luka's also possessed tremendous archival value—in telling the history of Sumba. Not only did the textile embody a wealth of privileged motifs, but it told a specific story through time—as a woven reification of "Sumba culture." He promoted his cloth by announcing in English, "This is only one like this here today. Longest cloth and longest story. Here you have whole story of Sumba. You have whole culture of Sumba! From first people here! Only I give this story. Only I use these colors [a claim to the originality of his dyes]."

The tourist continued to offer his price, but Luka retorted that his piece was worth much more. He reemphasized its value in not only telling the "whole story of Sumba" but also in the number of rarified symbols it employed—motifs until recently forbidden to anyone below *maramba* rank. The Dutchman appeared unmoved by such historical and sumptuary claims and began to walk away, after raising his offer slightly and declaring that this was his "last price." As Luka refused the offer, he huffed off and Luka called angrily after him, "You have history of Sumba in this cloth, Mister! Even the first people here! You can't have all that for cheap price!" Indifferent to Luka's claims, the tourists disappeared from sight.

Luka grew sullen after the passing of the Dutch couple and commented on how stingy (*kikir*, I.) Dutch tourists always were. He complained that the quality and meaning of local fabrics were of no importance to such people, who were only concerned with cheap prices.[5] Because of these tourists and their stupidity, he went on, the number of good fabrics was declining, while inferior textiles were everywhere. Several other tourists looked at his narrative *hinggi* during the hour allowed for touring the village, but there were no buyers on this day. To each prospective customer Luka stressed the same qualities of his piece: its links to a history of the island and the profound meanings inherent in its motifs.

Cultural Capital

Beyond Luka's selling territory stood Umbu Pari, dressed stylishly in a T-shirt and jeans and an *ikat* headcloth (*tera*). He was displaying fabrics of varying qualities from Parai Mutu. Smoking and leaning against a hut with an air of nonchalance, Umbu Pari observed the activities around him and studied tourists approaching his area. When the two Australian women who had originally looked at Luka's piece paused to see his fabrics, Umbu Pari began speaking to them in English. He casually uncoiled the headpiece he was wearing and held it at full-length for the women to see. The central section was decorated with a schematic design typical of local cloth; the ends contained several kangaroos. Umbu Pari explained his upcoming textile exhibition in Australia to the women. As they showed interest, he went on to boast of his connections with foreign galleries and collectors.

136

Exhibiting but a few pieces on this day, Umbu Pari commented to me that he had actually come to pass the time and look at the tourists. Selling at a *pameran* is not a prestigious undertaking for high-ranking Sumbanese. In fact, it is demeaning for nobles to actively participate in a local marketplace, even one that involves foreigners. Genuine prestige is achieved through off-island transactions, and Umbu Pari's demeanor at this local event let it be known that he was accustomed to far more grand milieus.[6]

Umbu Pari had designed his own business cards (which featured a stylized skull tree), and he distributed these freely to tourists he spoke with, asking for their cards in return.[7] At this *pameran*, he obtained the business card of an American woman living in Bali and later showed the card proudly to other Sumbanese men standing nearby. Because of their relative wealth and accessibility, Westerners living in Indonesia were valuable acquaintances. Resident Americans in particular were often hospitable to itinerant traders from the eastern islands, unlike most well-to-do Indonesians of Bali and Java.[8]

Vendors and Variables

Most vendors at the *pameran* were men, although a few Lambanapu women were visible and vocal in marketing their cloth. One local woman loudly groused that too many outsiders had flooded the village to compete with local people in sales to tourists. She lamented that the people in her village were suffering the imposition of the foreigners, but not profiting from the invasion. Others largely ignored her and went on, sometimes aggressively, peddling their fabrics. Latecomers without their own selling spaces followed the Westerners and doggedly thrust cloth at them, beseeching them to make offers. As the hour progressed, some tourists became visibly flustered by the growing ranks of vendors encircling them.

Typically, much of the cloth displayed at this *pameran* had been rapidly designed and produced and was of low quality. Derivations of historical designs of East Sumba faced in every direction. Sometimes the woven human and animal figures were misshapen to the point of being comical. Skulls impaled on spikes of trees "smiled" impishly, their eyes misaligned in jaggedly irregular heads. Warriors engaged in battle tottered on exceedingly short legs protruding at odd angles from their bodies. In some cases, their heads were larger than their torsos. Horses on one *hinggi* were missing legs, which staggered several centimeters to the sides of their bodies. In many of these cloths, the colors of one motif ran into the others, almost erasing parts of the design. Pieces had been over-dyed in yellow (see plate 19) or had been washed repeatedly to appear "old." Such cloths were selling at the low end of the day's market prices, and tourists seeking inexpensive souvenirs were hastily buying a few of them.

Vendors selling more expensive fabrics were displaying and conversing about their pieces in manners emphasizing quality and distinction. Intensely conscious of their presentations of themselves to foreigners, these sellers offered their personas as part of the bargain—attesting to the value and authenticity of the cloth they sold. After a purchase, a tourist would often be photographed with the seller, establishing a visual certification of the cloth's connection to a specific village "noble."

Igor Kopytoff has recognized a certain drama involved with commodities: "as with persons, the drama here lies in the uncertainties of valuation and of identity" (1988:90). Uncertainties within the tourist-local space of the *pameran* (involving the commodities of fabrics and culture) fueled a profusion of improvisations as Sumbanese traders vied for profitable connections with the visiting foreigners. The limited time the tourists were to be at the *pameran* intensified the social atmosphere. Uncertainties of value and identity became enacted in a number of ways.

Gendered Spaces

A wide range of fabrics bounded one commercial partition. Several complex *hinggi* filled with animal forms were the most prominently positioned. In the midst of these cloths stood the Wandi shopkeeper Hasan,

137

earnestly trying to communicate with a middle-aged American couple from the tour, assisted by his nephew who knew some English. Hasan's approach was almost demure, and the tourists appeared to be interested and unhurried. The motifs Hasan was explaining were said to be from antiquity.

At some distance from this arena, but nonetheless visible, Biba sat on the edge of a verandah, watching the transactions. While local women were dressed in simple cotton blouses and long, black, tubular *laus*, she wore a bright pink blouse embellished with sequins, and a matching flared skirt. Moreover, unlike the long, oiled, and tied back hair of the village women, Biba's was unbound and chin-length, and it gleamed from the color she had used to cover areas of grey. Although her appearance distinguished her from the half dozen other women who also sat on the verandah, Biba was engaged in conversation with her companions. One younger woman was asking the Wandi textile entrepreneur a series of questions about places she had been in Java and Bali. As Biba described some of her adventures and impressions, all of the women listened intently.

While Biba held audience with the fascinated women, Hasan was dealing with foreigners. In salient ways, this situation typified a kind of social propriety involving men and women in the textile trade. Although Biba had certainly ventured beyond conventional female realms, she reenacted them to some extent publicly. That is, she engaged in verandah-and-gender-bound behavior while her husband served as a merchant bridge to the outside world. Each respective area of demeanor and discourse (the commercial global and the social local) was in contrast and interaction with the other.

138

Hasan sold six cloths on this day and exchanged business cards with each of his customers. Two of the buyers (Americans) lived in Jakarta, and the connections would prove valuable in the future.

Heroic Spaces

In a bordering area of the village yard, immense scenes of heroic battles glowed in the morning sun, attracting a steady number of tourists. These were among the largest and most flamboyant cloths at the event, and a few people were taking photographs of them. Beneath them Umbu Taniku of Wandi, handsomely clad in traditional garb, bargained patiently with interested foreigners, with the help of an interpreter. His wife Kata was nowhere to be seen. Umbu was avidly collecting business cards from foreigners and talking to them about his enterprise. Umbu Taniku referred to each *hinggi* on display as an example of a particular "model" (he used the English-derived term) he offered.[9]

Three of his *hinggi*s eventually were taken down from the tree, ceremoniously folded, and handed to foreigners in exchange for money. The buyers had all been impressed by the rampant activity of Umbu Taniku's designs. The Dutchman who had refused to raise his price for Luka's historical *hinggi* earlier in the day settled upon a fabric in Umbu Taniku's arboreal inventory—which he obtained for the amount he had previously offered the offended Luka. As the *hinggi* was lowered to change owners, a stout, sedan-borne Queen Wilhelmina[10] collapsed into the visceral confrontations of scores of Sumbanese warriors. The fabric was folded into a tight bundle, and the elderly Hollander walked off smugly, pleased at obtaining regal symbols of his national history into the bargain.

After his departure, Umbu Taniku lit a cigarette, leaned against the tree supporting his remaining cloths, and spoke of initiating a "world leaders" series of fabrics:

> This is my plan. I could put presidents from different coun-
> tries in my cloth, presidents like Bill Clinton. If I could know
> long before a *pameran* what kind of tourists were coming, I
> could design *hinggi* with their leaders in them. Each group of
> people would have their special *hinggi*!

A few months later Umbu Taniku did just this. The late Dutch Queen Wilhelmina had been appropriated into eastern Sumba's textile iconography for decades; Umbu Taniku expanded the fold to include Bill Clinton, demonstrating his knowledge of world powers and hoping to appeal to an American clientele.

139

Hedging the Boundaries

Ana Humba of Parai Mutu sat in the shade of a sprawling mango tree, dressed in her best satin clothing, and her face glowed pale in the shadows from the makeup she wore. She had come to the *pameran* with a young male cousin, who was attempting to expedite the sale of her fabrics to interested foreigners. She was communicating intermittently with her young vendor by means of hand signals and facial expressions.

Her fabrics proceeded along a clothesline as a tableau of styles. Among these were several *halenda* resembling those made by the evangelical Martha of Hawewa. Asexual white figures upon black backgrounds danced in the wind several yards from Ana Humba. She had collected the textiles she displayed from wide-ranging households and villages around eastern Sumba; none were of the quality produced by her gifted and reclusive sister, Madai.

Ana Humba sat self-consciously poised, framed within a space reflecting a certain gendered decorum. Not content to sit at the same distance from the tourist activities as Biba, however, Ana Humba had chosen a selling area near a small house. In this way, she could somehow conform to local propriety in remaining verandah-bound, yet sit a few yards from where her fabrics were displayed. This position gave her the advantage, it seemed to me, of being able to interact (however indirectly) with foreigners and also to be seen by them.

One middle-aged American man showed interest in her cloth, and in the jewelry she wore around her neck. He attempted to bargain for her gems, through Ana Humba's young cousin, and then through me. She was not willing, however, to part with the carnelian and gold necklace that had attracted the American. The foreigner also commented on how pretty he thought Ana Humba was and asked about her age and marital status. As she realized that inquiries were being made about her, Ana Humba listened intently, while assuming an air of detached dignity. I translated the man's comment and questions for her. She would wait to give her answer.

Assessing the Scene

After the *pameran* was well under way, the noble Umbu Ama of Wandi arrived and circled the grounds on his motorbike, assessing the situation. He eventually parked his vehicle in an area bounded by Luka's cloth and keenly observed the passing foreigners. He joked that it was time that Luka got a wife and asked if there were any young women in the tour group that day. He then noticed Ana Humba sitting at some distance and jested that perhaps she was casting her eyes on foreign men at this late stage of her unmarried life.

Stories had been circulating that Ana Humba's most recent beau had married someone else in Java. A few people, including Umbu Ama, had teased her about this. The rumors had caused speculation on village porches. Women who did not care for Ana Humba, such as Umbu Ama's wife, Rambu Hamu, were especially critical of the Parai Mutu woman's failure to marry. For her part, Ana Humba had publicly affected a nonchalance toward the whole affair.

Umbu Ama had no cloth to sell—but he was not one to engage in public commerce in any case. He and Rambu Hamu had established links with Javanese markets (and had further secured their prominence in the episode described in chapter 4, in which they appeared together on television), and he would certainly not publicly demonstrate a need to participate in a local event for commercial reasons. Umbu Ama had arrived to watch the goings on and to socialize. As the highest-ranking nobleman present, he enjoyed the status of supreme commentator on the event. Eventually, he was ushered to a clan house. For the remainder of the *pameran*, he sat elevated on the front verandah of the *uma kabihu*, drinking coffee, smoking, and making fun of the tourists and locals under his gaze.

"Sumba Primitive"

The Chinese-Sumbanese entrepreneur from Hawewa, Sing Ha, had claimed his area of ground and sat in the background as several young men (all ethnically Sumbanese) acted as agents. The cloths did not reflect recent narrative influences (as evident in those of Luka and Umbu Taniku), but, rather, accentuated more "primitive," archetypal forms. The Sing Ha fabrics proclaimed an unmitigated paganism to the foreigners, trading on a variety of primitivistic interpretations of the human form.[11]

Sing Ha sold several pieces with long, stylized male forms rendered in the *pahikung* technique. He interacted little with the foreigners, relying instead upon an English-speaking Sumbanese to explain and expedite the sale of the fabrics. The youth told potential customers that the pieces had been produced in traditional villages and that some of them were very old. He also emphasized the uniqueness of many motifs, claiming that they denoted a specific village, family, and rank. These claims appeared to convince the foreign customers, who wrote down the names of places and terms associated with the fabrics they bought. Among the tourists were several who claimed to be collectors, including a podiatrist from California unabashedly seeking textiles with sexual motifs. He found what he was seeking in the "primitive people" being offered by Sing Ha.[12]

The podiatrist told me that he was collecting examples of "tribal art" that revealed genitals, and he described the carved wooden "gods" he had obtained in Bali: they flaunted erect penises larger than the rest of their bodies. These artifacts, he said, would be added to his growing collection in Palo Alto, which featured Tibetan Tantric paintings and Maori canoe prows carved with genitalia. He valued sexually explicit ethnic arts, he explained, because they revealed "the openness of simpler peoples to such matters."[13] He was also looking to buy a *mamuli* in Sumba—a traditional gold item fashioned in the shape of a vulva that is used in marriage exchange.

Exhibition and Lore

Across the woven backdrops of skull trees, battles, and primitive men with upraised arms paraded tourists in shorts—confused, irritated, or sometimes charmed. From verandahs issued continuous commentary marveling at the dress and anatomy of the foreigners. Villagers clucked in amazement as women in their sixties passed by in shorts and sleeveless blouses. Women of the same age among the village observers wore ankle-

141

length *lau* and cotton blouses with sleeves to the wrists; they chewed betel nut with long-blackened teeth and gums.

Village discourse in Sumba regarding Westerners incorporates stereotypes gleaned from television, magazines, and posters on the insides of *bemos*, as well as from visitors at *pamerans*. Moreover, tales of the amorous adventures of Sumbanese men with Western women arise not only from casual encounters upon the island with visiting tourists, but also from the intrigues of Bali. Such lore bears upon the construction of Western Others to a considerable extent, particularly regarding the positioning of women.[14]

Interaction between foreign men and Sumbanese women is locally discouraged in most contexts. Women often appear to avoid male tourists who enter their compounds. Although eager to profit from the purchases of their textiles by outsiders, Sumbanese village women, in my observation, usually were reticent and often critically scrutinizing toward foreigners. This particular day in Lambanapu was no exception. Commenting on the dress or manners of the tourists, the verandah-bound villagers also mused about their sexual mores—whether couples were married and what types of men the foreign women were permitted to go around with. On this day, Ana Humba assumed an air of moral superiority as she answered the male tourist's question about why she was not yet married. She emphasized the selectivity involved in marriages of high-caste women like herself as she stated, "We *maramba* women in Sumba only marry men of very high level and accomplishment. We do not just go around with anyone!"

142

Contested Authenticities

Two men were promoting a large *hinggi* they claimed was handspun. Hanging from a tree limb, the piece had obviously been overdyed a yellowish-brown to make it appear old. Several female tourists were examining the piece, and one was considering buying it. The *hinggi* had actually been woven from thick, factory-made thread, but it had something of the rough quality of handspun cloth.[15] Seeking the advice of an expert, the women had scouted around the village to find an old, accomplished weaver. Two elderly women were eventually escorted to the *hinggi* in question, and they were then asked (through a translator/guide) if the piece was "really a handspun" one (*benang kapas benar*, I.). One of the village women appeared shy and confused, but her companion scoffed openly and replied, *"Tidak mungkin!"* (I.; Impossible!). Her assessment was translated by the nervous guide, and the Western women then began to walk away. The crestfallen merchants immediately tried to win them back by greatly reducing their price, to no avail.

The elderly village matrons scurried back to the verandah from where they had been dislodged, covered their mouths with their hands, and giggled at what they had just taken part in. Others seated nearby commented that the two vendors who lost the sale were not "true Sumbanese" (*Tau Humba langataka*) and knew little themselves about cloth, but only tried to "deceive" (*tipu*) tourists. The merchants were descended from Arabs, the villagers said, and were looking to make money in any way they could.[16]

Unraveling

The hour for browsing was drawing to a close, and the chartered bus sounded its horn to summon the tourists for departure. Vendors knew that time was running out, and some frantically bargained with the foreigners. As the tourists began to drift back toward the bus, bands of vendors followed them, each man wrapped in several cloths and holding out fabrics and artifacts pleadingly. Some of the foreigners moved blithely through the swaddled merchants, while others impatiently waved them away. Numerous vendors pressed their goods to the bus windows in last attempts to make a sale. By this time, most of the tourists appeared disenchanted with the village life they had experienced, and several complained about the aggressive commercialism of the Lambanapu event. Looking out at the frenzied merchants around the bus, tourists expressed disappointment in the quality of the interactions they had endured, and one woman commented that it was obvious that this village had been "spoiled."

As the Party Doll pulled away from Lambanapu, many vendors were hastily folding and packing their cloths. Several men had chartered a *bemo* and were preparing to go down to the Waingapu harbor, where the tourist launch was moored. There they would congregate on the dock and attempt to sell their fabrics for a few hours, until the boat left for its next port of call.

Convergence

The *pameran* frames subtle and blatant aspects of the nature of encounters between tourists and locals in Sumba. Rather than being merely a staged (and thereby artificial) event, a fair such as this can be a crucible of desire, improvisation, and agency for participants. In such cases, interactions between foreigners and locals occur not in "empty meeting grounds" (MacCannell 1992) but in arenas of overlapping prestige systems—where culture is reproduced in sites in which difference is an impetus for creativity. People perform for others as they enhance themselves.

143

Thus the postures of Luka, Umbu Pari, and Umbu Taniku each claimed positions in relation to others. This was also true of Umbu Ama, in his explicit distancing of himself from the event, while redefining it through his own critiques from an elevated perch. And while Ana Humba and Biba maintained semblances of customarily gendered spaces, each framed on a verandah, they also enjoyed tactical positions from which to assert themselves and command attention from others.

Strategies, positions, and viewpoints at *pamerans* are infinite, as they interweave multiple, shifting realities. Such realities converge in any gathering of people, whether "staged" for a particular audience or not, whether incipient or obvious. As Fred Myers concludes (in reference to an Australian Aboriginal performance for a New York audience), "however troubled and imperfect they may be as incidents of representation, their effect outlasts the moment" (1994:691). *Pamerans* are incidents of representation that instigate ongoing effects. Such gatherings momentarily distill the social worlds involved in the commodification of Sumbanese fabrics and culture while illuminating the nature of local people's imaginings and involvements with outsiders and with each other, creating new political fields.

This converging of worlds, with whatever artifices or ironies emerge, is meaningful in its uncertainties. Within such spaces we might glimpse ways in which people are defining themselves; what kinds of behaviors, symbols, and discourses are being employed; and what is involved in personal stakes, satisfactions, and disappointments. A *pameran*, with its many human wiles and serendipities, is a scene of encounter between people of various social and cultural backgrounds. It is as genuine as any other form of social interaction and can reveal much of the imaginations and motivations of all involved, within a multivalanced, intensified economy.

144

Through these events, people partake of not only a global, monetary economy but also of an economy of experiences and an authenticating of selves (see Abrahams 1986:56)—certain politics of international collecting affects local politics of identity. In a *pameran* setting, where much is predicated on performance and backdrop, people also demonstrate their "experiences" as personal resources—indeed, they wield them as a kind of currency. Thus knowledge, finesse, and alliance all become attributes of a prowess that can be manifested by Sumbanese traders through their interactions with foreigners.

Moreover, the (largely Western) tourists assert sophistication and knowledge by venturing into an exotic locale, such as a Sumbanese village, adding to their own repertoire of experience. For them, the quality of such experience rests upon certain preconceived notions of non-

Western village life—
ideal images they
have bought into by
joining their tour
group. Although for-
eigners may find
something of value
to them in such ven-
tures, such as tex-
tiles or interaction
with village char-
acters, they often
become disillu-
sioned by the
nature of commer-
cial exchange involv-

Figure 35. Vendors displaying textiles at the entrance to a Waingapu hotel.

ing local people. When evident to locals, such disappointment becomes another risk of such encounters, to be taken into account. In this way, awareness of foreign ideals of local culture and identity and of the performance of these for outsiders becomes even more important to Sumba's entrepreneurs.

Relations of power are frequently played out overtly in the Sumbanese textile trade, with social status becoming evident in the situation of people. In Sumba, power and status manifest through encounters involving tourists and locals, men and women, Sumbanese and other ethnic groups such as Chinese and Arabs, and high- and low-caste people, as can be glimpsed in the previous pages. Yet power and status are also often challenged or even altered through unforeseeable or hidden circumstances. Transmutations in social life can emerge through enfolded subtleties, as in the vignette to follow.

145

The Hotel Orchid

> *Not only does laughter make no exception for the upper stratum, but indeed it is usually directed against it.*
> —Mikhail Bakhtin, *Rabelais and His World*

Later the same day of the *pameran*, at the Hotel Orchid in Waingapu, numerous vendors converged who had earlier been in the village of Lambanapu. The day's activities had provided some men with cash and had whetted the appetite of others to seek further commerce with tourists at the hotel. The hotel environs were an ultimate indicator of the status of the vendors who approached them: high-ranking Sumbanese were admitted to the restaurant/bar; lower-caste people sat on the patios or walkways surrounding the building.

A few noblemen drank beer or coffee in the restaurant and waited for opportunities to engage foreigners. Those excluded from the hotel interior sat on its fringes and smoked cigarettes as they passed the time. At the threshold between the hotel lobby and the front patio sat Luka, at one end of his five-meter *hinggi* laid out upon the floor. As people entered the Hotel Orchid, they walked the length of his woven fable.

The men who entered the hotel were dressed in self-consciously stylish mixes of Western attire and Sumbanese fabrics, sporting blue jeans and *ikat* sashes or scarves. They included Umbu Pari and Umbu Taniku, who cunningly eyed the foreigners sitting at various tables. Those who sat on the outer margins of the premises were clad in well-worn simple *hinggi*s and cheap market shirts or slacks; some were shoeless.[17]

In terms of local contests, the movement and behavior of village men at the Hotel Orchid typified any of many nights. Yet events that would affect the prestige of one locally powerful man would occur not within the restaurant, but on the walkway hosting poor vendors. On this particular night, business was slow for the outdoor sellers, and the men were talking among themselves and discreetly sharing whiskey bought with profits from the *pameran*. As the evening progressed, most of these vendors took their leave; the few remaining became very drunk. Finally, all left the premises in tottering states of inebriation, save one elderly villager who had passed out.

The following morning, the man remained unconscious on the walkway near the hotel's front entrance. He was in this state when the first of the day's vendors began to arrive. The proprietors of the hotel were becoming nervous, and after it was determined that the man was alive, attempts were made to resuscitate him. The man slept on, limp and unresponsive to stimuli. Hotel staff and tourists began to congregate around the scene.

Eventually a local official happened by and sternly appraised the situation at hand. This particular official was despised by the villagers who peddled their fabrics in the Waingapu area. He had often attempted to extract "commissions" from the vendors on their sales because they were operating on a terrain he seemed to consider as his own domain of authority. Moreover, this man long had been a prime suspect in a grave robbing that had taken place in a village years earlier. Stories had been circulating for years about the officious man's offenses in Waingapu and also at the airport (where many vendors went to sell fabrics to departing tourists). Not a native of Sumba, he had come from another island, and locals resented his imposed, abusive authority.

On this morning, the official began giving orders to the five textile vendors who were present, commanding them to move their comrade from the walkway to the driveway, where he could be taken away. The hoteliers had called the local hospital to come and remove the man, not knowing any other way to be rid of him, as his village home certainly had no telephone. The vendors had been reticent in response to the orders, and the official grew impatient.

The unconscious villager, though a slight man, seemed inexplicably heavy for the five who labored to move him from the walkway. He sagged onto the ground as the men attempted to drag him by his wrists and ankles. The agitated official barked his orders, growing angrier as the vendors failed to obey them. He demanded that the vendors pick up their drunk friend and carry him out. The men were noncompliant, adopting attitudes of dumb confusion. About thirty people had gathered around the scene at this point, including local passersby, the hotel staff, and foreign guests, including me.

Finally the official lost all patience. He bolted into the midst of the group, thrust his hands under the man's rump as the others were holding his limbs, and with a shout and a jerk elevated the limp victim off the walkway. No sooner had the passively resistant man gone up when he rapidly came down, with the stunned official holding out his own hands in horror and shrieking for a basin of water and a towel. Some of the gathered bystanders stifled their laughter, looked away, or dispersed in embarrassment, while a few children squealed and several foreign tourists laughed openly.

147

Shifting Status through Lore

This episode became a relished "Hotel Orchid tale" (*cerita Hotel Orchid*, I.) in Waingapu and surrounding villages and thus entered local lore. In weeks to come, many verandahs would ring with the laughter of people listening to a rendition of the story, which generally came to be called *hinggi tai* (feces cloth). Textile vendors who had been at the scene of the event enjoyed a novel popularity as orators, holding audience with groups of rapt villagers. One repeatedly offered a moral at the end of his tale: "For years [the official's] hands were soiled by stealing our profits from cloth. Now let them be soiled from our cloth!"

In this manner, through his humble *hinggi*, an elderly inebriate had unwittingly left an indelible imprint on a local power elite, compromising the latter's prestige as he lost face publicly.[18] The official's drunken nemesis (who eventually recovered from his night of revelry) inadvertently emerged from the margins of cloth sellers to gain a certain heroism, in having soiled the image of a despised local official.

CHAPTER 8
VILLAGE ENCOUNTERS

It is this particularity that is the essence of all history.
      —Paul Radin, *The Method and Theory of Anthropology*

Kenapa orang Barat datang ke sini? Mereka jalan-jalan ke mana-mana,
kasi keluar banyak uang. Buat apa?
*(Why do Westerners come here? They walk all over, spend lots of
money. What for?)*
                              —old woman in the village of Wandi

Besides the tour groups attending *pamerans*, there were various
foreign visitors to Sumbanese villages, many seeking to experience
something exotic or pristine. These tourists (usually traveling in couples
or alone) might meet any of a collection of locals at a Waingapu hotel
and be invited to a village. Foreigners also meandered through villages
uninvited and were usually extended someone's hospitality. Never predictable, the more prolonged or eventful encounters generated vivid
accounts among villagers. Moreover, such visits occasionally produced
disputes, displacements, and reevaluations in local lives.

The Eco-tourist
   One fateful visit in 1994 involved a middle-aged Danish tourist. Her
actions created a general tumult that interwove notions of the foreign and
the local in Sumba-
nese imaginations.
This tourist was
referred to as The
Lone Woman (Na
Wani Mandari[1]) by
villagers who knew
about her.
   The arrival of
tourists in the
plateau village of
Wandi sent children
throughout the vil-
lage calling, *"Turis
di atas!"* (I.; "Tour-
ist(s) above!").[2] This

Figure 36. Dutch tourists considering a *hinggi* containing
motifs of Queen Wilhelmina.

heralding prompted most households to dispatch agents with stacks of fabrics to display. One afternoon, the children's cries were incited by a tall, fair-haired woman carrying a large backpack. Instead of browsing for fabrics from house to house or photographing megaliths or high-peaked homes, the woman commenced to purposefully clear rocks and leaves from a yard near the home of a high-ranking noblewoman. She then laid out a tent on the ground.

Many villagers observed the woman as she set up her tent, tying lines to a nearby tree and then pounding stakes into the hard ground. After watching in confused alarm from her verandah, the noblewoman in the nearby home sent a child from her household to summon Luka (who was often used as an intermediary when English was needed). Luka arrived as the Dane was moving articles into her tent. Approaching the tourist with a practiced calm, he cordially asked what she was doing. The woman replied that she was going to camp for the night and had selected the site because of its proximity to the megalithic graves.

Luka explained that she was camping upon royal as well as sacred land and that people in the noble house nearby would be angry if she remained there. Furthermore, it was not customary for people to sleep on the ground in the village in any case.[3] He attempted to convince her of the earthly and ancestral spirits (conflated with the ground on which they both stood) and local notions of propriety, and the woman finally agreed to move and began to take down her camp. Luka assisted and then led the tourist to his home up the road.

When they arrived at Luka's household (followed by a pack of curious children), Luka offered his home for the night, explaining that the woman could sleep in a small alcove near the front of the *uma*. The visitor became disturbed by this offer and insisted that it was her intention to camp out of doors while traveling and also to provide and prepare all of her own food for herself. This, she asserted, was the way she always traveled. Perplexed, Luka tried once more to explain that people of the region simply did not sleep on the ground, especially if space within a home was available to them.[4] Unyielding, the tourist became increasingly irate. Acquiescing, Luka said that she could camp under a bougainvillea bush several yards away from his home.

Following this, the Dane once more pitched her tent and then entered it, not to emerge until dusk. Villagers watching were baffled, and children began to speak in whispers. At about six o'clock in the evening, as the day grew dark, the tourist reappeared and, sitting on a collapsible camp stool, proceeded to light a small gas stove and prepare her evening meal. This consisted of what villagers described as a soup, made with dry bits that looked like bark and came from a plastic bag, mixed with bottled water.

149

Luka attempted to sit and talk with the visitor as she ate, but she was largely uncommunicative. She did reveal to him that this was her first trip to Indonesia and that she had come by way of Australia. Shortly after eating, she reentered her tent and was not seen again for the rest of the evening.

In the hours between her disappearance and reemergence, the area surrounding her campsite was filled with uneasy speculation. Afraid to sleep, people from each of the six households in view of her tent stayed awake all night on their verandahs, watching and speaking in murmurs. Chewing betel nut and leaning against house posts, people punctuated their comments with the "tsk" sounds by which Sumbanese express perplexity.

For those holding vigil through the night, a prevailing worry was of witchery. People suspected either that the woman was a *mamarung* who might prey on people's spirits at night while they slept or that she might attract such forces stemming from local evils. In the first light of morning, the woman emerged and boiled water on her small stove. After drinking tea, she quickly packed up her gear and left Wandi. At no time, in the roughly fifteen hours that she had been at her campsite in Luka's yard, did she leave the area of ground her tent stood upon.

Villagers were distraught at her behavior. The fact that she would not socialize, behavior unthinkable for Sumbanese, was unusual, even for a foreigner. Tourists who spoke no Indonesian nonetheless usually engaged in sign language with locals or spoke in English to Luka. Further, people thought it most odd that the Danish woman had shown no interest in the suspended fabrics that were always part of the Wandi visual environment; villagers took for granted that foreigners came to see textiles. People expressed puzzlement at why the woman had come to their village, and even more why she had insisted upon sleeping there in such an unorthodox manner.

It particularly disturbed the residents that the woman had never wandered from the immediate vicinity of her tent. They found it inexplicable that the tourist had not gone into the bushes or to a privy at the rear of the house to relieve herself for the duration of her stay. This mysterious aspect of her visit lent credence to suspicions of an alien and peculiar sorcery, as some speculated that the woman may have tended to her eliminations within the tent. In this way, she had challenged notions of common sense and propriety regarding boundaries of not only the social landscape, but also those of the body (see Douglas 1966).

Yet another cause for alarm was that the Dane had not bathed during her stay.[5] Luka commented that the morning after her final emergence from her tent, the tourist emitted a strong, foul odor from her mouth.

This, he said, was indicative of a witch—someone with an evil essence, palpable in the "scent of spirit through breath" (*ngahuna wau*).[6]

In the wake of her ten-day tour of Sumba, a trail of speculations followed the Lone Woman. Tales of her oddness circulated through all communities she had entered, and in some villages people had been especially fearful. As discussed in previous chapters, a woman traveling alone, without clear indication of purpose and destination, is considered dangerously deviant in Sumba. Secretive, singular venturing is associated with madwomen and witches. While eastern Sumbanese villagers are accustomed to seeing lone female tourists, the behavior of the Dane was particularly unsociable and bizarre, giving rise to numerous suspicions. Moreover, she had been unresponsive to the multitude of local fabrics that had hung in her view—a visual indifference that ignored a primary link between locals and foreigners. In her inexplicable aloofness, she defied the local category of "tourist" that had normalized the presence of foreigners in the village.

The Danish woman had a contrasting but equally esoteric interpretation of the happenings above. I encountered her a few days later at a hotel restaurant in Waingapu, and recognizing me from Wandi,[7] she was surprisingly eager to talk and give me her assessment of what had happened. As she spoke, I suspected that she was a kind of renegade "ecotourist." She preferred outdoor camping, she said, because she wanted to be "close to nature" and deplored the unhygienic conditions in Indonesian hotels. She had once suffered food poisoning in Africa and thus had established a personal policy of seeing to her own meals and water. Moreover, she claimed to have endured many unwanted sexual advances by men while traveling and so was wary of accepting hospitality when men extended it (as had Luka). All in all, the Dane maintained an aversion to what any social group might have to offer her and resisted most overtures of the inhabitants of the villages she visited. She camped within villages, she said, only because they seemed safer than the wild. Regardless of this last concession, her visit to Sumba was a quest for "nature" that consciously resisted "culture."

Nelson Graburn defines "ecological tourism" as that "wherein the tourist tries to leave as little effect from his visit as possible" (1989:31). The Dane's ecological focus had left little trace of her visit upon the physical landscape but had created havoc upon the sociological one. Her steadfast and inexplicable singularity and unsociability, to Sumbanese villagers, was a hubris indicative of madness or evil.

A Clan Home (Nearly) Becomes a Gallery

Two days after the Dane vacated the bit of ground under the bougainvillea bush at the front of Luka's house, two German men arrived in

151

Wandi. These were tourists Luka had met in the lobby of the Hotel Orchid the day before and had invited to visit his home. Loud base rhythms of rock music from a *bemo* announced the arrival of the guests, who emerged from the vehicle carrying backpacks.

Luka greeted the two as old friends, and as they sat on the verandah together the men offered their host a cigarette. The tourists (in their thirties) were traveling "on the cheap" across Indonesia, on holiday from their jobs in Germany, where they worked for an urban entertainment magazine. The couple conversed with Luka in English, and the three seemed to have struck up an easy friendship. Beguiled by the village of Wandi, and obviously charmed by Luka, the visitors asked questions about local megaliths, customs, and architecture as they sat on a palm mat on the verandah. Luka described aspects of village life and "tradition" to the men in English. The Germans were as receptive as the Danish tourist had been resistant to Luka's hospitality and the immediate social milieu it afforded.

It had been decided before the men arrived that they would be houseguests for the night, and Luka took their belongings into his small room. The arrangement was that the men would sleep in Luka's bed (a mattress on the floor) and that he would sleep in the center of the house on a mat. The Germans were genuinely excited about spending the night in an *uma kabihu* and experiencing the ambience of village life. They were also pleased to have met the cordial Luka, who could explain local culture to them. Well into the night all of the men (including two of Luka's brothers) sat up drinking wine, smoking cigarettes, and engaging in a pantomime conversation punctuated by laughter.

The next day, textiles were ceremoniously shown to the guests in the house in which they had slept. After some consideration, the foreigners decided upon two cloths designed by Luka's older brother (and produced by his wife, who sat at her loom on the front verandah)—*ikat hinggi*s that each contained one large male figure the length of the cloth. These were among the most rapidly created pieces in the region and were specifically designed for sale to tourists. They had been colored chemically and had been overdyed yellow to appear old, although their seller was touting them as the newest of his productions. The yellow tint in many of the lower-quality cloths produced in Sumba often lend the fabrics a muddy look. The pieces the Germans selected were no exception to this tendency, yet the men had expressly liked them, they said, because they looked "primitive" and "muted" (see plate 19).

Luka hid his disappointment at the visitors' lack of interest in fabrics of his design. Yet he expressed no disdain for the men's insensitivity to quality in local textiles (a disdain he had voiced wholeheartedly at the *pameran* described in chapter 7). He appeared to accept quietly his brother's shoddy textile line as part of communal life in the family compound.

The men were taken with what they perceived as a kind of ethnic stylishness in Luka and his surroundings. They appreciated the fact that the Wandi entrepreneur spoke English, showed a quirky awareness of Western fashion trends through his dress, and extended seemingly unconditional hospitality to them. One remarked to me:

> Luka was a lucky find for us; otherwise we would have been afraid to stay in a primitive village. He is from a primitive society, and that has much value to us in its philosophy and arts. Now it is a global style, and Europeans are very interested in it. Luka is sophisticated and seems to know something of our world too.

As a mediator, Luka had succeeded. In negotiating a tension between "traditional" and "contemporary" modes of self-presentation, he had finessed an appealing persona for himself in the eyes of the foreigners, capitalizing on the way his guests viewed his world as "stylish" and playing—to the extent of his awareness—with a certain reflexivity between a number of worlds and viewpoints.[8]

The men stayed on for two more nights. During that time, they inspired Luka to redesign the large, central room (*bai uma*) of his household into an exhibition gallery for "ethnic art." The three men commenced to reorder the space within the *uma kabihu* to permit a new wall partition (constructed of plaited palm leaves) in an attempt to transform the section into a showroom. Wandi homes are the sites of much weaving, and fabrics are often within reach on looms or suspended for display at the front of houses. However, no organized, permanent showcase in the visibly open central room of an *uma* had yet been created, as far as I knew. Then one morning in 1994, Luka was inspired to remodel his cosmological center into another kind of center for outside viewers: a gallery-like space displaying and marketing objects of value to foreigners.

153

The decision came about after some discussion. Finally, Luka and his older brother decided that they would restructure something of the inside of their home to create an atmosphere more modern, stylish, and attractive to tourists. The brothers began to partition off sections and to hang a few fabrics on the walls. The central room of the house, in which ancestral spirits had been summoned and propitiated on numerous occasions, became ordered and decorated with an attention to the walls that bounded it. The German tourists enthusiastically gave directions as Luka and his brother hung and took down various fabrics. Other artifacts, such as a large, carved stone crocodile and plaited rice containers, were brought into the space and experimentally positioned on the floor. Mats, boxes, and looms were cleared from the large room in an effort to provide space in which to accent particular items deemed valuable. The following day, the two brothers whitewashed the new wall partitions of their house. When the walls dried, they installed a display of eight *hinggi*s.

This transformation did not proceed without contention. The cloth-making women of the household, which included three sisters, two sisters-in-law, and an elderly mother and aunt, had grumbled at the changes. Luka's mother protested:

> A clan home is not the place to make a modern, empty room for the tourists to see. What use is this? We must live here like always! What is all this about? This will bring problems for us! This will create troubles [*rawa*]!

Several days after the installation was completed, Umbu Ama, the village's highest-ranking nobleman, stopped by to view the room. As he surveyed the stark gallery space and the sulking women at its margins, he pronounced the transformation a "mistake" (*manjala*), and one that went against custom (*huri*). The German guests had since departed, and original enthusiasm for the innovation had subsided. Their resolve weakened from the passage of time and the censure of their female kin, the Wandi brothers became resigned to allowing things to proceed naturally.

The impending death of an elderly uncle and the subsequent arrival of numerous kin impinged on any remaining efforts to maintain the pristine isolation of the gallery. Reclaimed by the exigencies of local life and death,[9] the house was filled by dozens of relatives as they ascended the porch and sat on the floor, surrounding the dying man. Now sheltering an emotional, human contingency, the rarified exhibition space the German tourists had imagined was not to be. Scents and sounds once more humanized the room as one recently painted white partition was spattered with the red spittle of betel nut.

A Woman Houseguest

That same season, a woman skilled in textile techniques came to stay in Wandi. "Jane" (an Australian) had gained fluency in Indonesian through a long stay in Java (where she had studied *batik* processes) and was able to communicate well with her initial hosts, Rambu Hamu and Umbu Ama. Jane had met Rambu Hamu at the large Sumbanese textile exhibition Rambu had been part of in Jakarta the year before and had been issued an invitation to visit Wandi. During her two-month sojourn in Sumba, she also came to enjoy the hospitality of other households and stayed for lengths of time at the home of Rambu Nina and Tabi in Hawewa. Her extended visit and language skills enabled her to relate to village people and set her apart from most tourists to the region.

Jane studied the *ikat* and *pahikung* techniques for some weeks and took extensive photographs. Congenial and humorous, she was generally well liked (although not entirely understood). Locals remarked on her good looks, yet were perplexed at her clownish antics and dramatic gesticulations in conversation. Such behavior went against local notions of feminine social grace.[10]

During her stay in Sumba Jane had two misfortunes that (in increasing her emotional and physical vulnerability) made her more accessible, especially to the women around her. Her Australian boyfriend broke off their relationship by letter, and then remained unresponsive to her telephone calls. Following this, while attempting to take a photograph of a *lau pahudu* being woven on Rambu Nina's porch, she backed up too far and fell off the edge, badly spraining her ankle.

Jane's troubles were the focus of much discussion during the few weeks she stayed with Rambu Nina and Tabi in their Hawewa home. During this time she confided in her hosts and sought their advice on her own ill-fated romance. The cousins and other village women were curious about the Australian woman's freedom and asked many questions about her life. Jane was thirty years old, which by local standards was dangerously advanced in years in terms of marriage prospects. Although they had remained unmarried themselves, Tabi and Rambu Nina came to feel sorry for Jane. For as they expressed it, she was someone "floating" (*berapung-apung*, I.) in the world, and they wondered why she had no distinct place she called home.

155

As Jane lay recovering from her sprain and her emotional loss in their home, Rambu Nina and Tabi commented to me on the sad state of their Australian convalescent. Tabi asked, "What good is it to travel so freely if there is no place to go home to? She doesn't live with her parents anymore, but she doesn't have a husband's house either."

Rambu Nina remarked that she was glad (as always) to not have men determining her life. Moreover, Jane had come purposefully to her home because of the reputation of its textiles. It was clear that Rambu Nina considered herself at an advantage: she had a secure sense of social place and enjoyed a renown through her fabrics that drew international guests to her home. The weaving cousins, nonetheless, expressed an affection for their guest, and the three women confided often together. Yet Jane's misfortunes had reinforced a belief in the rightness of the Hawewa women's lives and places in the world.

Although befriended by Rambu Nina and Tabi, and in the good graces of Rambu Hamu of Wandi,[11] Jane unintentionally created some bad feelings in Parai Mutu. When she visited the home of Ana Humba and Madai, the sisters felt that Jane ignored them and behaved too effusively toward their brothers and male cousins. The two had watched critically as Jane clowned and laughed with the men of the clan.

Although Madai seldom conversed in any case, she nonetheless felt slighted when Jane photographed one of her best *hinggi*s with crayfish motifs and then did not question her about the fabric afterward but instead directed her inquiries to Madai's male kin. In response to this, Madai mimicked Jane, flapping her arms rapidly and throwing her head back in an impression of monkey-like laughter. And Ana Humba, whose sojourns had teased customary bounds of female travel and propriety (chapter 5), was notably vocal in her critiques of Jane's unbridled mobility and expressiveness. In Ana Humba's opinion, Jane had been "acting too much like men" (*berbuat terlalu macam laki-laki*, I.), transgressing proper public modes of behavior for women. Jane was uncontrollable. She moved between realms irrespective of their margins, and she did so with evident pleasure.

Madai and Ana Humba came to resist Jane's overtures of conversation and ultimately shut themselves off from her when she visited, retreating further into the recesses of their family home. Gender had become a gulf, not a bridge between the women, and as Jane socialized with the men of the house, the sisters remained in the innermost room with the best of the household fabrics. In the right inner portion of their *uma*, a room symbolically associated with men, Madai and Ana Humba bound themselves off from the unwanted Westerner and sat in proximity to the bundle of fabrics enfolding their deceased father—the patriarchal center of their household.

Jane's response to the taciturn Parai Mutu sisters was to cease visiting the household and the village. She surmised that the two had snubbed her because she had neglected to buy fabrics from them. She did not realize how her presence had reinforced or challenged the women's gendered postures. One day, when I was at the sisters' home, talk of Jane's unwitting offenses stimulated a household discussion of a scandal in Waingapu —one that exemplified to the women the recklessness of Western women.

In recent months, a European schoolteacher (living in Waingapu) who had befriended Ana Humba had become romantically involved with a young local man who worked at a hotel. It was rumored that he had been living with the woman in her rented home—a place Ana Humba had been invited to months before but had not dared visit because it had been out of the range of her permitted stopping points.[12] Ana Humba related this tale of cohabitation to me with a moralistic verve, emphasizing how disappointed (*kecewa*, I.) she was with the woman's character (*sifat*, I.). What especially puzzled her was why the woman had been so shamelessly public in her affair with the local man, behaving as though no one was watching.

The actions of the foreign women prompted local women to reassess their own lives and moral values. Jane initially had inspired Rambu Hamu (chapter 4) to reflect on relationships between men and women and offer her ideas on ideal situations. She also roused Ana Humba to define her own morality aloud. Despite her sometimes cryptic circumvention of local norms, Ana Humba maintained certain postures regarding public behavior. Madai's assessment of the Australian visitor was the most truculent. Quietly, she voiced, "She is not a real person [*tau mema*]. A crazy kind of bird, maybe." She then flapped her arms and shook her head dismissively.

The Crazy Dutchman

A stout, middle-aged European ambled out of a hired jeep in Parai Mutu one morning. He immediately began distributing thousand-rupiah notes (about fifty U.S. cents at the time) to entice the shy children who observed him from behind house posts. Draped with shoulder bags and camera gear, the man found his way to the family compound of Madai and Ana Humba, following the sounds of the banging shuttles of looms. Jovially greeting people in Indonesian, "Hans" took a seat on the verandah, overlooking Mia and others at their looms.

Hans had lived in Bali for fifteen years and operated an export business to Holland. He periodically made trips to some of the outer islands to buy fabrics and handcrafts and had visited Parai Mutu several times in the past. It was rumored among people in Sumba's villages who knew him that Hans had several very young Balinese wives. It was also rumored that he at times behaved like a homosexual. Two young men from the village of Wandi had told many people of how Hans had invited them one evening to the restaurant at the Hotel Orchid and bought them bottles of beer. Afterward he had invited them to his room and asked them to kiss him. The young men had run out of the room, but they repeatedly told the story with a humorous relish. Hans acquired the name Belanda Toba (Crazy Dutchman) in areas of eastern Sumba, and it was this name that Madai muttered upon his entrance into her compound in Parai Mutu.

Hans sat recovering from the heat of the journey, then asked to see the fabrics the household had to sell. Folded *hinggi*s were draped over clotheslines in the courtyard for the visitor to examine. As he sipped coffee, he removed an indigo blue and white Japanese-style shirt (a kind of jacket laced to one side) he wore and placed it to his side on the

157

verandah. Wiping his brow, he sighed, "That's better," and now clad in his undershirt, examined the textiles before him. Sitting nearby, Madai looked intently at the removed shirt (which actually came from a boutique in Bali), focusing upon an embroidered geometric design on its sleeves. For several minutes she studied the border, appearing oblivious to everything else.

After quite some time and haggling, Hans agreed to buy four of the fabrics when the mother of the household conceded to a lower price for the lot. He cheerfully packed away the cloths and bid farewell to the people in the compound, which included Madai, her mother, a younger sister, and the servant Mia. After he left, Madai began impersonating the Dutchman, pantomiming his hot and puffing manner upon arrival and the way in which he had taken off his shirt. As usual, everyone responded with laughter, especially Mia, who was always a receptive audience for comedy.

Later the same week, Hans encountered Umbu Pari at the Hotel Orchid. The Dutchman's original contact with Parai Mutu villagers, Umbu Pari had invited him to his village after meeting him in Bali years earlier. On this current trip to Sumba, Hans was bearing two catalogues from European museums containing pictures of various non-Western arts, which he presented to Umbu Pari in the hotel bar. The two sat drinking beer for a few evenings at the hotel, and during the days the Dutchman hired the hotel van and visited villages. Umbu Pari accompanied him on a few of these jaunts.

Insistent upon serving as a guide for Hans, Umbu Pari jealously guarded against others who might be wanting to establish a connection with him. It happened, however, that Hans one morning wandered on his own to Wandi and purchased several fabrics from a commoner family in the village. When Umbu Pari learned of this, he went to the seller's home and, angry and drunk, he struck the villager in the face for intruding upon his clientele. This caused an instant uproar in the area, and the village *raja*, Umbu Ama, was called in to intervene. He scolded Umbu Pari harshly and shoved him toward the road. Umbu Pari stumbled into the side door of a stopping *bemo* and rode back to Waingapu.

That evening at the Hotel Orchid, Umbu Pari recounted the incident before other Sumbanese textile traders sitting in the lobby, denouncing the Wandi commoner who had sold cloth to the Dutchman. As he expressed it, "The Dutchman was *my* tourist. That's true. I first invited him to Sumba. The connection was mine. A low-caste person can't just take the business from me. He can't! I won't allow it!"

Hans, in the meantime, had checked out of the hotel and returned to his home in Bali.

Resonance of Lives

Meetings between people in eastern Sumba and foreign visitors prompt reassessments of local knowledge and norms, and many Sumbanese often view foreigners as aberrations upon normalcy. However impressed they might be by the visitors' cameras and clothing, villagers often consider tourists as oddly displaced people, sometimes bordering on madness. At best their dislocation is cause for humor or pity (as in the case of Jane); at worst it incites fear (as caused by the Danish woman).

Whatever prestige traveling brings to local people, a sense of rootedness and place is also crucial to their sense of well-being. Not belonging to a distinct geographical place is a generally frightening condition for them, an anomie to which few Sumbanese would aspire.[13] At the least, foreign visitors inspire local people to reevaluate their beliefs and conventions, which fundamentally involve issues of place and mobility. A dramatic contrast between Sumbanese and foreigners is evoked in local imaginations by the mobility of women, and the implications of this mobility stir reflection in villages.

A tension between moving about and staying in place is magnified by the presence of foreigners in Sumbanese villages. Outsiders become axioms around which locals realize anew their own senses of location or their desires for expansion of their social worlds. It is not by chance that most tourists entering village households are hosted by men, and many move through Sumba accompanied by local male guides. Exceptions occur when a foreigner is a woman and is able to communicate on her own, such as Jane, who was hosted by Rambu Nina and Tabi. Jane, however, fell into a category other than "tourist." Because she spoke Indonesian and had studied extensively about textiles, she was viewed as a scholar. Hosting her conferred an amount of prestige on households despite whatever miscommunications arose.

159

Foreigners also incite local contests of authority that are sometimes overt and fierce, as when Umbu Pari accosted a lower-caste man for infringing upon his interests. His behavior, in turn, called into question authority in the village of Wandi, and Umbu Ama was compelled to demonstrate his social control in the village. He wielded this same command in declaring the "art gallery" beginning to evolve in Luka's clan home a mistake—a travesty upon the proper use of a dwelling place rightfully a center of ancestral powers and family activities.

The presence of outsiders draws a web of local positions into play and often re-situates people, if only momentarily. The Parai Mutu sisters, slighted (and perhaps threatened) by Jane's unabashed behavior, retreated into the recesses of their family home, to the very center of their kin-based world, where they remained next to the body of their father.

Luka's female kin became temporarily dispossessed from the central room of their *uma kabihu* by his "gallery"—sitting listlessly at the margins before the intervention of Umbu Ama and the ultimate death of a kinsman redefined the space in immediate, human terms. And the recalcitrant Dane's campsite under the bougainvillea bush became a locus of fear for those living nearby, impelling people to position themselves as guardians against danger. The effects of such consequential visits reinforce or challenge Sumbanese epistemologies regarding proximal and distant worlds.

The next chapter moves away from Sumba to other regions of convergence and redefinition involving the local and the foreign. Following traders and fabrics to other Indonesian islands, we can glimpse expansions in their worlds involving multicultural, transnational social landscapes as they manifest themselves in Indonesia.

160

CHAPTER 9
ON OTHER ISLANDS

Are there affinities joining these iconic extremes, which themselves suggestively invent a correspondence of creatures and cultures?
—James A. Boon, *Affinities and Extremes*

O ne evening in 1994, an itinerant textile trader from Sumba stood spellbound on a street in Kuta Beach, Bali. Bending under a backpack stuffed with *ikat* fabrics, Luka gazed upward. At that moment, a half-naked tourist jumped from a tower constructed on the roof of a disco-pub, then bounced wildly as the bungee cord he was attached to stretched and recoiled. Days before, the spectator transfixed by this event had traveled four hundred miles west from Sumba to Bali, where he entered into the cosmopolitan and often baffling community of locals, traders, and tourists. When he returned home, his travel tales would increase his prestige and enrich the lore regarding foreigners that animates village porches and urban alleys throughout Indonesia.

Figure 37. Postcard from a boutique/gallery in Bali.

Bali

Over the past two or three decades, Bali has been the prime destination of the increasing hordes of international tourists traveling to Indonesia. Regions of southern Bali are now globalized bazaars of fashion, food, and arts. Cosmopolitan streetscapes, bustling with international commerce and motorized traffic, are permanent economic and social environments on the island, sometimes eclipsing the palm trees, temples, and village architecture portrayed in tourist brochures.[1]

Western writers (such as the American novelist Alice Walker) and media stars have promoted a lushly pristine, paradisiacal picture of Bali, emphasizing the artistic creativity and "spirituality" of its unique Hindu-animist culture.[2] Some years back, with extensive media attention, British rock star Mick Jagger was married in Bali, setting a trend for Western celebrities to follow. In the late 1980s, a New Age seminar leader from California led a group of spiritual seekers to the island, where they embarked upon a quest to relive their "past lives" as Balinese—within a span of two weeks.[3] As an international, postmodern[4] holiday resort, Bali has been colonized by leisured, "first world" people, often seeking a primordial authenticity in its culture and natural setting. Such seekers frequently appropriate Balinese cultural elements into their own identities —whether through buying artifacts, studying local dance, reconstructing their personal histories within Bali's history, or attending local rituals clad in native *sarungs*. Bali is, in salient ways, a late-twentieth-century depot of orientalism (cf. Said 1978), where disenchanted Westerners might reinvent their worlds.[5] While such reinventions are laden with the power relations intended in Said's term, a more finely nuanced universe of contests is also taking place.

As we have seen in previous chapters, Bali has increasingly drawn in people from other Indonesian islands, and an eclectic mix of agents and entrepreneurs enlivens the island's tourist enclaves. Just as tourists might inhabit "reinvented" worlds within certain eclectic and malleable social settings of the island, locals and people from other Indonesian islands also experience Bali as a kind of social free-zone in which to experiment. In this chapter, we will follow a few foreigners and Sumbanese as they navigate the town of Kuta Beach, Bali's busiest "tourist ghetto." First, however, I will describe the crucible environment that attracts them, putting them in the company of millions of others who migrate to Bali annually.

162

Correspondence of Creatures and Cultures

The bustling tourist region centered in Kuta Beach occupies a portion of Bali's southern coast and has spread to engulf the area for several kilometers to the north, south, and east. A wide, white beach bounds the area on the west and is especially popular because of the quality of its Indian Ocean surf. For roughly three decades now Kuta has been frequented by hippies and surfers, and before the most recent growth in tourism to Bali (largely due to an increased number of international airline carriers coming from North America and Europe), the beach town had hosted a mixture of largely young, budget travelers. Most were from Australia (especially the surfing crowd), with Europeans and North Americans also frequenting the makeshift resort.[6]

Along with this youthful, recreational set, markets developed for T-shirts, shorts, and various handcrafted articles produced by local Balinese entrepreneurs. With the eventual arrival of a larger and more affluent international crowd, however, came demands for more sophisticated and expensive items. The Balinese, whose inventive responses to influences and demands from the outside world are now legendary,[7] began to invent and diversify specific products for foreigners, and a number of talented entrepreneurs became exceedingly successful. A permanent and creative community of innovators and merchants developed, a community characterized by a constant influx of foreigners and a resulting local compulsion to elaborate continuously upon itself.[8]

This elaboration proceeded through a maze of roads and alleys dedicated to cross-cultural commerce and containing a profusion of new goods and services for outsiders. Shops and restaurants catering to tourists appeared everywhere, offering international cuisines and all manner of carvings, paintings, and locally designed fashions. A wide-ranging commercialism evolved to include the import of goods from other Indonesian islands in response to a growing tourist demand for "ethnic" and "primitive" arts. Over the years, the streets radiating from Kuta's global hub became clogged with motorcycles, *bemo*s, tourist buses, taxis, vintage cars, and Land Rovers. The roar of traffic grew constant in an atmosphere in which engine fumes mingled with tropical heat.

163

Currently, along the lanes of Kuta Beach stroll young surfers, elderly Westerners, groups of Japanese, scores of hawkers, local schoolchildren, village matrons in sarongs carrying baskets of fruit, and numerous young men (Balinese and those from other islands) dressed in the globally chic costume of jeans and T-shirts. The Balinese live their everyday lives within this sociocultural medley of the Kuta region, with its overlay of a commercial, multicultural, "global ethnoscape."[9] Within this environment, Balinese women make regular offerings at any of hundreds of small temples along thoroughfares as scantily clad tourists stop to take photographs or blithely pass by.

Along the main strip of the area, hawkers of all ages add to a mercantile climate of incessant persuasion. Carrying flat wooden boxes, which they open to every passing (and often harried) tourist, the traders ask, "Watch, Mister? I give cheap price. Okay?!" Vendors selling "fanny packs" and braided leather bracelets approach the numerous foreigners who walk by them, occasionally finding an interested customer. The chant-like call of "TrrrrrrranSPORT!" can be heard every twenty meters, and numbers of men stand against their jeeps, taxicabs, and motorcycles, offering to whisk tourists away to other sites on the island.

English is the commercial lingua franca of Kuta Beach, and the word "primitive" regularly punctuates the streetscape. One passes a Primitive Art of Borneo shop and soon another that reads Antiques and Primitive Art. People walk by (tourists and locals) wearing "Bali Primitive" and "Lombok Primitive"[10] T-shirts featuring bold, *tiki*-like graphics of human figures below the written messages.

Accommodations in the Kuta region range from basic, budget hovels to four-star hotels, and tourists in the area reflect this range of expenditure. Many young, penny-wise foreigners eat at the simple, stand-like restaurants (*warung*) the Balinese frequent. Numerous, more costly eateries along the lanes offer a range of international fare, from Thai to Mexican cuisine. The posher hotels feature elegant restaurants, in which aspects of Balinese culture—such as orchestral performances (known as *gamelan*) and accompanying dances—are performed in palm-fringed, air-conditioned settings.

164

The wide range of tourists in the hotel compounds facing the beach is striking. Topless, thong-clad European women (many the parents of accompanying small children) sit at poolside, as do families of sunburned Australians and small groups of elderly Dutch, conservatively dressed. Balinese masseuses rub the oiled bodies of near-naked tourists on hotel lawns.

Enfolded Pastiche

Of the relatively clad tourists, many wear stylish outfits created by local designers and artisans. *Batik* fabrics in myriad forms, as well as *ikat* and various types of woven cloth from other Indonesian islands, enfold the bodies of foreigners, creating a voguish parade of colorful shawls, shirts, pants, and dresses along Bali's tourist lanes. Of these visitors, a notable proportion are women,[11] from young adults to late middle-aged women, tanned and sparsely or smartly dressed in assorted fabrics— making up a distinctly female modeling of an Indonesian-fashion-chic that has had its genesis in Balinese tourist enclaves. In this manner, textiles from distant islands of the archipelago clothe tourists in all sorts of combinations, with their wearers uncertain of the origins of the fabrics.[12] The slippage between the "ethnic" and the "primitive" into "modern" dimensions of fashion is seamless as it complies with international tastes. Thus pieces of cloth from far-flung isles become ready-to-wear in a Balinese setting (see plate 20).

Indeed, popular fashions in the tourist zones could be metaphors for the kaleidoscopic composites Bali is famous for and the peoples it pulls in. The Sumbanese textile entrepreneur Biba (chapter 4) told me of a tall, blond woman she sighted in Kuta Beach wearing a jacket Biba described as being made up of "parts from all over Indonesia." The frontal bodice looked like Balinese temple scenes. The sleeves were of woven *songket* (supplementary weft) from Sumatra. The floral hem was of Rotinese *ikat*, and the back panel displayed a bold Sumba crocodile. The jacket was buttoned with carved bones, Biba said, "probably from Irian Jaya." The garment—composed of fabrics of multiethnic origin spanning the Indonesian archipelago and worn by someone from another hemisphere—suggested to Biba an intricate network of crafts and cultures and the arbitrary nature of their refashioning in current times. These novel combinations—ready-to-wear versions of a kind of "overstimulating ensemble" Jameson (1994:93) characterizes as typifying postmodern urbanism—are mixtures of pluralism, appropriation, and opportunity, in a threadborne community of commerce, however loosely woven. Such congeries are common sights in Balinese tourist zones, which have developed into trade diasporas[13] where everything often seems to just come together, in what might be characterized as "transnational capitals of an art without frontiers" (Williams 1989:51).[14] Biba marveled at the ensemble she saw the tourist wearing, pieced from assorted frontiers. "The jacket was such a mix! Like the park Beautiful Indonesia in Miniature,[15] but one that a person could wear."

An economy of cloth again unfolds as an economy of experience, animating a distinctive "borderzone" region rife with invention.[16] Sumbanese textile traders become enmeshed in this multilayered economy, and their goods and presence become part of the environment described above. They also are affected by situations such as those to follow.

Latter-day Memsahib

A tall European woman in her thirties, adorned with heavy silver and amber jewelry and elegantly dressed in a rayon *sarong*-like skirt and a short, sleeveless blouse, stood in a posh, gallery-like shop. In the midst of Indonesian arts from around the archipelago—fine cloth, modern ceramics, and stylish clothing—the European delivered stern orders to a Balinese salesgirl, who appeared chastened after the woman briskly left. The inventory of "Island Designs Gallery" includes a mixture of outer-island textiles and carvings juxtaposed with Balinese "traditional" and novel designs. As in a showroom in a metropolitan gallery, articles are accented on walls or floor spaces: an old and intricate Javanese batik hangs on one wall, a woman's red leather jacket (of sleek, contemporary design) is suspended and spotlit nearby, minimalist raku pottery sits atop an ornately carved teak tabletop from Irian Jaya, brightly painted wooden Balinese goddesses descend from invisible cords overhead, and a white skull tree within a deep indigo *hinggi* from Sumba dominates the wall at one end of the room.[17]

I initially sought Olga out after obtaining her name and the location of her shop from a Sumbanese I knew: Umbu Pari from Parai Mutu. She is the same woman who had once consorted with the roguish nobleman, and a couple of years before I had witnessed her public admonishment of him in the lobby of the Hotel Orchid in Waingapu (chapter 5). After this, Pari had lost touch with Olga, but he passed her address on to me as someone who sold fine things in Bali. When I eventually mentioned my acquaintance with the Sumba noble (among others in the textile trade I thought Olga might know), she responded by rolling her eyes and commenting on the dishonesty of certain Sumbanese she had dealt with.

The European had been the proprietress of this shop for several years; she spent part of the year in Bali and the remainder in Europe, where she owned what she describes as another exclusive Indonesian ethnic art gallery. When in Bali, she resided in a house she had built on the property of a Balinese "partner" in business; the house sat on a private lane not far from her shop.[18] The Island Designs entrepreneur ("Olga") became an acquaintance during my several stays in the Kuta Beach region between 1993 and 1994.

Olga was drawn to Bali in the late 1970s, arriving originally from Europe for a vacation and then repeatedly returning to the island. Since then, she had married and divorced a Balinese man, had traveled widely across Indonesia, and was both informed and cynical when speaking of its numerous cultural manifestations. Her terse behavior toward the young girl in her shop might partially be explained in a statement she once made to me on the realities of living as an expatriate in Bali:

> When I first began to live in Bali, I was married to Made [her ex-husband] and I was in a kind of romantic bubble. After a year, we separated and I continued the business alone. I learned to deal with the people and had to be hard so as not to be taken advantage of. Indonesians will really abuse kindness if you let them. It is sad, but I have become this way through experience, and I must say I don't enjoy it here as I

did once. But that is what business does. And I do a good
business, especially with what I can sell in Europe.

Olga's shop attracted a steady clientele of well-to-do tourists. A
magnetic quality of the shop was its elegant organization: an eclectic mix
of Indonesian arts was displayed in an evocatively Western gallery setting,
one that emphasized *distinction*. If, as Pierre Bourdieu claims, "taste
classifies, and it classifies the classifier" (1984:6),[19] discriminating foreigners entering the Island Designs Gallery enjoyed a redoubled prestige.
A taste for "primitive" or "ethnic" arts had extended the classificatory
reach of such collectors to the exotic, global level; this reach was then
reframed within a familiar and affirming context of exclusivity: the
museum-like gallery, with its authority over the certification of objects
and their suspension in time.[20]

Moreover, in its vastness, the Indonesian archipelago invites an intensified mystique of remoteness among foreign tourists. There are forever
islands, mountains, and peoples remaining out of reach—beyond the
travel and time constraints of any particular holiday. In this way, an eternally elusive "elsewhere" beckons, from which tourists seek objects of
value. Dean MacCannell (1992) sees tourism as celebrating "distance,"
which I regard as an essential ingredient in a type of tourism character-
izing that to Indonesia. Through distance, a "timeless ethnographic
present" (Fabian 1983) remains uncompromised in the imaginations of
foreigners, and arts gain in value in being from unreachable lands—as do
those of Irian Jaya or of Sumba in a Balinese context. As James Clifford
claims, "Any collection implies a temporal vision generating rarity and
worth" (1988:13). In gallery environments like those in Kuta Beach, such
vision reifies ethnic groups at the same time that it fragments them.

Johannes Fabian defines an ideology by which Westerners position
themselves in relation to the exotic Other as perpetuated through distance. This relationship is "conceived not only as difference, but as distance in space and time" (1983:147). In its present state of (often brash)
commercial development, however, Bali offers disenchantment to foreign seekers of the pristine. Currently presenting a dazzling infinity of
products and services, Kuta Beach is a region of garish overproduction.[21]
For this reason, arts and cultures of unreachable Indonesian islands
become more intriguing reminders to international tourists of pristine
Others and enticements for a truer alterity.[22] This exoticism promises
compensation to tourists seeking the unattainable in a Balinese context.
As the "essences" of Balinese culture prove opaque or spoiled to tourists,
they often seek such essentiality from unreachable locales, with yet
greater fervor.[23]

167

Memsahibs *and* "Bali Boys"

About two kilometers west of the gallery described above, the exclusive Bali Oberoi Hotel stretches along the beach. Entering the grounds, one comes into a sanitized parody of Bali, a smug reinvention of the island's culture in a lavish theme park for the affluent outsider. The hotel acres evoke an idyllic travel brochure writ large. Ocean views become a backdrop for a constructed domain, which includes an immense swimming pool with a gushing fountain in its center. Thatched pavilions shelter pool tables, giant chess sets, and upholstered rattan furniture. Accommodations consist of thatch-roofed, stone cottages, walled and cloistered within their own gardens, set along winding paths that seem to follow an endlessly lush, tropical maze.

One day I found my way from the beach through the hotel grounds and eventually exited the premises through a driveway leading to what remained of the surrounding landscape of rice paddies and grassy fields. A Western woman in her twenties, wearing a short T-shirt and a "thong" bathing-suit bottom, which exposed most of her lower body, also exited several meters ahead of me. The woman ambled hastily, nakedly, down the hotel driveway, passing a large sign at the entrance that stated "The Bali Oberoi—the way you want Bali to be."

I lost sight of the woman but later spotted her again, sitting at a table at a sidewalk cafe. Two things had been added to her personal inventory: she had evidently purchased a *sarung,* which wrapped her lower body, and a young Indonesian man sat with his arm around her shoulder. They appeared to have recently met; the man was asking numerous questions and the American woman was answering; they both smoked cigarettes. What seemed to be transpiring was a kind of tourist enclave social phenomenon many people (locals and foreigners) have come to refer to as the "Bali Boy" syndrome.

Adrian Vickers noted the existence of this phenomenon in the 1980s, describing it as a "small-scale gigolo industry as part of the Kuta Beach scene, rumored by both Westerners and Balinese youth to depend mainly on the large numbers of unattached Australian women visiting the island" (1989:193). By the early 1990s, the numbers of unattached women included those from a variety of industrialized nations, including Japan. While riding in a taxicab from the airport on one trip to Bali, I was asked by the driver if I wanted a Bali Boy for the duration of my visit. After that, I became even more attuned to a tendency I had already noticed, and I began to see foreign women of all ages with young, Indonesian men—eating in restaurants, emerging from hotel rooms, or strolling along the beach in the evening.[24]

Looming large in the imaginations of many Sumbanese men, Bali

168

promises sexual adventure and perhaps ongoing, lucrative relationships. A foreign girlfriend in Bali is not only a potential means to financial gain, but also a badge of sophistication and conquest for Sumbanese men, who often accent their ethnicity to impress women eager for exotic experiences.

Transcultural Heroics

A popular meeting area for Indonesians and foreigners is the Warung Kopi (Coffee Restaurant), on Kuta's main commercial strip. As the woman just described sat with her Indonesian suitor at the restaurant's sidewalk cafe, other patrons occupied a cloistered courtyard filled with tropical foliage. Tables at the Warung Kopi are situated around a small pond, and the bill of fare is international, offering Balinese dishes along with European and Indian cuisine. A portion of the menu is also devoted to "health foods," including vegetarian entrees and brown rice. Through a compression of diverse ethnic cuisines, the restaurant is a globalized "everywhere" in offering a culinary variety to its patrons.

One day I encountered the Sumbanese textile entrepreneur Umbu Taniku of Wandi village sitting in the courtyard restaurant, sipping coffee and wearing an *ikat* scarf around his neck. Umbu had been in Bali for several weeks on a textile-selling mission, lodging at a small hotel in Kuta Beach frequented by Sumbanese traders. Poised and watchful, he was surveying the patrons of the restaurant. Surprised by my entry, he rose and invited me to sit with him.

169

In chapter 4 I described something of Umbu Taniku's home life, primarily focusing on his wife, Kata. Umbu, it may be remembered, had become accustomed to taking trips to Bali to sell textiles, staying for indeterminate periods. This had been a source of conflict with Kata, who continuously produced the fabrics yet never accompanied Umbu on his travels. This was now such a venture, but one on which he had met with bad fortune. Umbu told me his version of what had happened and only later on returning to Sumba would I hear the commentary of others on the fateful events in Kuta Beach.

Along with textiles produced in his household, Umbu Taniku had also brought to Bali a number of cloths made by villagers in the Wandi region, which he had planned to sell on commission. Over the course of a month, he sold most of the fabrics. He was joined at the hotel by a younger friend on his first trip away from Sumba. As Umbu told the story, he had amassed a total of four million rupiah (then about two thousand U.S. dollars), which he hid in his hotel room. One day the money was gone and so was his friend, and he could only assume that he had been robbed. Since that time, Umbu had been attempting to sell his remaining fabrics (the thief had also allegedly taken off with much of his remaining inventory) to make enough money to return home. He had written to his wife in Sumba of his predicament. Although he appeared composed sitting in the Warung Kopi, Umbu was in desperate straits, at the margins of his experienced world.

Three German women he had met earlier had agreed to meet him at the restaurant to consider buying some *hinggi*s. Umbu Taniku had attempted to sell these fabrics to some of the shops in Kuta (and had ventured further to the other tourist regions of Sanur and Ubud) but had not been offered a price he felt was duly profitable. He had approached Olga at the Island Designs Gallery a few days before I met him, but she told him that the colors of his fabrics were too chemical in appearance. Finally, a Chinese-Sumbanese boutique owner offered to buy the lot of his textiles, but Umbu was holding out to get a better price on his own from tourists. While Umbu and I conversed, the German women appeared. All spoke English and one spoke rudimentary Indonesian. We had coffee and then Umbu asked if the women would like to see the fabrics he had at his hotel. He invited me to come along to assist in the translating. (Umbu was hampered by knowing limited English; the friend who had stolen his recent profits had also been acting as an interpreter for him.)

Arriving at the hotel compound, I saw it was a kind of ghetto for outer-island traders in Kuta Beach, and I was greeted by several other men I knew from Sumba. One was a Muslim merchant from Waingapu; the others were textile traders from several villages. A few men were cooking rice in a small kitchen; another was laundering clothes at one end of the courtyard. In addition to the men from Sumba, I learned that dealers in arts from Timor, Irian Jaya, Sulawesi, and Flores were also staying at the hotel. To minimize their expenses while staying in Bali, the traders stayed two or more to a room.

Umbu Taniku led the three of us through the hotel courtyard to a bench outside his room, then entered the room to retrieve his textiles. The German women were pleased at making Umbu's acquaintance (they had initially met at the Warung Kopi, where they said they had been taken with Umbu's *ikat* scarf) and began to ask me questions about his village and life in Sumba. One asked if Umbu was really a nobleman, as he had claimed to the women. I was relieved to be able to answer truthfully that he was, and even more relieved when Umbu emerged from his room, preempting any further, more personal questions about him. I had little idea of what he may have told the women about himself.

The *hinggi*s Umbu Taniku presented to the tourists were characteristically large and boldly designed, and as he opened them he related the stories they contained, speaking slowly and simply in Indonesian, flour-

170

Figure 38. One of many ethnic arts boutiques in Kuta Beach.

ished with an occasional English word. Umbu Taniku enthusiastically re-
lived the story of the hero within one woven piece. Claiming the monarch
as an ancestor, he told the women of his bravery in battle and of the
huge megalith that marked his grave site in Sumba. He connected the
diorama of the cloth to his own family and history, noting the powerful
symbolism embodied by the horses and crocodiles in the design. Emphasizing valorous content over technical merits in the *hinggi*, Umbu seduced
his customers with the grandeur of his design and his narrative.[25]

171

The three tourists marveled at his cloth and his story. One agreed to
buy the *hinggi* and did not bargain with the price Umbu asked for it.
Eight hundred thousand rupiah (roughly four hundred fifty dollars)
changed hands, and the woman asked Umbu Taniku if he would like to
have dinner with the three later in the evening. He agreed and they set a
time to meet at an up-scale restaurant on one of Kuta's back lanes. After
they left the hotel grounds, Umbu was visibly excited and thanked me
repeatedly for my help in translating his Indonesian into English for
the women. I had been complicit in his presentation of self and in his
commerce with the tourists.

"Sumba Primitive"

On the main thoroughfare of Kuta Beach, the "Sumba Primitive" boutique sits among numerous such enterprises. The shop's sign features an

iconic male figure, like those typical in textiles of the Hawewa region in eastern Sumba. Ibu Ana, sister of Sing Ha, the Chinese-Sumbanese entrepreneur described in chapter 6, owns the shop. It was at her shop that Umbu Taniku finally sold the remainder of his depleted fabric inventory, enabling him to take a ferry back to Sumba.

By 1994, Ibu Ana had become the successful proprietress of this "art shop." Soon after she first greeted me, Ibu Ana led me into her household behind the boutique, where she and her husband lived. The dwelling looked out on a small courtyard, in which Ibu Ana kept a pig and some chickens. Brightly lit with fluorescent bulbs, rooms of the home were crowded with stacked boxes of textiles amidst the furnishings. Ibu Ana proudly took me into a small, modern kitchen and pointed to a micro-wave oven she had bought since coming to Bali. Reveling in a techno-logical modernity unattainable to her in Sumba, she was far more zealous in showing me her electrical appliances than the arts in her inventory.

The interior of the Sumba Primitive shop was densely stocked with folded fabrics, and on the walls hung pieces that looked like Sing Ha's most lavish productions, replete with multiple, "primitive" male figures often seen in the Hawewa region and wide borders of contrasting *pahikung* weaving. Viewing the distinctive combinations, I recalled the clois-tered Quiet One of Sing Ha's factory and mused on the contrast between the environment in which she produced her fabrics and the one in which they were eventually sold. Observing cloths reframed within the environ-ment of a tourist shop in Bali gave me a sense of their biographies and disjunctures, particularly the ones whose creators I thought I knew.

172

Igor Kopytoff notes that biographies of things can make salient what otherwise might remain obscure (1988:67). The cloistered women of Sing Ha's enterprise in Sumba, or women such as Madai or Rambu Nina weaving on their village verandahs, are far removed from the commercial spaces their fabrics might eventually occupy in Bali. This remoteness characterizes the distances involved in not only the biography of "things" such as textiles, but of people. By noting the various places these fabrics travel from and to, we get a tangible sense of the scope involved in their production, trade, and consumption—and a certain definition emerges from an obscurity created through the distances they cross.

Ibu Ana told me that she had prospered since moving from Sumba to Bali in 1993, and although there was much local competition, her busi-ness had fared better than it had in Sumba, where her small store had been overshadowed by the hotel shops of Waingapu. In Bali, she had capi-talized on being from Sumba and (commanding some English) could talk to tourists about her fabrics and their places of origin. A monthly ship-ment of textiles arrived from her brother's workshop in eastern Sumba, and other fabrics made their way to her shop via any of a number of itinerant traders from the island. Traces of various villages, designers, and trends were visible in the cloths in her shop.

A loom sat at the rear of her shop space, and when not engaged with customers, Ibu Ana would tend to her own weaving of combined *ikat* and *pahikung* fabrics. The sight of her actually producing textiles like those from a distant island made her shop and inventory appealing to many tourists. Moreover, she continued to dye yarns in her courtyard and could take potential customers to see firsthand how her own cloths were colored. Some foreigners had taken her picture after buying one of her textiles, and she displayed a collection of photos of herself with various tourists she had done business with. Among these, on one wall of her shop, were pictures of Ibu Ana in the village of Hawewa: standing next to traditional homes, weaving, and standing in front of a funeral megalith beside her brother, Sing Ha.

Ibu Ana belonged to a small diaspora[26] of Sumbanese textile merchants living in Bali by the mid-1990s. Her relations with other immigrant Sumbanese were varied: with a few she enjoyed a friendly, commercial cooperation; with others she felt a grudging enmity, most particularly with certain Chinese-Sumbanese, whom she regarded as ruthless competitors. One such rival operated the "Andung Primitive Art"[27] shop on the next block.

As she was able to recount who had recently come from Sumba with textiles to sell, when in Bali I would often find out who was in the area through Ibu Ana. She peppered such news with commentaries on the follies of many of the Sumbanese traders, who often mismanaged their profits from trading in Bali to the point that they relied upon relatives in Sumba to send them money to return home. Like her enterprising brother, Sing Ha, Ibu Ana credited the Chinese part of her lineage as having given her a head for business. Simultaneously, she was proud of her textile knowledge and weaving skills inherited from her Sumbanese mother. Sitting in her shop in Bali, Ibu Ana once reflected aloud:

> Bali is a perfect place for someone like me. Very busy and modern and I am the right mix to be here. In Sumba I never fit [*mencocoki*] and could not succeed. Here everything is all so mixed together that I fit.

Displacement, for Ibu Ana, had become a positive means to "fit" in the world—in the multicultural commercial setting of a Balinese tourist enclave. It was from Ibu Ana that I eventually learned that Umbu Taniku had sold his remaining textiles (to her) and soon after had returned to Sumba. Ibu Ana had her own suspicions regarding Umbu's "misfortune."

173

She speculated that Umbu had squandered all of his profits himself, as did many Sumbanese traders in Kuta Beach. Umbu Pari (of Parai Mutu) and Luka (of Wandi) had visited her shop in the same week and were still at large in Bali.

Cavorting in Kuta

Some days later, while wandering the commercial strip of Kuta Beach, I saw a familiar face peering out from a restaurant window. Framed within a large plate glass pane of a Kentucky Fried Chicken franchise, Umbu Pari gazed out at the noisy thoroughfare, not yet seeing me. This was an ironic portrait, as the noble from Parai Mutu maintained a renowned penchant for augury in Sumba using the entrails of chickens (described in chapter 5). Disporting in the motley landscape of Kuta Beach as a patron of this particular restaurant, he posed a displacement as typical of Bali as it was poetic in the terms of my study. Umbu Pari's affinity for poultry as a means to divination corresponded with what was, for him, a prestigious culinary venture—and his visibility from the street was no accident.[28]

A ten-year veteran of the Balinese tourist scene, by 1994 Umbu Pari's English enabled him to interact easily with tourists. He did not stay at the hotel frequented by most Sumbanese traders, however, but at a slightly more up-scale accommodation, where he could more easily mingle with foreigners. By day he frequented restaurants and shops along the commercial strip; by evening he went to bars and discotheques. He especially enjoyed a large disco called "Peanuts," and in a smartly eclectic costume composed of wrapped Sumba *ikat* and tailored denim, he would enter the mixes of foreigners and Indonesians crowding the place nightly. It was upon such meeting grounds that he had made a number of international connections, including Hans, the "Crazy Dutchman" (who appeared in Umbu Pari's village in chapter 8), and the Australian who was ostensibly sponsoring a textile exhibit of his pieces.

Wearing a "Parai Mutu" T-shirt, with his own whimsical design of a skull tree on the back, Umbu Pari had commodified his village and identity into a logotype, marking himself within the multiethnic commodity flow of the Kuta Beach community. Thus displaying ethnicity, design savvy, and male prowess, Umbu Pari enjoyed a combined "cultural capital" (Bourdieu 1984),[29] which gained in its combination and (dis)-location. Reflecting a practice long outlawed in Sumba (by Dutch and then Indonesian authorities), headhunting resurfaced as a trope in a present fashioning of culture—to paraphrase Janet Hoskins, moving from a domain of traditional practice to a modern mythology constructed by external powers (1996:37). Umbu cavorted in the space of this transformation in Bali, playing through an infinity of desires, tastes, signs, and

174

encounters. Moreover, his T-shirt skull tree bore a restyled ferocity that perhaps—talismanically—also countered certain perils in travel. *Ikat* cloth and a reworked village motif conjoined jeans and a position at table in a Western fast-food franchise as Pari sat poised in his Balinese haunt. Later he would be going to a disco-pub to meet some Australians he knew, and he issued a casual invitation to me to join the group that evening.

That night, I went to the pub. Loud, bass-rhythm music made conversation impossible. The disco was constructed on two levels, the top of which was a dance floor filled with moving people. The social mix included slender Indonesians in well-tailored clothes and shirtless, barrel-chested Australians wearing sun visors. Tables in the lower level were crowded with people and large pitchers of beer, illuminated by flashing lights and neon beer signs decorating the walls.

I eventually sighted Umbu Pari sitting at a table with a group of Indonesian and Western men. He appeared to be very drunk and was talking intently to a heavy-set, middle-aged European. I stood at some distance, feeling reluctant to approach the table of inebriated men, but nevertheless curious to see how the evening would progress. I remained a voyeur in the pub. Finally Umbu Pari and the man he had been talking with arose, staggered somewhat, and ambled out to the street. This was the last I would see of the Parai Mutu nobleman on this visit to Bali. Later (in Sumba) he would tell me that the large man he had been with in the Kuta Beach establishment was a college professor from Australia, the one who had promised him an exhibit of his textiles sometime in the following year.

175

Foreign Affair

Luka knew the hotel I stayed at when in the Kuta Beach region and called at the front desk one morning. He looked sheepish as I approached him and obviously uncertain of the proper decorum in calling on me away from Sumba. He had been in Bali for two weeks, having come with Hasan and Biba after their joint tour of Java. The couple had flown back to Sumba, and Luka remained alone in Bali.

Events in Java had strained Luka's relationship with the Wandi couple, and Luka spoke of their venture with some reserve, saying that things had not gone as he had wanted them to. Now, Luka confided, he was in Bali to enjoy himself after weeks of travel and work in Java. He added that he did not want to be responsible any more for other people, as he felt he had been regarding Hasan and Biba, but wanted to travel freely (*jalan bebas*, I.) in Bali, making his own decisions.

He had been going out every evening, he told me, to night spots in the region, and had made some new friends. The night before I saw him, Luka had once more witnessed daring Australians jumping off a tower on the roof of a pub attached to bungee cords. Luka marveled at the risks of the stunts. He also wondered aloud to me whether the Australians had some sort of special power (*kuasa*, I.) or knowledge (*ilmu*, I.) to protect them from accidents. The bungee jumping event had further impressed upon Luka the idea that Westerners delighted in perilous sports, including surfing. It was in Bali that he fully realized this.

Luka carried several *hinggi*s he had been showing to shops and tourists in the hopes of eliciting orders for future pieces. The fabrics told tales that included archers from the Indian epic, the *Mahabarata*, and two others revealing historic battles in Sumba, proceeding unidirectionally in cloth. On two occasions in Bali, I witnessed Luka unfolding his cloths to interested tourists and then narrating the *hinggi*s, linking them to heroic historical events. In this manner, he, like Umbu Taniku, positioned himself by claiming descendence from noble heroes celebrated within his woven tales. In Luka's case, however, he was asserting a nobility in Bali's tourist zones that eluded him in Sumba because of his mixed-caste birth. Through his fabrics, Luka enframed tradition, folklore, and realism, supporting claims of "authenticity" in encounters and spaces rife with hybridity.[30] Luka summarized his knowledge of Western tastes:

> Westerners like tales of bravery. In Bali I see them jumping from high towers and surfing in dangerous waters. In my *hinggi*s, they get daring events from Sumba history. Events where a man comes close to death, but then lives, wins [*menang*].

Hasan and Biba had profited handsomely in Java, and Luka had been given a percentage of their earnings for his assistance in the sales. Now in Bali, Luka wore smart new clothing purchased at a Jakarta department store. After I complimented his outfit, he ventured nervously:

> It's like this: I want to ask you about a problem. Don't be angry. Do you think it's possible that I might get a Western girlfriend? I thought maybe on this trip I could meet one. But there is another problem. Excuse me, but I'm afraid of the AIDS sickness.[31] Do most Westerners have it? How do people take care not to get it? Please excuse me. Please tell no one I said this.

I advised Luka to be very careful about encounters in Bali, as AIDS was a deadly illness spreading around the world. I then urged him to go to a nearby clinic for advice, which he agreed to do that day. This was the first time that he had ever spoken to me of intimate matters, and he periodically excused himself profusely, insisting he knew of no one else who might be able to counsel him. As he left, Luka bid his farewell with a recently acquired expression: "*Ciao.*"

I sensed that Luka was on the brink of new adventure. His attitude also suggested a general imagining of Bali by Sumbanese men—as a place of unlimited possibility and personal bounty, a social arena of "unlimited good."[32] Yet the intrusion of a disease that had become an international epidemic had begun to temper the imaginations and actions of some Indonesians by 1994, and Luka had been affected by a growing atmosphere of caution.

Several days later I saw Luka in a restaurant in the company of a mixed group of foreigners, laughing as he spoke with a couple of women at the table. He was enjoying himself, and we exchanged brief greetings. The following evening, I spotted Luka from a distance on the beach, but this time he did not see me. He and a young European woman I recognized from his table the evening before were strolling together along the water, and after they passed, I noticed a segment of a battle scene on the *hinggi* wrapped around the woman's back.

Java

Hasan and Biba had been accompanied by Luka on a selling mission to Java. As described in chapter 4, the couple's textile holdings had begun modestly (just a few years earlier), stored in a basket at the rear of their small shop in Sumba, from which they initially sold sundries to villagers of the Wandi region. By 1993, their fabric inventory and sales had grown tremendously, largely through Biba's enterprise. In November of that year, they left Sumba on a ferry destined for Java. Their travels would last six weeks.

The three eventually arrived in Jakarta, where they were taken in by a Sumbanese civil service worker (a distant relative of Hasan) in a small, rented house in a working-class area of town. In a back room looking out on an open sewer, they began their urban sojourn. During the day, they would take buses or taxis to galleries and boutiques they knew of or arrange meetings with Western residents in the city. Most of these foreigners they had met in Sumba, either at *pameran*s or when the tourists had visited Wandi. During their Jakarta stay, I was also in the city, and met up with them several times.

Although Biba had been to Bali on her own, this had been her first trip to Java, and Hasan's first time away from Sumba. In their company, Luka easily took on the role of guide and translator inasmuch as he had been to Jakarta once before and the couple spoke no English. When the three entered the large, modern home of an American oil company employee, carrying textiles to show to his wife,[33] they were overwhelmed by the things they encountered. Even the comparatively well-traveled Luka had never visited such a residence. After they were led into the kitchen by their American hostess, Hasan asked if the electric range, with its four coiled burners, was a mosquito repellent machine (*mesin obat nyamuk*, I.), for he had never seen such an appliance and mistook the burners for the coils of bug-repelling incense burned throughout Indonesia. Everyone laughed at his question.

Newfound Celebrity

For five weeks, the threesome entered homes unlike any they had ever visited. They ate and drank with their hosts, and Luka constantly translated between Hasan and Biba and the English speakers. In the environments of American collectors of Indonesian arts, the congenial and self-effacing Sumbanese were a charming trio of "natives." At one point, they were all driven to the private school attended by the children of American expatriates living in Jakarta. There they participated in Indonesian Cultures Day by dressing in eastern Sumbanese traditional garb and exhibiting their fabrics. Luka performed a short dance and sang a traditional Sumbanese song for the children and their parents. Biba spun cotton balls into yarn on a spindle she was given. After the performances, they sold a number of textiles to parents attending the event and were astonished at the celebrity status they had achieved.

Following the ethnic fair at the private school, their acquaintances increased, and the three were invited to a number of homes, where they sold their fabrics at relatively high prices. They were all given gifts of clothing by their hosts, and it was at this point that Biba went to a beauty salon for the first time in her life and had her long, graying hair cut and dyed black. During the Jakarta stay, she took on something of the style of the Western women she was meeting. She continued, however, to wear her traditional carnelian and gold necklace, and the short sleeves on her new blouses revealed tattoos of birds and crayfish on her arms (sources of great interest for foreigners, who saw similar symbols in her fabrics).[34]

During their weeks in Jakarta, the couple also met (through gallery owners) some elite Javanese, and one took a special liking to them, inviting them to his home when he had foreign visitors. At some point in the Jakarta sojourn, Hasan and Biba began to surreptitiously go places without Luka and to conceal certain meetings with people from him. Biba told me that this was because they had realized that they needed to establish connections on their own and that Luka had been often too imposing in his attempts to translate and control their sales strategies and behavior. Almost all of the fabrics they had brought to Java and sold had

178

been their own and those they had bought from other Sumbanese villagers. Luka had but six samples of his designs he had been showing to potential customers. Eventually, Biba and Hasan had tired of Luka's company and at having to give him a percentage of all that they sold.

Parting of Ways

Tensions had developed between the Wandi couple and Luka. Biba especially felt that Luka was demanding more than his share of profits. Luka considered that he was not only making the couple intelligible to foreigners through his translation, but was also lending them ethnic credibility through his position in Sumbanese society and knowledge of traditional culture. He felt he brought valuable cultural savvy to the traveling partnership.

As has been noted, Luka's father had been of the *maramba* caste, although his mother was of low-ranking *ata* ancestry. Biba admitted to coming from poor parents in the hinterlands, the descendant of commoners. As a Muslim, of mixed Sumba-Sumbawa ancestry, and of a commoner Sumbanese line, Hasan could not claim (in the presence of his Sumbanese neighbors) to be of high-ranking or even purely Sumbanese descent. In their company and in presentations of themselves to foreigners, Luka had a clear sense of his own ethnic validity and relative rank. In a heated argument with Biba in Jakarta (regarding a difference of opinion about sales tactics), he had appealed to the authority of his caste standing to subjugate her. Both Luka and Biba related this confrontation to me later (separately), the former feeling within his inherent rights, the latter feeling unjustly bullied and humiliated.

Their relations strained, the three traveled by bus and then ferry together across Java to Bali, and shortly afterward Luka ventured out on his own. In Bali, Hasan and Biba proceeded to the Sanur[35] region (about fifteen kilometers northeast of Kuta Beach), to a small hotel owned by a successful textile merchant from Flores Biba had dealt with on a former visit. Luka took a room in an inexpensive, small hotel behind a pub in Kuta Beach.

The Jakarta trip secured a number of valuable connections for Hasan and Biba, who sold many fabrics and earned in excess of nine million rupiah (close to five thousand U.S. dollars). This was well over twice the income they had formerly known in a year's time. Although Luka had participated, his had been the role of middleman, and his profits had been ten percent of what the couple had received (as had been initially agreed upon). Realizing the extent of their earnings, and feeling left out of some of their final dealings in Jakarta, Luka became embittered and expressed resentment that he had not been given his due. Moreover, he had been

179

left to take a ferry back to Sumba (a voyage of three days), whereas his traveling partners had bought plane tickets for their return trip. This, he felt, was a symbolic indignity. Tensions would erupt again in Sumba.

During their week in Bali, Hasan and Biba sold the remainder of their stock to galleries in Sanur. Then they went shopping in department stores in Denpasar and purchased a television set, a stereo system, items for their kitchen, and clothing for themselves and their children. Their appearances had changed remarkably during their trade venture away from home, and they boarded a plane for Waingapu looking like a cross between affluent Javanese and Americans. Biba, as already mentioned, had adopted a metropolitan stylishness, and Hasan wore an expensive *batik* shirt given him by a wealthy Javanese. As they ascended from Bali, Biba reassured her nervous husband that their plane would not fall into the sea.

CHAPTER 10
UNFOLDING PASSAGES

Life consists of retellings.
> —Edward Bruner, "Experience and Its Expressions"

Art is part of a man's quest for grace; sometimes his ecstasy in partial success, sometimes his rage and agony at failure.
> —Gregory Bateson, "Style, Grace, and Information in Primitive Art"

Selalu begitu di Sumba! *(It is always like that in Sumba!)*
> —Biba

In the last months of 1994, a relentless heat weighed upon East Sumba as people awaited the overdue monsoon. Late in the dry season (*ndau wandu*), this was a listless and sweltering time of the year when most activity ceased during the afternoon hours. Rain had not fallen for months, and villages were dusty and parched. This was also the season known as *musim lapar* (I.; hungry season), when food stores from the year's harvests were depleted and many people were stretching their resources until after the rains, when gardens could grow again.

Figure 39. Calling down the rains.

Shifts

During this time, fewer foreigners visited the villages than in the months between April and September, and there were fewer *pamerans*. Sumbanese who traded textiles in Bali or Java often chose this season to do so, and it had been a year earlier that Biba, Hasan, and Luka had embarked upon their joint venture to the other islands.

By this dry season, there had been shifts in people's lives. Changes in fortunes, reputations, and relationships were evident to me at the end of my time in Sumba. With the rains, I left the island to return to California, where I would ponder for many months before attempting to account for the tapestry of lives I had entered into. What follows are summaries of some conditions in Sumba as I then experienced them—episodes within processes of living in, moving between, and interpreting worlds.

Prosperity

The ambience had changed as I approached Hasan and Biba's home in late 1994. Whereas a year before playing children had filled the front yard, the amplified sounds of a television program now wafted across it. The usual heralding calls of children to their parents when anyone arrived at the house had been supplanted by electronic noises. Visible through the open front door of the house, most of the children sitting on the floor were transfixed by a televised event and oblivious to my arrival.

182

The increased affluence of Biba and Hasan over the past months was striking, as was the frequency of callers to their home. Relatives arrived asking favors and loans. Along with the growing numbers of local visitors to their household, rings of a newly installed telephone brought more-distant voices to the family. One morning, some months after they had returned from their first trip to Java, an American woman living in Jakarta called Biba to inform her that she was planning to bring a tour group of women to Sumba. She asked if Biba would help her coordinate certain aspects of the tour, such as a demonstration of dyeing and weaving. Biba readily accepted the offer, and thus a broadened career in tourism began.

Soon after this, Hasan constructed a large, thatch-roofed pavilion big enough for twelve to fifteen people in the front yard. The couple planned to entertain tour groups in the structure and suspend fabrics along its sides. When the first group arrived some weeks later, they were seated and fed in the pavilion. The arrival of the foreigners (and eventually other tourists to follow) established Hasan and Biba's household as a new center of activity and commerce, a kind of one-family *pameran* zone. Nonetheless, others from the Wandi region would arrive on the heels of the tourists and hedge the borders of the family yard, opening and displaying their cloths. The couple did not put up resistance to their competitors but went about their business, seemingly unfazed.

The designs in Biba's fabrics were now mostly inspired by pictures from museum catalogues and were quite complex. During their Javanese trip, she had collected illustrated publications from galleries and from American customers. Although Biba continued to produce some of her own designs, the angel motifs of a few years earlier (which had signified a religious sentiment) were now supplanted by more intricate imagery. Following their broadened commercial and social scopes, Biba and Hasan had developed an increased knowledge of and concern with the "traditional" in Sumbanese motifs. And such tradition, for them, was defined by pieces in prestigious foreign collections.

Other changes in the household included a live-in housekeeper (*pembantu*, I.). The woman was a poor widow from Waingapu who had been seeking employment, and her presence in the home freed Biba to tend to her textile business. Biba acknowledged the irony of this latest domestic arrangement. Having originated from a poor family, she now commanded a servant. In the village, a stir followed the arrival of the woman into the couple's household, and gossip began to circulate. Someone speculated that Hasan was taking the woman as a second wife, and rumors of this possibility spread through the village. One day, Hasan countered the rumor publicly in an uncharacteristically loud and adamant voice: "This talk [the rumors] is all false, all empty talk [*omong kosong*, I.]! During our travels to Java and Bali my wife got prettier! I never wanted another wife in the past! I want one less now!"

Jealousies of neighbors and relatives continued to beset the couple, and their lives became filled with an endless balancing of the fruits of their successes with the sentiments of resentful villagers. One day, after she related a story of how certain people in Wandi village had been slandering her, Biba proclaimed with exasperation something she had said to me more than a year earlier: "*Selalu begitu di Sumba!*" (I.; "It is always like that in Sumba!").

Jealousy

The year had produced an assortment of bad feelings among Sumbanese I knew, and some such sentiments, particularly involving the household of one textile entrepreneur in Wandi, were directed against me. Because of my friendships in the village, this household had taken a dislike to me, and the resident fabric entrepreneur, "Kula," was casting blame on me for his having been less prosperous than others in the village. He had spread stories that I was writing a book promoting Sumbanese textiles that would publicize the actual names and addresses of my

Wandi friends. This publicity would bring them commerce from foreigners who would come to Sumba specifically seeking them out. I was singularly suspect in facilitating the recent affluence of Hasan and Biba.

One day when Biba was walking to the home of Rambu Hamu, someone called out an insult to her as she passed Kula's house, in what she described as the affected voice of a child. The heckler taunted, "How can you sell cloth? You are only allowed to wear bark!" Laughter filled the house as Biba walked past. The insult inferred that as a slave-caste person, Biba would in former times have been allowed to wear only pounded bark as clothing. Now she was a successful textile entrepreneur, a bitter irony that irked Kula's household. Of higher caste, they felt entitled to riches they had yet to realize.

Over the time I had been in Sumba, no amount of explaining on my part could convince certain people that my interests were not commercial. Most foreigners (in recent years) who had prolonged dealings with eastern Sumbanese people were involved in the textile business, and many local people could not imagine it otherwise. I came to accept the inevitability of being disliked by some people, as my friendships with some would almost certainly alienate others. And, whether the tales were positive or negative, accurate or fabricated, I also knew that I had entered the lore of village verandahs.

184

Passage

In the spring of 1994, Luka had proclaimed to a number of people sitting upon his family porch (including me) that he was ready to become a man (*lalei*), a status fundamentally involving marriage and fatherhood. Later in the year, after months of negotiation among relatives of both clans, Luka finally married a young woman from a village several kilometers from Wandi; she was also of parents of mixed social caste.[1] The marriage, however, had not been completely formalized, as Luka had little to offer for the bride price. Consequently, he could spend nights with his bride in her family home, but could not bring her back to his village to reside. Following custom, any children to come out of the marriage during this period of indebtedness would be considered descendants of Luka's wife's patriclan, not his.

Although he now slept in his wife's village, Luka usually returned to Wandi most days. Inspired by his new status, he demonstrated a renewed vigor in designing fabrics. To become a true householder, and take his wife to live permanently in Wandi village, Luka would have to become more prosperous and pay off a portion of his marriage debt.

In recent times past he had often sold his cloth through Hasan and Biba, but Luka's textile enterprise was now wholly singular. Still at odds with the couple, he vowed never to interact with them again. Luka was irreconcilably *ndewa paita* (bitter of spirit); he reserved his fiercest vitriol for Biba. Moreover, although he had resolved to gain prosperity (*tambah makmur*, I.)[2] in the coming year, he blamed an abiding rage against Biba for consuming his thoughts and sapping his energies. Luka told me of an incident that had occurred after the three had been back in Sumba (from Bali) a short time.

Needing cash to begin another textile venture, he had openly asked Hasan and Biba for money. Biba had answered for the couple, refusing his request in the presence of several neighbors. This had shamed Luka publicly, calling into question his status in the community. The incident also reinforced his own sense of economic failure in his enterprises with fabrics. Regarding himself as of superior caste standing to Biba and Hasan, he considered their public denial of his request insulting. It was after this encounter that he vowed never to reconcile with his former friends. If their names were mentioned, Luka would express long, angry diatribes against them.

During this time, Luka produced several detailed pencil drawings, which he intended as plans for future textiles. The designs were a continuation of the unidirectional, narrative pieces he had done in the past, but the central themes were unusually graphic with bloodshed. Slaughtered water buffalo shed pools of blood at the hands of men wielding sacrificial knives. These scenes, Luka claimed, vented his anger somewhat, as violent impulses became enacted in pictures:

185

> I'm half crazy with hatred for them. It's true. I think about
> them [Biba and Hasan] at night and my blood becomes hot
> and I can't sleep. So then I make pictures like this. These are
> my feelings. My spirit is bitter! It's like that.

Images he created on such nights would later take form in the threads and colors of cloth. In this way, experiences and emotions were inscribed into fabric, reflecting events and relationships at a juncture in his life. As a kind of woven chronicle, Luka's cloth persisted as an expressive medium.

Hoskins' article on violence and sacrifice in West Sumba addresses something of the "complex social relations between persons (represented through animals)" (1993b:166) and their transformations in sacrificial rites in which violence is central. Transformations also occur through visual expressions for people in East Sumba, and the complexities of social relations find emotional outlets in artistic practices. That is, images such as Luka's sacrificial buffalo draw from local ritual idioms to bridge the realms of reason and emotion and afford a certain transcendence to their creator. By rendering scenes of bloodshed, Luka not only vented his fury, but reempowered himself through the creation of a new design. This design eventually resulted in an unanticipated commercial victory.

One morning a Japanese tourist appeared in Wandi. Seeing the man on the central lane of the village, Luka approached him and invited him in English to visit his home. The man followed to the verandah, and after seeing the sacrificial drawings Luka had completed, took an interest in his work. The tourist told Luka that he was also an artist, on holiday from Osaka, and was interested in buying fabrics in Sumba for his gallery. The visitor eventually commissioned a series of textiles from Luka, giving him money in advance. And so it was that by the end of my fieldwork period in Sumba, Luka was once more realizing some measure of prosperity from his creative endeavors, as he prepared to produce his cloths for a Japanese client.

Loss

Several months after his return from the calamitous business venture in Bali, Umbu Taniku had not recovered from his losses. What is more, Kata had been severely ill with dengue fever while he was away, and the family had incurred debts resulting from her hospitalization. Now Kata, pregnant with their third child, worked sluggishly on her binding, coloring, and weaving of warps.

186

Umbu Taniku had returned to Sumba amid serious controversy. Some villagers who had entrusted their fabrics to him to sell in Bali were doubtful of his claim that he was robbed by his assistant in Kuta Beach. Local men who had been trading in Bali at the time of Umbu's misfortune reported that they had seen him gambling recklessly in card games and going to nightclubs every evening. A few villagers voiced openly their surmise that Umbu had squandered and gambled their profits away and had then concocted an alibi to protect himself. One neighbor said that Umbu Taniku had been guilty of such deceptions in the past, but never on such a grand scale. She pronounced that being away from Sumba and the village of Wandi had affected Umbu Taniku in ways similar to what she had witnessed regarding other local men who had carried out Balinese ventures. That is, the sojourn had loosened Umbu's reason (*akal*, I.) and responsibilities (*tanggung jawab*, I.) to others. While in Bali he had gone money mad (*gila uang*, I.) without thought to the consequences.

Umbu Taniku's losses were all the more grievous in the face of Hasan and Biba's gains. Although there was no overt hostility between the households, Biba said that she felt undercurrents of resentment from Umbu Taniku after they had all returned to Sumba from their travels to other islands. She also noted Umbu's dilemma as an example of the follies of many Sumbanese men in handling money, especially when the sums and stakes were large. Umbu Taniku, however, consistently attributed his economic fall to sheer fate, not to any mishandling on his part.

Kata continued to produce fabrics, but she was more sullen than the year before. Some of the women who had formerly frequented her home had stopped visiting. Several families in the neighborhood had lost fabrics or money through Umbu's mishap in Bali, and this misadventure had created a rift between households. Not only had Umbu's losses created economic hardship for her family, but Kata had also been deprived of the company of some of her former women friends through the alienation of several families. This loss was a severe blow to her social life.

Before I left the island in 1994, Umbu was brought to account publicly, around the issue of his largely outstanding bride price. Kata was carrying their third child, yet he still owed her father a considerable portion of the initial marital debt in livestock.[3] His fortunes spent, and owing those who had forwarded him their fabrics for his Balinese enterprise, Umbu Taniku was in no state to repay his long-standing debt to his father-in-law.

One day there was a funeral at a village not far from Wandi. Perhaps three hundred people were present. Numerous pigs were slaughtered and stewed in pots, and caldrons of rice were prepared to feed the guests. As people sat eating on platforms and chairs in a yard bordering a clan home, loud, mournful cries carried above the buzz of conversation. Hearing the laments, the people near me and I paused and looked across the yard from where we sat. There, crouched on the ground, Umbu Taniku sobbed uncontrollably, shuddering as he raised his face from his father-in-law's lap. Having no other means to make amends for his long-standing debt, Umbu had been impelled to demonstrate shame publicly. Those witnessing his humiliation spoke in hushed tones as the father-in-law sat impassively, looking beyond the humbled man at his feet. Recalling his boldly emblazoned fabric designs and his grand commercial schemes, I saw Umbu Taniku as a fallen hero of sorts, led to ruin in the cosmopolitan byways of trade.

187

Reflections

At the hottest times of day, Rambu Nina and Tabi reclined on a raised bamboo platform underneath a bougainvillea bush in their yard. In 1994 they were producing three complex new fabric designs to be woven in *ikat* and *pahikung* methods. A Chinese merchant from Waingapu had recently delivered a large sum of money in exchange for their cloth and had then taken the fabrics to Bali, where they would be sold among the more expensive Indonesian arts. The Hawewa cousins invested some of their profits into their household, repainting the inner rooms in pastel colors and repairing the roof. They also bought a satellite dish (*parabola*, I.); sitting ten feet from their clan home, it looked like an extraterrestrial device. As was the case with Biba and Hasan, the economic gains of the cousins were reflected in a newly acquired access to global media.

The anomaly of the metal dish poised within the family compound corresponded to contrasts between images transmitted from the new television set and scenes of daily life of the Hawewa household. By day the women[4] sat embodied by looms and warps, looking downward toward their yarns and motifs, or reclined languidly while gossiping under the shade of their bright floral canopy. In the evenings, lounging in the blue light of television, they viewed broadcasts of variety shows and soap operas from Jakarta—or (to them) linguistically unintelligible but visually interesting programs from the American network CNN (Cable News Network). Through the television, they encountered a new imaginative scope, while their daily activities proceeded much as before.

The cousins were creating more complex fabrics by the end of 1994. Still reworking ancient motifs, they sat at their yarns purposefully, chatting among themselves and with others on the verandah or occasionally looking up to note a passerby. On my last visit to them, the village *raja* rode by on his motorbike, and derisive jokes by Tabi—referring to his physical sloth—followed his passing. Later the evangelical weaver, Martha, walked by on the road, skeins of black yarn in one hand and her Bible in the other.

Rambu Nina commented on Martha and her zealousness for the Bethel Church. A few nights before she had seen a Christian choir singing on the Jakarta television channel, and she reflected on the world religion that had yet to convert her:

> It seems as though they get strength from the book [Bible] and through their singing. But we don't feel a need for that. We continue things as they are and try to prosper. We have our own ideas and a place to be. And it's true that this suits us.

Village Ensembles

In the noon heat radiating off the dry, white ground, Parai Mutu sat shadowless and parched before the rains. Even the eternal banging of shuttles sounded faint and listless, and walking into a family compound I could feel a lethargy weighing on its occupants. Mia, the servant, worked on a weaving as she sat on the ground in the middle of the courtyard, shaded by the overhanging eaves.

Madai, the resident fabric artist, sat listlessly nearby, one foot resting on the back of a dozing pig. Ana Humba had been passing most of these hot days in a kind of torpor, seldom venturing out because of the heat and spending a good deal of time in slumber. Indeed, the pan-Sumban travels of Ana Humba had come to a seasonal halt.

"She's lazy!" ("*Mayauna!*") her mother pronounced, adding that if there was no excitement, Ana Humba would continue to sleep. Madai mimicked her sister in a collapsed, unconscious condition and laughed. After some time, awakened by our chatter, Ana Humba emerged from the house onto the verandah, clad in a colorless *lau*, her face still sleepy. She sat dazed and moody for some time.

That day a tour group arrived in Parai Mutu and drifted from house to house. The fifteen Westerners edging their way through the village were noticed by people on the verandah as a momentarily interesting but nonetheless commonplace procession;[5] an odd human breeze that wafted between households and then left without a trace. After an uneventful hour, the tourists boarded their bus and departed.

Umbu Pari arrived some hours later in a jeep, in the company of a Frenchman. We exchanged greetings, and the tourist sat waiting for fabrics to be brought out for his inspection. His manner was impatient. He told me that he had been to several islands in eastern Indonesia looking for quality fabrics, but had found nothing.

189

> In Flores there was nothing. In Sumbawa there was nothing. I am looking for good quality textiles. I sell them in Paris. But I can find nothing of any value. Timor? Oh, nothing! Absolutely nothing!

Exuding the ennui of a connoisseur, a spent aesthete, the man examined the fabrics the family had arranged for him on the clotheslines. Overlooking the finest cloths, he focused upon the most boldly designed. He bargained for one *hinggi*, and when finally an agreement was made, the man solemnly put the cloth into his shoulder bag.

At some point I asked Umbu Pari about the upcoming textile exhibit in Australia he had now been talking about for two years. Pari answered evasively that the date for the event was not yet set (*belum tentu*, I.) and that he was still awaiting news from his Australian friend, the curator. The "professor" who was promising the exhibit had recently come to Sumba and had created some controversy. Some young men in villages were saying that the Australian was really just a merchant (*pedagang*, I.) and got drunk (*mabuk*, I.) every night at his hotel, clad in odd clothing (short shorts and open shirts with no buttons) made of silk. Recently, three men from Wandi had sighted him in the restaurant of a hotel on the

Western part of the island. The villagers reported that the Australian was intoxicated to the point of being unable to walk and that Umbu Pari had to half carry him back to his room. This was the same man Umbu Pari had been with the last time I had seen him in Bali, at the pub in Kuta Beach.

Later the same day, the Chinese owner of the Andung Art Shop[6] in Bali arrived in Parai Mutu and bought several *hinggi*s from the household. The intractable Madai refused to lower her price on one fabric the dealer especially wanted. After hours of haggling, she still held onto her best piece, having persisted in keeping what was hers. Madai then took her *hinggi* back into the house, to join the pattern guides (*pahudu*) and heirloom fabrics still locked away. Inaccessible to outside eyes, the cloth would join others, hidden in the high peaks of the home or around the still-present body of her father.

As I was soon to return to the United States, Madai presented me with a gift—a folded *hinggi* she had recently completed. As I opened it, multiple images of crayfish unfolded. The colors were natural, indigo blue, and *kombu* red, and the dyes were deep and rich. The fabric was beautiful. The center panel, however, was unlike designs I had seen. Against a *kombu*-red background, Madai had crafted a strangely geometric *pahikung* pattern, woven in undyed and indigo threads.

"*Ingat?*" (I.; "Remember?") she asked in a barely audible voice. I looked carefully at the pattern, but I couldn't come to terms with it. Madai looked mischievous, and then began a pantomime. She puffed and panted, wiped her brow, then sat on the verandah and went through the motions of taking off a shirt and thrusting it down beside her. When I failed to react, she slapped me hard on the arm. Ana Humba covered her mouth and laughed. So did Mia. I rubbed my smarting arm as I remembered: the one called the Crazy Dutchman who had visited the family when I was there months before. Madai had taken this pattern from the embroidery on the sleeves of the shirt (created in Bali, of "Japanese" style) he had taken off in the heat and set on the verandah next to him. She had memorized the pattern during her long contemplation of it. Then later she had incorporated it into cloth along with her crayfish, entering it into the realm of the sublime.

Hedging the Margins

Late in the day, as dusk fell, Ana Humba, Mia, and I descended to the river to bathe. Mia was afraid to come into the water with us, and crouching under her black *lau*, splashed herself with a dipper at the river's edge. Mia's sense of place was delimited not only by her low-caste standing, but also by her fears of certain perils in spatiality. The river had proved a

190

nearly deadly place in the past, and beyond it was a world dangerously unfamiliar.

By contrast, Ana Humba's privileged position and impetuousity had propelled her along whatever routes were available to her, following buses and *bemos* around the island. Between the two women bathing at the river were two very different ways of experiencing themselves within their own peculiar geographies.

Yet despite her advantages, Ana Humba had suffered a humiliating disappointment over the past few months. The man she had talked of eloping with (a Sumbanese working in Jakarta) had unexpectedly married a Javanese woman. Ana Humba had learned of this through relatives. Adding to her indignity, the man had recently brought his new wife to Sumba for a visit. The couple had socialized at various households and at one large funeral. The Javanese wife was a professional woman with a university degree. Sumbanese who met her during her visit commented to me that she was very refined (*halus*, I.) and also clever (*pintar*, I.).

Everyone knew of the marriage, and Ana Humba was aware that she was at the center of village gossip in having been jilted in such a manner. She also realized that, inevitably, some people were comparing her unfavorably to the new bride. A group of people from the village of Wandi had praised the woman's appearance in Ana Humba's presence, noting her youthfulness and her thick, straight hair (which contrasted with Ana Humba's kinky hair). Despite her humiliation, Ana Humba nonetheless publicly maintained an insouciance toward the whole episode, claiming aloud that she had never intended to marry the man. To me she said, "It was something both of our parents had arranged, not what I wanted. Besides, he didn't excite me. He bored me and that's the truth. I know someone who works in Kupang who is much more lively and suits me better. It's like that." Ana Humba and I waded several feet out into the water, next to a rock on which we set our shared bar of soap. She wet her face and began in a low voice, "I'll tell you a secret. This time next year I'll be living somewhere else."

191

More Passages

The rains were so long overdue in late 1994 that an immense ritual was organized in the hopes of calling them down. This was called *hama-yangu wai urangu* (rain prayers) and involved men from villages around eastern Sumba meeting at an ancient grave site in the Kambera region and then walking five kilometers along a river until they reached the sea. Near where the river met the sea, auspicious omens were expected. The trek coincided with the time of year when men of the region have historically ventured out in search of food and beneficial exchanges, purposeful travels called *mandara*. Early in the morning the march began, led by four *ratu* on horseback. Thousands followed on foot, a human stream in *ikat* fabrics, with some *maramba* leaders traveling by motorbike. The parade embodied men, cloth, and mobility.

After circling a large tree eight times, the four *ratu* and numerous men went down to the riverbank to look for signs of crocodiles, whose presence would indicate the imminence of the monsoon. There was much tension and excitement surrounding this activity. Few women were present, and I was scolded by a group of men for attempting to approach the river. This was a male realm and I was transgressing it. I remained behind, at some distance from it all. Shouts and warbling from the riverbanks indicated that crocodiles had been sighted, and the vast crowd became wild with excitement. Frenzied men ran to and fro from the water's edge. A water buffalo was killed and butchered. As night fell, fires were made and rice and meat were cooked. Men began to drink palm wine.

One week later the rains came and I departed. Rambu Hamu, Biba, and Ana Humba came to my house early in the day, and we boarded a *bemo* to go to the airport. Catching a last glimpse of my three friends on the edge of the airfield, I rose into the clouds on a plane bound for Bali.

192

CHAPTER 11
CONCLUSION

". . . a kind of natural history of signs and symbols. An ethnography of the vehicles of meaning"
—Clifford Geertz, "Art as a Cultural System"

I n 1996, almost two years after I left Sumba, I coiled an *ikat* headcloth around a Styrofoam form to be included in a glass case in an ethnographic exhibit I was curating at the Hearst Museum of Anthropology at the University of California at Berkeley. The case, labeled "Eclectic Wear," displayed a costume once worn by Umbu Pari from Parai Mutu. Reconstructing what he had constructed of himself, I was continuing a chain of inscriptions involving images and fabrics from East Sumba. Next to the

Figure 40. Posing at the entrance to a home.

ensemble—consisting of a *hinggi*, a headcloth, and a T-shirt with a skull tree motif on it—was an enlarged photograph of the nobleman, staring roguishly as he sat holding a cigarette, wearing an outfit similar to that in the display case. Others I had written accounts of were represented in photographs and cloth throughout the gallery, in ways that seemed to me as characteristic of them.

Draped in fabrics from several villages, Ana Humba posed facing the camera proudly. Biba crouched intently over a warp she was unbinding in a photograph taken in her shop, with packets of coffee, sugar, and other sundries visible on the shelves behind her. Luka, while absent from another photograph, was evident in a complex cloth suspended from a tree, peopled with a narrative tale in its length. Umbu Taniku stood self-assuredly next to a collection of fabrics on a clothesline, his head held high. Mia, absorbed in her work on a cloth, sat in faded clothes at her loom on the ground of the courtyard of the family she served. Her shuttle was weaving the fabric of an elegant piece designed by Madai, who always stubbornly had refused to be photographed—maintaining a control over her own image as she did of her cloth. In another photo a simplified, "primitive" human form (which looked as if it might have been woven by the evangelical Martha) had been fashioned into a handbag displayed in a boutique in Bali. And an intricate *pahikung* and *ikat* cloth with finely rendered motifs by Rambu Nina—the most complex in the exhibit—hung in a case at the gallery entrance.

194

Ethnography: An Open-ended Endeavor

The museum exhibit provided interventive glimpses of moments in the lives of certain people. Yet these moments were never anyone's to hold. At this writing, in 1998, stories of those in the photographs have continued well beyond the ones in this book and perhaps even defy some of them. I have traced conditions, exploits, and encounters involving specific people to grasp something of the unwieldy human stuff that fabrics enfold. This might include an inebriated textile vendor's unconscious soiling of an Indonesian official's local status or a village woman's venting her amorous desires along trade routes of cloth.

While participating in a global economic system, people continue to live in immediate terms, responding to exigencies of day-to-day worlds. Such worlds contain many sites—geographical, social, and imaginary—stirring a constant "shuttling" between them. While this shuttling might suggest a postmodern picture of fragmentation, it also compels a study that follows such movement, a condition not best understood as "post" to any former realities, but as myriad ways that people are grappling subjectively in a current world. Throughout this book I have intentionally avoided conclusively casting people's lives within analytical rubrics such as "modernity," "postmodernity," or "postcolonialism," instead endeavoring to allow any such conditions (if indeed they are relevant to the people and places I describe) to emerge through the chapters.

I also have tried to depict, tangibly, certain social processes that create and shape what might either work into or challenge tradition. In East Sumba, these processes include a consciousness of the concept of "tradition" as a value in the international market for arts. Thus the term bears manifold meanings in a recent history of eastern Sumba that involves an ongoing conversation with outside influences.

There has been no typical village, villager, or outsider in my account, although patterns appear concerning them all. The cosmopolitanism affecting many from Sumba also accents specifically local beliefs and practices, throwing into relief precedents (see Fox 1997) of village environments, family histories, or ethnic, rank, and gender identities. In their overlapping complexities, regions in this analysis defy "marginality," in terms of the validity of social life within them. Commercial zones in Bali or hotel grounds in Waingapu are as inhabited as traditional villages in East Sumba, in the lively and consequential phenomena they contain. One location is as ethnographically real as the other, and transpositions between them demand an open-ended ethnographic vision.

195

Losses, Revivals, Inventions, and Conquests

Laments of loss in eastern Sumba relate to more than the quality of fabrics. Following in the wake of previous social and economic changes (such as religious conversion, an Indonesian state system, global market influences, tourism), the contemporary textile market has prompted some people to sidestep local, historical strictures through new social avenues. A formerly privileged domain of material culture—cloth—became a channel to upward economic mobility for those of lower social rank in East Sumba. While some have increased their fortunes and certainly expanded their social horizons, they must contend with local reactions to their stepping out of historical place. The erosion of social, symbolic, and economic control of textiles formerly the privilege of historical elites has facilitated formerly impossible opportunities for others—resulting in new struggles in arenas of fabric creation and trade.

Anthony Giddens writes that "the more tradition loses its hold, the more daily life is reconstituted in terms of the dialectical interplay of the global and the local, the more individuals are forced to negotiate lifestyle choices from a diversity of options" (1992:19). A diversity of options in Sumba include some formerly unknown, imported from around the world. But increased options might also stimulate a resurgence of local constructions, allowing "traditional" forms to skip through changing contexts—as do Biba's *hinggi*s of "antique" design or Umbu Pari's T-shirts emblazoned with skull trees. And life choices might also reassert the historical, in efforts to hold onto past means of control. Rambu Nina's attachment to family home and ancient clan motifs in the cloth she creates suggests this, as does Umbu Taniku's insistence upon his wife's housebound position as his own fabric trading takes him far afield. And Rambu Hamu's ventures to Jakarta to participate in a textile exhibition reinforced her husband's noble status in Sumba by conquering new ground, ultimately through appearances on national television.

Autonomies by Design

Even though the national government through the Suharto era focused its representations of the numerous ethnic cultures within Indonesia upon variously "typical" aesthetic forms,[1] this effort did not necessarily stifle the verve of specific arts and the range of local choices they contained. In East Sumba, as people live under state rule, they do so with a vivacity often beyond the ken or control of external authorities. People create arts or devise strategies for promoting them with passion and ingenuity. Aesthetic expression is a highly elastic realm for cultural or personal resurgence, thwarting domination in the audacity of its play. This play often involves teasing peril through extraordinary experiences— as people venture to other islands, enjoy trysts with foreigners, break norms of gendered behavior, or plot themselves in designs of their fabrics and the social opportunities these fabrics facilitate. Scenes of encounter between people from Sumba and those from afar generate relentless vigor, producing many sorts of artistry and display. An engagement with the global allows more leg room for the local, when considered in a nationalistic setting.

Moreover, elements of risk historically surfacing in eastern Sumbanese society through actions such as war, travel, or gambling currently also manifest through contemporary trade-based adventures. Former prestige symbols now take on life and significance suffused with new dangers and passions. As Luka walked the beach in Bali with a European girlfriend, he wrapped across her shoulders a *hinggi* that contained scenes of a Sumbanese battle he had designed. His valorous cloth now enfolded a new symbol of status for the designer from Sumba, and Luka's promenade with the young woman afforded him a prestigious display in a new arena of social life. Yet he also risked the loss of his very soul in his distance from Sumba, and he was aware that such perils haunted his adventure.

What is more, social and physical mobility involved in the textile

196

trade highlights areas of discrepancy in overt power and autonomy in eastern Sumba between men and women. Many women in Sumba are exploited, as conditions in the lives of the cloth makers Kata, Mia, and those in the Sing Ha workshop illustrate. Public political power and mobility are overwhelmingly the privilege of men. Yet stories such as those of Biba, Ana Humba, Rambu Nina, Madai, and others reveal how women constantly manipulate or evade social conventions, sometimes blatantly, sometimes under subterfuge. In doing so, they risk social censure and accusations of immorality or witchery. Amid such difficulties, people strategically swerve along unpredictable paths, perpetuating the uncertainties of life.

As individuals portrayed in this book push beyond former conventions of customary space, they defy singular authorities by their multiple positions and itineraries. Following their cloth, many people have now slipped out into the world, not to be "retrieved" under former social conditions. Exercises of power from historical controls in eastern Sumba are now often impossible to carry out among subjects who are no longer easily "surveyable" (see Foucault 1977), in their whereabouts or in their creations. Entrepreneurs such as Luka and Biba claim their own fields of sovereignty, controlling new products and interacting with others on grounds where rules are ambiguous. Conversely, others, such as Madai, Mia, and Rambu Nina, have found a kind of refuge in their variably constrained social lives. While affected by the international textile market, their worlds remain centered in customary spaces, wherein they forge their own victories.

A persistent contrast through these stories involves emotion and entrepreneurship in the design of fabrics, which in some instances overlap. Images as often materialize from spontaneous whimsy as they do from prolonged or impassioned contemplation. An international audience for their cloth provides people with an enlarged social field in which to create, compete, and display. Local concerns resonate with new audiences in radically different contexts, wherein the artistic inventiveness visible in cloth is enhanced by the performances of those promoting it. We have seen this in the stories of Luka, Ana Humba, Umbu Pari, and Umbu Taniku, among others, in their tactical postures in diverse social settings as they have unfolded their cloth to others.

Art Cultures and Contests

As George Marcus and Fred Myers state, "Perhaps one of the most challenging properties of art culture as a field for theory is the extent to which the arts recognize the significance of culture as an area of contest" (1995:10). Textile art worlds of eastern Sumba teem with contests as they

197

mirror the productivity, controversy, and elasticity of culture as people live it. Always more than frozen symbols, motifs in cloth are often dialogic "nudges" to ongoing disputes. Thus image making and viewing never merely reproduce what was before, but are alive with intricacies of personal motivations and reactions—and "the relationships through which objects are constructed as social forms" (Miller 1987:11). Pierre Bourdieu concludes that "among all the inventions which accompany the emergence of the field of [cultural] production, one of the most significant is probably the elaboration of an artistic language" (1993:260), and some in this book have grappled with such language.

Further, in elaborating their artistic language, people conceptualize, move, and "image" within and between places well-known to them and sometimes regions far beyond. Following the breadth of such activities, "biographies of things make salient what otherwise might remain obscure" (Kopytoff 1988:67, as noted in chapter 9) as they map out relationships of people to things and to each other. I have tried to demonstrate something of this here, not only along the multiple trajectories Sumba textiles travel as they parallel ventures of people who make and trade them, but in biographical moments or passages their imagery sometimes crystallizes.[2] People articulate these through narrative expressions, religious iconography, foreign commercial symbols, or infinite other designs. There is power in manipulating pictures, which at least metaphorically conquer dilemmas in individual lives and redefine the world, shaping an ontology that satisfies the times. Indeed, if the fundamental event of the modern age is the conquest of the world as a picture,[3] then some in eastern Sumba have partaken masterfully of such an event.

198

Considering objects and lives in a western region of Sumba, Janet Hoskins recently argued that "objects are used as vehicles for fantasy and imagination because they are saturated with both conventional and subjective meanings"; this argument might apply to current and past times, challenging the notion that imaginativeness surrounding the production and consumption of objects only arises in moments in "the 'special expressive space' of art, myth, and ritual" (1998:196). The expressive spaces giving rise to East Sumba's fabrics can exist in the most mundane of circumstances yet produce deeply inventive moments and forms, with ongoing effects.

In this book, I have attempted to give the reader a profound sense of the complexities of provenance of eastern Sumba textiles: some aspects of the actual processes of creation; people's awareness of stimulations and modifications involving cloth; the pains and pleasures of cloth design, production, and schemes of its trade; and ultimately individuals' views of the purposes to which their creations and actions might be put and how these might affect their positions in the world. I have tried to show why people sell or do not sell their cloth, their views on buyers, and what they gained or lost from individual efforts, whether through production or trade. There is much more to know about provenance of arts and artifacts than has formerly concerned most Western provenancial interests, which have largely ignored the personal.

Values of international collectors play directly—and often personally—into the lives and arts of eastern Sumbanese. Historical complexities and shifts involving global art discourses and trends affect people in Sumba who, although unschooled in art worlds of the West, have nonetheless become aware of demands emanating from them. Textile traders and producers have reinterpreted foreigners' idealized notions of "primitivism," "traditionality," or relentless quests for the "authentic." Whether by direct contact with foreign consumers or through possession of museum literature, eastern Sumbanese have a seasoned knowledge of how others in the world portray them and what they seek in local arts.

Beyond this, through observing what they often regard as an inexplicable recklessness, people in Sumba form opinions about the nature of foreigners. Risky behavior such as singular travel, bungee jumping, sexual promiscuity, or even sleeping on the ground are consequential phenomena in the construction of typologies of the foreign. As world travelers and collectors seek a certain "wildness" in Sumba and its arts, sometimes they unwittingly are cast as wildly exotic by eastern Sumbanese. While such characterization informs designs in fabrics to appeal to a foreign market, it simultaneously shapes ideas of people in East Sumba about their relative places in the world. Mutual constructions between "insiders" and "outsiders" (see Morphy 1991) are in constant volley, complicating the interplay of cloth and identities in contemporary times.

199

The multiply heroic stories unfolding through the narrative cloths of Luka or Umbu Taniku—which portray idealized selves of their designers in linear, sequential perspectives—are glimpses of conceptual worlds that differ from those of a generation ago. Networks of Ana Humba's itinerant textile trade map out an often urgent movement beyond conventional bounds and a selfhood responding to fluctuating possibilities. As Mia walks from her loom to the river, her footsteps trace the grounds of a circumscribed and intensely experienced village world. Her terrifying struggle with a river spirit at the limits of this world eventually influenced ghostly imagery in cloth— which ultimately travels far beyond the place of its origin. And Rambu Nina devotes herself to cloth making as an exemplary way of life, conservative in some respects, liberated in others. As she creates intricate pieces with ancient motifs, she continuously assesses contemporary life and her place within it.

Innovated forms in fabrics may be born of the emotional turmoil of agonistic relations (such as Luka's sacrificial water buffaloes) while others arise from sublimely inventive inner worlds (as do Madai's crayfish). Still other images respond to recent cosmological and moral realities, as glimpsed in the evangelical Martha's sexual neutering of a "pagan" human figure to render it "moral." As Biba's angels grace a local king, they enact a modern, cloth-bound parable for social harmony in bringing together, pictorially, Marapu and Christian sentiments. Moreover, serious tactics for increased social prestige are attached to creatures like the kangaroos Umbu Pari appropriated from commercial decals stealthily peeled from the doors of a tourist hotel.

This cloth-based account is a glimmer of eastern Sumbanese worlds. In their threads and dyes we find traces of people's lives, their travels, their visions: reemergent patterns of royal fabrics long removed to remote foreign museums; ancient human figures now sexually neutered in a response to a Christian god; a kangaroo flaunting a foreign alliance; heroic battles in fabric reflecting grand schemes involved in trading them; and the pattern on a sleeve of a "Japanese" shirt created in Bali and worn by an overheated Dutchman, then casually dropped on a Sumbanese verandah one morning.

1998

When I returned to Sumba for a brief period in July and August of 1998, people were faring better than I had anticipated in the midst of political and economic crises across Indonesia. Most had returned purposefully to their gardens, and food shortages had not yet become crucial for the people I knew. Yet a decline in tourism and an awareness of national crises were prompting people to redefine what they had come to view as a recent era of local prosperity through the international textile trade. At this point, my discussion of their situations can only be tentative, but I will conclude with a few notes on particular people in previous chapters, as of late 1998.

Ana Humba finally made it to Jakarta, fulfilling her hopes of years before. In August she had been there for almost a year. Some in eastern Sumba said she was visiting a relative and selling cloth sent to her from Parai Mutu; others rumored that she had become involved with a Jakarta man. Mystery and scandal followed her absence, and Ana Humba—whose travels had extended perilously beyond local bounds—now was spoken of in hushed tones in Sumba. It may be some time before I catch up with her.

Her sister Madai had grown prouder in bearing and wore more gold jewelry than in years past. According to her mother, she spoke even less these days, and had become increasingly *sombong* (I.; arrogant), refusing to acknowledge most people. She continued with her cloth creations, which were as elegant as ever, and the servant Mia still assisted her. Three European women visited her home in August and bought several of Madai's *hinggi*s at her first asking price.

Rambu Nina and Tabi were producing even more complex *lau* pieces with the most intricate *pahikung* sections I had ever seen in Sumba. They were still selling them to selected Chinese merchants in Waingapu, who continued to export them to shops in Bali. The two cousins had prospered since 1994, to the extent that they had financed an impressive concrete building, devoted to dyeing processes, next to their home. A blue-tiled bathroom sat at one end of the structure. While creating exquisitely detailed fabrics based in motifs from Sumba's past, the women were now regularly engaged electronically with depictions of a global present as they watched televised events in the evening. The Indonesian national channel (TVRI) and the American-based CNN brought scenes of riots, fashions, and natural disasters into their home nightly, and they discussed world news by day as they worked on their cloth.

Sing Ha's textile workshop was operating in late 1998, although the only remaining cloth maker from years before was the silent woman. New workers had taken the place of former ones, but there were fewer than in the past. Sing Ha still supplied fabrics to his sister in Bali, Ibu Ana, whose business persisted through the current economic crisis and decline in tourism in Indonesia. After the Jakarta riots of May 1998, many Indonesian Chinese closed their shops in Bali, fearing the kinds of violence that had befallen Chinese merchants in Jakarta. Ibu Ana remained open through the year, telling her brother Sing Ha that she would face any problems that might confront her in Bali. She proceeded with her enterprise much as before.

Biba continues to prosper through recent times, more than anyone else in her village region, by carrying cloth to Jakarta and often selling it for U.S. dollars. During the May riots, Biba and Hasan stayed on at the Jakarta house of their recently evacuated American hosts as guardians of their friends' lavish home and possessions. They bore witness to history-making political events and social unrest that has altered further their views of the world. As they watched the sky fill with the smoke of burning buildings and heard shouts and the sounds of breaking glass from a nearby street, they wondered if they would ever see their children in Wandi again. They returned to Sumba a month later, richer in profits and experience.

Umbu Taniku ultimately abandoned the textile trade, did not recover his losses of years earlier, and was attempting to make a living through trading livestock in 1998. Everyone in Wandi (including his wife, Kata) said that he still gambled with cards frequently and that he was rarely at home. Kata blamed Bill Clinton (who had enjoyed short-term glory as one of Umbu Taniku's "world leader" motifs in textiles) for her family's economic woes: in raising the value of the U.S. dollar he caused the fall of the Indonesian rupiah.

As far as I know, Luka may yet be in Bali on a textile-selling mission that has kept him there for many months. In September 1998, I saw the bungee tower in Kuta Beach that had amazed him several years earlier, but I have yet to see the most recent images and stories unfolding through his cloth.

Following social unrest and economic instability throughout Indonesia, East Sumba's fabrics and people will continue to mix in complex histories arising near and far from their homes—as they live through what are always modern times.

202

NOTES

Part One: Fabricscapes
Chapter 1: Introduction

1. As many have noted, "art" is a slippery term of analysis when applied to non-Western societies. For examples, see R. Anderson (1979); Clifford (1988); Coote (1992); Errington (1994b, 1998); Forge (1973); Graburn (1976); Hart (1995); Losche (1997); Maquet (1986); Marcus and Myers (1995); Sheldon (1992); Steiner (1994); and Thomas (1999). Not surprisingly, there is no word in eastern Sumbanese language that precisely means "art," in the Euro-American sense—that is, implying a discrete area of production of nonutilitarian aesthetic works and the historical institutions and public consensus that support it. I impose the shorthand term "art" in the context of Sumbanese textiles, however, to denote an aesthetic form that involves culturally shared (and contested) concepts of beauty, artisanship, value, and talent and that is a format for expressiveness. Such art in eastern Sumba is underscored by intense competition and public commentary, in which something of beauty is deemed *hamu*, which can also denote qualities of goodness.

2. I am certainly not arguing that this is the first time they have ever envisioned themselves anew, as undoubtedly throughout the past people in Sumba reassessed their places in the world based on ever-changing circumstances and new influences in their environments. My purpose here is to show something of how people are doing so in recent times.

3. Toby Volkman (1990) examines how a "tourist gaze" reshapes Torajan cultural realities in Sulawesi, revealing aspects of this "timelessness" as taken up in local contexts. See also Kathleen Adams (1999).

4. I use the term "tradition" throughout this book in multiple senses. Tradition proceeds as persistent yet mutable symbolic forms and practices, carrying local precedence and social power. But I also consider it as a quite separate concept, of which people in East Sumba are aware: "tradition" as a prized category wielded by international collectors to authenticate non-Western arts. In response to this latter, imported category, many people in eastern Sumba manipulate or invent traditions, but also reassert traditional forms they perceive of as esteemed by foreigners. Eric Hobsbawm notes how " 'traditions' which appear or claim to be old are often quite recent in origin and sometimes invented" (1983:1). Yet all tradition inevitably was "invented" (in the sense that it was constructed) at some point, whether gradually or rapidly. This does not necessarily mean that such invention was fictitious or false in relation to previous "real" models (see Jolly and Thomas 1992, Linnekin 1992). I concur with Nicholas Thomas' assessment that "indigenous cultures are simultaneously 'traditional' and 'contemporary'. They are 'traditional' in the sense that distinctive views of the world remain alive, but they are also 'contemporary' in the sense that they belong in the present (1999:17). The challenge is discerning something of how various notions and manifestations of tradition might play between the past and present, between the local and the foreign.

5. I consider "aesthetics" to mean generally a sense of beauty. In the context of the Sumbanese worlds I describe, the term almost foils a certain Western notion of aesthetics (as linked to art and going back to Kant) as characterized by an emotional disinterestedness, independent of moral spheres. Emotional interests pervade the conception, production, and reception of aesthetic objects in this account of eastern Sumba; all are entwined with moral positions and notions of the right ordering of things in the world. As Taylor and Aragon note, "Terms used in Indonesian languages to describe beauty usually include a moral component" (1991:30), and this is true in eastern Sumba.

6. For valuable information and analysis regarding history, former social realities,

and earlier textiles of East Sumba, I am indebted to the work of Marie Jeanne Adams, who carried out extensive research in the region in the 1960s. People I refer to in this book as "indigenous" Sumbanese (and who refer to themselves as Tau Humba 'Sumba People') are those who claim descent from ancient lineages in Sumba and who for the most part continue to regard clan villages as their homes. Their forebears may have arrived via a number of other islands, such as Sulawesi, Sumbawa, and Timor, bringing Austronesian and Papuan influences at various points in history (see Bellwood 1997).

7. Shelly Errington (1989) has noted the persistent, transgenerational quality of regalia in Southeast Asia, as it anchors and legitimizes spheres of political power. I will consider such spheres as not only reflected by Sumbanese fabrics, but as created by connections and transformations that transpire as Sumba's producers and traders of cloth interact with people from around the world. As Robert Hefner has recently written, "When examined by way of its organizations and meanings, capitalism proves to be a more diverse beast than was once thought" (1998:29). Movements and markets involving eastern Sumbanese cloth reflect this diversity, while they highlight former social and moral precedents to current economic conditions.

8. This echoes something of Janet Hoskins' findings (1987c) in the Kodi region of West Sumba, in which a hero and myths were taken away from local people and became reappropriated into Indonesian nationalist discourse. The slippage of Sumbanese fabrics and any historical authority they embodied is irretrievable, as cloth and various reinterpretations of its meanings are diffused around the globe.

9. I borrow this term from Howard Becker's *Art Worlds* (1982), a sociological account of subcultures and institutions underpinning art in the West.

10. Shelly Errington recently noted, "Like the discipline of art history itself, the discourses of 'authenticity' and 'the primitive' were made possible by the [Western] metanarrative of progress" (1998:5). Aspects of such a metanarrative, which issues not only from the West, have been interpreted and taken up by many in Sumba—in various responses and to numerous ends, which will emerge. Marianna Torgovnick, discussing Western attitudes (modernist and postmodernist) toward "the primitive" writes, "The real secret of the primitive in this century has often been the same secret as always: the primitive can be—has been, will be(?)—whatever Europeans want it to be" (1990:9). This implies a capriciousness on both sides of the foreign collector ("modern")–local producer ("primitive") encounter. Yet the guile and ingenuity of the subjects of quests for the exotic or the primitive have usually been overlooked in critiques of Western stereotyping. People in Sumba often possess an uncanny awareness of what people in distant places "say about them." This involves those other than Westerners, including authoritative voices from other parts of Indonesia. "Primitivism" can be a positive or negative attribute, depending upon who is speaking, and many in eastern Sumba know this.

11. Accounts in this book proceed for the most part through a four-year time span beginning in 1990, with most of the events and observations taking place in 1993 and 1994, in an extended fieldwork period. I expand this time period into 1998 in the Conclusion, where I provide glimpses of some of the people from the book under recent conditions.

12. See Sahlins (1994); Tsing (1993); Vickers (1996).

13. I borrow this term from George Marcus (1995).

14. Gayatri Spivak's (1988) assertion that the mere mechanics of constructing the Other structurally renders that Other mute (indeed creating a "subaltern" subject) has prompted much reexamination of representing subjects in Western ethnographic accounts, particularly those from the "Third World." This follows upon Edward Said's critique of hegemonic Western constructions of the "Orient" (1978).

15. For example, see how Gewertz and Errington's (1991) ethnographic exploration of New Guinea villagers in interaction with foreign tourists demonstrates the "global" and the "modern" as creatively negotiated in local terms. Similar types of interactions involving eastern Sumbanese and international tourists produce local reformulations of identity and

worldview. Tsing (1993) tells an individual story of a type of marginality (involving region and gender) responding to a state-imposed modernity in Kalimantan and the resourceful ploys for reconstructing identity and claiming social power that emerge from this. In eastern Sumba, there are many such ploys responding to "modernities" coming from various directions and manifesting as local "presents." Hoskins (1993a) explores intricate conceptual worlds in the face of modern incursions in a region of West Sumba, specifically focusing on local notions of time. I attempt to reveal changing social and aesthetic concepts in East Sumba, which are also in response to changing notions of history. Wikan (1990) elucidates multiple forces, strategies, and interpretations within one Balinese individual's life and the emotional complexities and ambiguities this involves. As does Wikan, I try to characterize the elusive nature of subjectivity through events in the lives of specific people.

16. The certainties of imposed anthropological structures were earlier challenged by Leach (1954). Recent studies of local terms in Indonesian settings further question Western analytical categories such as "agency" or "power" (see Atkinson and Errington 1990; Errington 1989; Keane 1997; Tsing 1993) and prompt reinterpretations of taken-for-granted associations (i.e., that power is equivalent with status, that individual agency is viewed as such everywhere).

17. Appadurai (1991); Bruner (1996); Clifford (1997); Gupta and Ferguson (1992); Lavie and Swedenburg (1996); Marcus and Myers (1995); R. Rosaldo (1989b); and Trinh (1991) (among others) all discuss currently hybridized environments the world over, which often confound local or scholarly notions of "place" and "identity."

18. Compare Feld and Basso (1996); Fox (1997); Morley and Robins (1995); and Rodman (1992) for a few recent approaches to defining "place." Margaret Rodman's consideration of place as containing multiple dimensions and "betweenness" is especially useful in this account. In his Introduction to *The Poetic Power of Place,* James Fox notes that (and I am paraphrasing) tree imagery—a branching out in many directions—might represent relationships of similarity and difference and links between social groups in eastern Indonesia. He concludes that "a comparative study of Austronesian 'pathways', as an active mode for relations and their transformations, should be the next step in the investigation of place" (1997:17). We will follow such pathways here.

19. As do other scholars (see E. Wolf, 1982), I regard the intrinsically hierarchical terms "Third World" and "First World" as problematic relics of the European colonial era and Cold War politics. I use them with reservation throughout this book, for lack of a better terminology. I do not think that alternative oppositional labels, such as "developed/undeveloped," "Western/non-Western," "industrialized/nonindustrialized," or "modern/traditional" describe regions of the world any more accurately.

20. See Babcock (1993); Ben-Amos (1977); H. Geertz (1995); Graburn (1976, 1984); Jules-Rosette (1985); Kasfir (1992); Morphy (1991); Myers (1994); Phillips (1992); Steiner (1994); and Thomas (1995, 1998, 1999) for discussions of a range of non-Western arts and artists in response to worldwide influence and market demand.

21. Recent scholarship has explored indigenous concepts of history and time in concurrence or contrast to imported notions. Janet Hoskins' account of changing perspectives of time in the Kodi region of West Sumba demonstrates how "revolutions in time are revolutions in consciousness" (1993a:363). Similar revolutions surface through my study as well, most perceptibly through the modifications eastern Sumbanese are rendering in textile designs. See also Dening (1996); Jolly (1992); Rodgers (1995); Sahlins (1985); Sears (1996); Steedly (1993); Tsing (1993); and Wiener (1995) for a variety of reconsidered histories.

22. Marcus and Fischer have characterized a recent era in anthropology as one of " 'postconditions'—postmodern, postcolonial, posttraditional" (1986:24) resulting from a current lack of master paradigms or metanarratives in Western scholarship. Yet this sense of "post-ness" reflects dilemmas in our own modes of discourse and representation and is not necessarily an overriding reality in our subjects' lives. Much postmodern positioning has often assumed a theoretical "panopticism" (to borrow a term from Foucault 1977),

incapable of touching down into specific sites of living. A denouncing of "ethnographic authority," while justified, might then claim authority on a higher register, forming a kind of analytical hegemony that is disabling in terms of talking about much of anything except itself.

23. Nicholas Thomas recently stated: "It is most important that we understand that transcultural exchanges are not in any sense novel processes and that they are not peculiar to any particular epoch. Many of these processes arose independently of European colonisation and, indeed, preceded it. While for many people there has been a dramatic increase in the density and velocity of global cultural flows, these flows themselves are not new" (1998: 107). I agree with Thomas' assessment and will attempt to show something of the nature of such flows in current times in specific places.

24. Fredrik Barth's (1993) ethnographic rendering of a number of village areas in Bali challenges the formerly dominant anthropological concept of "the Balinese" and shows tremendous variation in village structures and individual interpretations in Balinese worlds. He disrupts the concept of "the village" as a unified entity while challenging a long-held ethnographic trope ("Bali"). My account challenges unified notions of "village," of "East Sumba," and often of particular personalities.

25. Issues of the representation of peoples have been called into question not only in ethnographic literature, but in museum display—an area especially vulnerable to such critiques (see Clifford 1985a, 1988, 1991; Errington 1998; Handler 1985; Kirshenblatt-Gimblett 1991; Lavine and Karp 1991; and Stocking 1985). In terms of the latter, Lavine and Karp call for multiple perspectives and admitting to the highly contingent nature of interpretations offered (1991:7) in "exhibiting" cultural Others, which I also attempt to do here.

26. Durkheim (1965); C. Geertz (1973b); Stewart (1996).

27. Renato Rosaldo (1989a) has emphasized the cultural force of emotions and passions that animate human conduct.

28. Ruth Barnes notes in her study of island regions east of Flores, *The Ikat Textiles of Lamalera*, how a contrast between strongly traditional culture, which apparently emphasizes the indigenous and which seems largely self-sufficient, and the eager readiness to adopt new possibilities have created a community of great diversity and constant surprises (1989a:6). Such contrasts also bear out in eastern Sumba.

29. Herbert Phillips' insistence that "the mere existence of an institution says little about the behavior of people in it, toward it, or away from it" (1969:26) antecedes current arguments regarding "agency." Phillips urges that "as much attention be given to the study of nonparticipation and nonfulfillment of cultural forms as is given to fulfillment and fact of these forms" (1969:27).

30. Lila Abu-Lughod, in examining Bedouin women's lives, asserts the value of storytelling as a means to uncover social and emotional dynamics, while acknowledging that such stories are always situated between a teller and an audience and are partial in perspective and motivated in the telling (1993:15). Stories form a major part of my account of Sumba, and their partiality and the motivations of those telling them will become evident in places, along with the interactions they allowed me. Diane Losche (1997) suggests that we gain insight into local aesthetic systems if we are attentive—in what she terms "hybrid moments" of interaction—to what people ask of us, the outsiders/researchers, and to their responses to our design systems or categories of value.

31. Chandra Mohanty (1988) criticizes Western scholarship as overdetermining the non-Western world in its positioning of subjects. Below I try to shift the focus from any predetermined hierarchical centers and peripheries and allow varying subjectivities to unfold.

Chapter 2: Locations, Histories, Identities

1. Sumba spans about 75 kilometers north to south and 200 kilometers east to west. Its population numbers roughly 400,000, sparse by Indonesian standards. The region of my study, an area of the central coastal plains at the eastern portion of the island (see map), contains approximately 90,000 residents.

2. Terms noted parenthetically, unless otherwise indicated, are in the regional language of Kambera, which is general to East Sumba. Although there are variations in dialect between the village regions of my study, most terminology is shared by them. Dutch colonial administrators often spoke Malay (Bahasa Malayu, a language that was antecedent to Indonesian across the archipelago, but that is similar to it), and some Sumbanese learned to speak this during the colonial era. Following the institution of an Indonesian state school system, which began in Sumba in the 1960s (roughly a decade after independence from the Dutch), most Sumbanese are now fluent in Bahasa Indonesia, the lingua franca of the nation. Indonesian is used extensively between ethnic groups in Sumba and by villagers speaking with residents of other regions to avoid communication problems between differing dialects or even different languages. I will indicate in the text wherever the words or quotes are in Indonesian by a parenthetical "I."

3. European chronicles about Sumba began to appear largely in the nineteenth century and were authored by colonial officers, traders, and Christian missionaries, most of them Dutch. In East Sumba, ethnographic studies were first carried out extensively in the early twentieth century, by D. K. Wielenga (beginning in 1907) and by Louis Onvlee (beginning in 1925), themselves associated with the Dutch Reformed Church. Marie Jeanne Adams built upon findings of these authors and carried out fieldwork in the eastern, coastal region in the 1960s. Gregory Forth has written extensively from his research during the 1970s in the village domain of Rende, East Sumba. Rodney Needham's studies of Sumbanese customs and social structure (1980, 1984), while relevant to eastern Sumba, were largely carried out in the western portion of the island. This abbreviated account of literature regarding eastern Sumba will be supplemented throughout this book.

4. Such clan myths in eastern Sumba have been described by M. Adams (1970); Kapita (1976b); Lambooy (1926); Nooteboom (1940); and Wielenga (1937).

5. Women are usually dispersed from their natal villages through marriage, as they become part of a husband's patriclan, associated with his *uma*. In recent decades, people have often moved to other regions for employment, and many eastern Sumbanese villagers have resettled in or around the main town of Waingapu. Kinship links are generally widespread around Sumba.

6. As Louis Onvlee noted in Sumba, "A person must make apparent the fact that he has possessions" (1980:203). Such ostentation in social life perpetuates the elaborate material culture distinguishing the region. Peter Bellwood, referring generally to Austronesian societies, notes, "We have a kind of 'founder principle' that can be applied to the ranking of lineages . . . but this ranking is also open to constant rearrangement through individual cleverness and the manipulation of wealth" (1997:146). Stories in this book further substantiate this principle.

7. Ethnic groups are referred to as *suku bangsa* in such discourse and are labeled as part of a diversity across Indonesia that the national government seeks to subsume through its ideal of "unity in diversity."

8. While Sumbanese have been aware of numerous differences between themselves and outsiders for centuries, Indonesian government emphasis upon the "ethnicity" of groups across the archipelago and the obvious value of the ethnic in the tourist and local arts trades have intensified interest in this category of identity for people in Sumba. Moreover, a growing pluralism in Sumba through the twentieth century has prompted indigenous groups to

find ways of distinguishing themselves from Chinese, Arabs, and Indonesians from other islands.

9. Hoskins has addressed such reevaluations regarding the Kodi region of West Sumba (1987a, 1987b, 1993a).

10. My estimates were taken from statistical reports regarding the main town of Waingapu published by Kantor Statistik Kabupaten Sumba Timur (1993a), as well as from calculations of the numbers in their folds from various clergymen in the region. Figures regarding religious affiliation, however, are elusive in East Sumba, as many people, in compliance with Indonesian government ideology and pressures, simply state on paper that they are Christians, while continuing to follow Marapu beliefs and practices. This was also likely the case in the past, as Sumbanese attempted to profit from Dutch schooling and political assistance by complying with demands to convert. Based upon research carried out in the 1970s, Forth estimated that "despite several decades of missionary efforts, the majority of Sumbanese, probably more than two-thirds in East Sumba, still retained their traditional religion" (1981:9).

11. There are similarities to the Toraja of Sulawesi in the centrality of funerals to cultural life. See K. Adams (1985); Crystal (1985, 1989); Volkman (1985).

12. See M. Adams (1969); Fox (1973, 1975); Hoskins (1990); Kuipers (1990a, 1990b); McKinnon (1989); Needham (1980); Schulte Nordholt (1980); Traube (1980); and Valeri (1980) for examples in various Indonesian contexts.

13. Studies of dualisms throughout Sumba have focused upon ritual speech, which is typically organized into paired couplets (Clamagirand 1980; Forth 1981, 1988; Fox 1988; Hoskins 1988, 1993a; Keane 1991, 1995; Kuipers 1988, 1990a, 1990b; D. Mitchell 1988), social organization (I. Mitchell 1981; Needham 1980; Onvlee 1977), and architecture (Forth 1981; Keane 1995). Hoskins has related dualism in West Sumbanese thought to gendered ritual roles (1987a), religious deities (1990), and religious conversion (1987b), among other things. M. Jeanne Adams' numerous studies address dualisms in various manifestations in Sumbanese society, with a prevalent focus upon textiles. See also Geirnaert(-Martin's) (1989, 1992) studies of cloth and cosmology in western Sumba.

14. As Thomas has shown (in relation to contemporary Maori arts), complementarity creates no reassuring sense of balance or coherence, but an unsettling condition of tension (1995:25).

15. Benedict Anderson (1983) wrote of how a modern spread of literacy and print media facilitated an "imagined community" within Indonesia (and other nations). As people read of other ethnic groups in a newly founded nation, they might better imagine themselves as part of a greater political entity. While profoundly affected by literacy, pluralism, and state government, many people in Sumba seem to imagine expanded fields of social and economic opportunity in which to act more than they imagine national "communities."

16. Despite the fact that, since after World War Two, Sumba has been incorporated politically into a nation containing the largest Islamic population in the world, converts to Islam have been relatively few on the island and tend to result from marriages. Of the Muslim population of East Sumba, most descend from immigrants to the island (originally Arabs) and are not usually indigenous Sumbanese. Various reasons may account for the lack of following Islam has drawn, such as the importance of pigs in Sumba in exchanges and rituals and the centrality of caste divisions in social life.

17. The earliest conversions to Christianity on the island took place in West Sumba, initiated by German Jesuits in 1893 (Velden 1894). Dutch Calvinist missionaries established themselves in East Sumba in 1907, and between the Christian sects, a number of mission schools were set up on the island. For a detailed history of early missionary activity in West Sumba see Hoskins (1987b, 1993a) and Keane (1995a, 1996).

18. Similar motivations are theorized by Kipp (1995) and Steedly (1993) regarding Karo Batak of Sumatra in conversions from animism to Protestantism. See also Keane's discussions of forces and complexities involved in conversion from animism to Christianity

in the Anakalang region of West Sumba (1995a, 1996, 1997). Reid (1994) notes that generally throughout Southeast Asia local peoples likely saw foreign missionaries as having keys to a great source of power and were thus drawn to the Christian folds. M. Adams (1970:91) reports how the animist people of the Kapunduk region selectively adopted the sacred Muslim city of Mecca into their clan history as the site to which their first priest-deity descended from the heavens. This development, she postulates, resulted from interactions with Arabs living on Sumba and the subsequent realization of Mecca as a place of great spiritual force. While not in any sense a conversion to Islam, local adoption of Mecca into a clan myth became a link with great powers far from Sumba, including (the largely Islamic) Jakarta. Goody generally acknowledges the force of a newly introduced "written word" as an incentive in itself for religious conversion among nonliterates, irrespective of the content of the Bible (1986:5).

19. Through an early political and economic complicity with the Dutch colonial administration, certain noble families of East Sumba were able to greatly increase their wealth and ramify their social power within the region. This power persisted, to a considerable extent, through Sumba's incorporation into Indonesian statehood following independence from the Dutch and into present times.

20. John Pemberton (1994) provides a historical account of the original deployment of this concept in colonial Java under the Dutch and its transformation into a hegemonic discourse of Indonesian statehood. Adrian Vickers (1996) has recently written of the notion of *kemajuan* as it shapes Balinese modernity. A modern ideology of progress has many manifestations throughout Indonesia, as a force for cultural change. See Barth (1993); Hoskins (1993a); Kipp (1993); Kipp and Rodgers (1987); Pemberton (1994); Tsing (1993); Vickers (1996); and Volkman (1990) for a variety of examples. While rooted in Indonesian nationalist politics, the compelling force of "progressiveness," as I will demonstrate, goes beyond this, as people attempt to link themselves with international forces. In this way, Sumbanese sometimes circumvent state control and even enjoy autonomy in their relations with foreigners.

21. Monotheism is inherent in Pancasila—an ideological doctrine presented by Sukarno in 1945, stating five principles of Indonesian nationhood. The first of these principles asserts belief in one God.

22. See Hobsbawm (1983:265); also see Acciaioli (1985); Atkinson (1983): Crystal (1989); Hoskins (1987c); Kipp (1993); Pemberton (1994); and Volkman (1985, 1990) for discussions of how regional groups are drawn into a national system in Indonesia.

23. This ambivalent stance between modern notions of state citizenship and local hegemonic control is obviously an elite position in Sumba. It can be argued with equal validity that the notion of democracy (*demokrasi*, I.) and incorporation into a larger, national political entity might benefit people at lower socioeconomic levels. Indeed, as will emerge in later chapters, those socially marginalized by hierarchical systems such as exist in Sumba may themselves push the limits of their social worlds. In Sumba, however, the noble caste has for many decades had the benefit of schooling as well as ongoing social connections to imposed authorities and thus holds a clearer grasp of political realities than do people from lower ranks. In this sense, such elites might consider themselves within an "imagined community" (following B. Anderson, 1983) of Indonesia as a whole. Although there has been a state school system in effect in East Sumba for three decades, tuition and book fees beyond the means of many local people are still required for attendance. Moreover, it is general practice in the region to be exceedingly conscious of social caste and to behave accordingly; such behavior involves deference to nobility.

24. See M. Adams (1969); Needham (1983); Wielenga (1913).

25. See Forth (1981); Ricklefs (1993); Wielenga (1913).

26. Throughout Southeast Asia, Chinese long have established themselves as a merchant class. Seaborne commerce involving Chinese traders began many centuries ago, but most Chinese immigrants to Indonesia arrived during the colonial era. As middlemen in

port regions, they performed a complementary role in peasant economies. Most Chinese living in Sumba came to the island in the twentieth century from more populous areas of Indonesia, such as Java and Sulawesi. See Curtin (1984); Mackie (1976); Purcell (1951); Reid (1996); and Steinberg (1987) for histories of Chinese immigration in Southeast Asia. Van der Kroef (1954) discusses the history of Chinese and Arab merchants living in Indonesia. See van Leur (1955) for a history of Chinese, Arab, and Indian trade across the archipelago.

27. This traveling by men to gain or maintain prestige (a phenomenon called *merantau* throughout Indonesia) has been discussed by M. Adams (1969); Atkinson (1990); Errington (1989, 1990); H. Geertz (1963); Peacock (1979); Siegel (1969); M. Rosaldo (1980); and Tsing (1993), among others. It is something of a basic and pervasive idiom when considering differential modes of behavior and mobility between the sexes in the Southeast Asian world. The travels of Sumbanese men have not (until recently) been as far-flung or lengthy as those of men in other regions, such as areas of Sumatra. Yet men in Sumba have routinely traveled for a number of purposes, including trade, warfare, treaties, and the negotiation for brides. Although I know of no term in the eastern Sumbanese language with precisely the meaning of "*merantau*," "*palaku*" connotes journeying. The word "*danggangu,*" however, might better approximate the concept in current times, as it applies to wide-ranging travel for purposes of trade. The term "*mbawa*" implies traveling about for pleasure, but usually entails short distances. The phrase "*ndadik la tana tau*" denotes staying in a foreign place and currently marks a kind of status of off-island travelers.

28. See Maria Mies (1982) for a similar gap in mobility and access to outsiders between the sexes, involving female lace makers in India and male kin who sell their wares. Margaret Swain (1989) also describes this gendered tendency among the Kuna of Panama, although she notes that women have also claimed increased political authority in some instances through the weaving cooperatives created in response to the tourist market.

29. Forth notes a ritual couplet in which such death is described in parallel speech: *meti njadangu, na meti wenangu*, which means "the roaming death, the wandering death" (1991b:67).

30. As described by Joel Kuipers, "*podda*" in the Weyéwa region of West Sumba (1990a, 1990b) seems to be an analog to "*hanggamar*" in East Sumba. Current eastern Sumbanese quests and fears reveal moral precedents for or against modern capitalist enterprise. See Robert Hefner (1998).

31. This discrepancy in mobility and activity between the sexes is reminiscent of Nancy Munn's (1973) description and contextualizing of Walbiri iconography. The iconography of Sumbanese textiles, however, although reflecting manners of thought and social organization, does not read as a literal map of gendered mobility and concerns as do the creations of Munn's Australian women artists, but rather as a fluctuating tableau of prestige symbols. These prestige symbols, nonetheless, are connected in many cases to male mobility and prowess.

32. As a foreigner, I was given some leeway in such judgments, although my travels between villages in Sumba were cause for concern. Often people commented on how strong (*kaparu*) I was to be able to walk so much, but more often I was chastised for risking my health through overexertion. When I did fall ill at one point, people advised me that it was because I moved around excessively and that certain diseases fell particularly to women who were too physically active. Others, I heard, considered me *katoba* ("crazy") because I wandered about alone—to them, inexplicably.

33. In East Sumba, body movements and facial expressions of women should ideally be controlled and languid. People say that women tire easily and cannot walk long distances. This echoes the generally *lemah* (I.)—meaning "weak" but also "supple and graceful"—feminine demeanor conventional in much of Indonesia. The eastern Sumbanese call such bearing *tamainangu*, and many commented to me that by contrast, they found Western women too rapid and clumsy in their motions. It is through controlled, limited gestures that women

ideally move. Yet, as will emerge, there can be great dexterity in extending personal movement.

34. Although eastern Sumbanese speak hypothetically of matrilateral cross-cousin marriages as the ideal, few families I knew of were actually following this pattern to any degree. Clan alliances were important, but often much was negotiable. To my knowledge, daughters, however, were always married to a man of at least equal caste standing, while for sons a bride could be of a lower caste.

35. I depart somewhat from Foucault's (1984) generally top-down view of discourse and consider it as an aspect in less obvious manifestations of power and social control. A growing body of literature (much of it feminist) explores the power of voices from "marginal" or "subaltern" perspectives. See, for example, Abu-Lughod (1993); Hoskins (1989); Ong (1987); Stewart (1990, 1996); Tsing (1993); and Visweswaran (1994). Some of these studies raise the issue of "marginality" as addressed in scholarly literature, illustrating ways to bring the formerly peripheral to the center.

36. Kathleen Stewart (1990) demonstrates how "backtalk"—a telling of the way things are against dominant representations and narratives—becomes a mode of social positioning for women, creating a discourse that is not only a form of resistance to male dominance, but a mechanism that redefines reality and wields social influence in the process.

37. Vanessa Maher illustrates how Italian dressmakers used their symbolic and technical knowledge to subvert the social order they participated in, creating enclaves of anomalous social relations in which they enjoyed certain freedoms (1987:140). Similar conditions involving some of the Sumbanese women in this study will emerge.

38. The textile trade in Sumba reflects what Arjun Appadurai defines as a status competition between elite males in linking internal and external systems of exchange (1988:33). In this sense, a third-world patriarchal system is reinforcing itself through phenomena arising out of interactions and discourses involving the First World, but in ways that are leading to disjunctions between the sexes that are even wider than in the past (see Mies 1982; Ong 1987, 1991; Strathern 1990).

211

Chapter 3: Enfolding History and Flux

1. Some informative studies that follow cloth historically are those of M. Adams (1969); R. Barnes (1989a); Bayly (1988); Blum-Schevill (1993); Gittinger (1980, 1989b); Hamilton (1994b); Hitchcock (1991); Kahlenberg (1977); Maher (1987); Maxwell (1990a); Milgram and Van Esterik (1994); Nabholz-Kartaschoff, Barnes, and Stuart-Fox (1993); Niessen (1994); Veldhuisen-Djajasoebrata (1988); Weiner (1976); and Weiner and Schneider (1989).

2. Lisa Aronson (1991) has discussed biases in Western scholarly representations of African artistic forms and the cultures they emerge from. She notes the overwhelming attention most research literature has paid to male activities as being definitive of arts and culture. Annette Weiner (1976) makes a similar (and earlier) critique regarding Malinowski's biased focus in the Trobriand Islands, which set a standard for later studies that inordinately privileged male endeavors throughout the Pacific region.

3. See Forth (1981); Hoskins (1988); Keane (1991, 1997); Kuipers (1988, 1990a, 1990b); D. Mitchell (1988).

4. This is also the case in other areas of eastern Indonesia, where weaving and marriage eligibility are importantly connected (see R. Barnes 1992, 1994).

5. This follows what Needham (1980, 1984) terms "circulating connubium" in endogamous, patriarchal, and patrilocal marriage patterns, although it occurs in a more fluid and negotiable sense than Needham's system allows for, following my impressions and those of M. Adams (1969).

6. See Ruth Barnes (1989:129–135) for a discussion of evidence that influences in Indonesian textiles go beyond this, in both time depth and geographical origins.

7. It is not my purpose to go into a detailed technical description of cloth production here. The interested reader may refer to M. Adams (1969); R. Barnes (1989); Bolland (1956); Geirnaert-Martin (1992); Gittinger (1979); Hamilton (1994b); and Jacobson and Yaeger (1995) for more descriptive accounts of weaving techniques in eastern Indonesian contexts. For a general orientation to the mechanics and terminology of weaving, see Burnham (1980).

8. Cotton (*kamba*) has long been grown on Sumba as the sole material used for fabrics, although it is not clear when its cultivation on the island actually began. In other regions of the Indonesian archipelago (such as Sumatra) there is evidence that cotton was in use by the sixth century (Hitchcock 1991:29); it may have been employed by inhabitants of Sumba in a similarly distant past. A variety of species are grown in Indonesia (and within Sumba), but a common one is *Gossypium herbaceum*. Robyn Maxwell writes that cotton thread appears to have been in use in island Southeast Asia by the time of Christ (1990a:157).

9. Mattiebelle Gittinger marvels at the dramatically different expressiveness in motifs of Sumba textiles in comparison to other textiles woven in Indonesia (1980:157).

10. See M. Adams (1971a); Geirnaert-Martin (1992); Hoskins (1990).

11. In the Preface of this book, Luka forges a long detour around a village to avoid a sorceress given to spells using indigo.

12. M. Adams (1969, 1980) goes into extensive, diagrammatic detail in her structural analysis of *hinggi* cloths of East Sumba and how their designs reflect a basic intellectual and social ordering in village lives. Especially interesting is her interpretation of the central panel (which divides all pieces) as reasserting, through visual design, the centrality of the Sumbanese value upon mediation between social groups, including those living within the same village. This mediation reflects the importance of ritual speakers (called *wunang*, as are the central sections of fabrics) in Sumbanese village life and the extensive use of parallelism, as discussed by Forth (1981:18–20), but also demonstrates the value of a visual art in revealing something of how people conceptualize (or idealize) their social worlds.

13. Geirnaert-Martin (1992) links this binding in West Sumba to the practice of *ikat* in a larger socio-cosmic sense. That is, inasmuch as *ikat* dyeing is carried out on the two extreme eastern and western ends of Sumba, it metaphorically binds the island's waters, preventing rivers from completely flowing out to sea. I did not hear this idea expressed in East Sumba, but the image it suggests is compelling.

14. Forth (1985) discusses eastern Sumbanese numerical concepts in a more general sense.

15. See M. Adams (1969); Bühler (1959); Hoskins (1996).

16. See Fischer, ed. (1979); Gittinger, ed. (1989); Maxwell (1990a, 1990b).

17. See Fischer (1979); Hitchcock (1991); Kartiwa (1989); and Langewis and Wagner (1964). Ruth Barnes (1989:83–85) suggests that similar figures in eastern Indonesia textiles have existed for at least five hundred years, as local interpretations upon Indian *patola* patterns with ancient sources in Inner Asia. Barnes is speaking specifically for the Lamaholot region east of Flores, but similar influences evidently also spread to Sumba through trade.

18. For examples of woven human figures from other regions of Indonesia and Southeast Asia, see R. Barnes (1989); Fischer (1979); Gittinger (1980); Hitchcock (1991); Jacobson and Yaeger (1995); Langewis and Wagner (1964); and Maxwell (1990a). Photographs in an article by W. O. J. Nieuwenkamp, published in 1927, show various renditions of the human figure in East Sumba at the earlier part of the twentieth century, and they are similar to ones produced today.

19. See Onvlee (1980) for a detailed discussion of the history and importance of horses in Sumba.

20. For the extent to which the *patola* cloths circulated through Southeast Asia and the ways they were adopted and valued across an enormous geographical and cultural range, see R. Barnes (1989); Bühler (1959); Hamilton (1994b); and Maxwell (1990a:206–237).

21. The most obvious examples of this might be seen in the warm tones and vivid contrasts employed by Rembrandt, Vermeer, and Jan Steen.

22. See M. Adams (1969). Witold Rybczynski (1987) describes the historical development of a specifically Dutch attitude toward domesticity and comfortable decor beginning in the sixteenth century.

23. Robyn Maxwell (1990a) notes a greater degree of realism in textile motifs of regions such as Java and Sarawak through the late nineteenth and early twentieth centuries, largely in response to foreign influences. This change resulted in more humanly representational (and frequently personified) figures than in the past. And some Javanese batiks of the period contain stories from European fairy tales (see Maxwell 1990a:382–383).

24. Such as J. A. Loeber (1901, 1902) and especially the artist W. O. J. Nieuwenkamp (1920, 1927).

25. See M. Adams (1969:96–100) for more details of this period of Dutch collecting, which spread to other cities of Europe.

26. I mean by "realism" the attempt to depict things with some accuracy as they appear in nature.

Part Two: Between the Folds

1. The organization and atmosphere of Waingapu echo some of Clifford Geertz's descriptions of Modjokuto, Java, in its then recent stages of an "urbanization" that had not completely incorporated the social life within and around it. Thus, "lacking a truly dynamic core, life becomes makeshift in quality, gathers around it an air of exigency and insubstantiality, and although there is a great deal of hubbub, the over-all effect is one of agitated stability rather than growth and change" (1963:134).

2. There is little domestic tourism on the island, perhaps because Sumba is considered primitive (referred to in Indonesian as *primitif*, implying wild, unsafe, and unclean conditions, and largely devoid of the romanticism the term "primitive" often carries in the West) and unappealing to the largely metropolitan Indonesians who can afford to travel for pleasure.

Chapter 4: Wandi

1. Young men from these groups are the ones most often migrating to Waingapu to seek employment.

2. Velocity in itself has been long emblematic of modern development and its displacements and is currently no less so in Sumba.

3. Similar stories appear throughout the Indonesian islands (and across Southeast Asia) to account for the intentions and prowess of outsiders. See Drake (1989); Erb (1991); Forth (1991a); George (1991); Hoskins (1996b); Metcalf (1996); Pannel (1992); and Tsing (1996) for examples in various regions.

4. The population of the area surrounding the elevated village is approximately two thousand.

213

5. This is the Sumba Christian Church, which originated with the Dutch Reformed Church in the colonial era.

6. Roxana Waterson writes of landscapes of myth and history in another region of Indonesia (Tana Toraja), "The visual perspective is thus only one among many dimensions by which landscape can be known or comprehended" (1997:63). The new visual perspective of Wandi's landscape (coexistent with numerous other dimensions) reordered comprehensions of its citizens through permitting new vistas and forms to emerge and be transfigured through the years to follow.

7. Flights on the two domestic carriers to Sumba from Bali were increased in 1992, bringing more tourists to the island. This was in addition to tourists arriving on flights from Timor or Flores. With this increase in arrivals came a greater market for local fabrics in Sumba.

8. Giving money as bride price (*wili tau*) is rare in East Sumba, as animals and gold items are the commonly agreed-upon wealth (*banda*) that seal a marriage negotiation. Rumors that Biba was obtained by her husband for cash—whether true or not—may also have helped reinforce her marginal status among Wandi villagers.

9. Eastern Sumbanese lore states that a Marapu ancestor issued an edict to certain inland villages that they were forbidden to weave. Hence, weaving skill is rare in such regions, and historically the inlanders have traded agricultural goods for textiles produced by the coastal peoples. Forth (1981) notes this, as does M. Adams (1969).

10. This might parallel what Christopher Steiner discovered about the influence of European publications about African art on local traders. Informed by foreign catalogues of African creations, such traders regard "authenticity as something which emanates directly from the pages of a book" (1994:103). The picture in the book then becomes the prime reference for future copies, and such copies are judged by their accurate depiction of the picture.

214

11. Biba's economic success epitomized a certain growing belief in East Sumba that women are better money managers than men. As men historically have been the traders and venturers of the region, and as there is no long-standing institution of the marketplace as in Java (and thus Sumbanese women are new to such trade), such skill in Sumba on the part of women is something of a paradox. Yet enterprise and resourcefulness have strong antecedents in the domestic sphere, and Biba said that she merely applied the same principles of household management and common sense to commerce at large. (See Strathern's discussion of Sexton [1982] on the tendency in Melanesian society for women to safeguard money and men to be concerned with only short-term goals and consumption [1990: 84]).

12. This suggests George Foster's "image of limited good" (1965) observed in peasant societies with distinct nuclear families. At the same time, ideas in Sumba about prospering through the fabric trade incorporate images of limitless abundance by way of commerce with the outside world. What are "limited" are the knowledge, finesse, and contacts with which to continue to profit within the transcultural market.

13. That Hasan was a Muslim did not appear to me to present problems with the Wandi villagers (whether animist or Christian). Although he eschewed pork and observed the fast during Ramadan, he did not practice daily prayers or express religious convictions to others. Many of Hasan's ideas and overt practices corresponded to those of other villagers, as he attended weddings and funerals of all sorts and extended hospitality to people dropping by his home. The skill of his mother, wife, and sisters at producing fabrics situated them firmly in local modes of behavior, despite Biba's business prowess.

14. To avoid irking the Wandi nobility, Biba tried to employ designs that had originated in more distant village regions.

15. See Hoskins (1989).

16. "Culture" is referred to in Bahasa Indonesia by such critics as *kebudayaan* or simply *budaya*. This term relates to Indonesian state discourse involving various ethnic

groups across the archipelago. The eastern Sumbanese have developed a consciousness of the values ascribed to "culture" by outsiders (be they state officials or foreign tourists), and it has become realized as a kind of commodity by those who attempt to claim control over it.

17. Speaking of a region in the western part of Sumba, Joel Kuipers notes that "among Weyéwa, the political nature of gender relations appears most clearly in the context of misfortunes, when the perpetration of the patrilineal society is most seriously challenged" (1990b:156). Good fortune can also make such relations salient. Biba's successes presented a corresponding misfortune for some men in the region because they were surpassed by a woman who had transgressed boundaries historically within the realm of men. Her offense was thus doubly "unfortunate" for her critics, whose commentaries, in turn, articulated something of the nature of gender relations and the tensions emerging from them in current times.

18. Many villagers say these sorts of storytelling *hinggi* designs began to appear at this time. I have seen no evidence of similar narrative pieces in outside collections or publications, although pictures of *hinggis* with different design fields in each end of the cloths have appeared in various publications (see Maxwell 1990a:391 for a good example). While these other sorts of asymmetrical *hinggis* are unusual, they do not depict events sequentially from one end to the other, as do the fabrics I introduce here.

19. Studies have noted the development of spatial perspective in European visual art as indicating a shift in social and ideological perspective (see Baxandall 1972; Damisch 1994; Edgerton 1975; Gombrich 1969; Kubovy 1986; Maquet 1986; Panofsky 1991). Hildred Geertz (1995) discusses the emergence of a type of "perspective" (similar to what I describe in cloth above) in Balinese paintings beginning in the 1930s—that is, the depiction of actual "scenes" connecting events and surroundings and viewed from specific vantage points. In Bali, as in Sumba, this constitutes a move to naturalistic realism that reflects an altered consciousness of the world. This new consciousness—in its multiple forms—also implies new types of subjectivities. I do not consider such a shift in perspective as evolutionary in any ideal sense of art, such as from "simple" to "complex." Rather, this shift reflects changing social conditions and views of the world. A major ingredient in this change in Sumba, as it was in Bali, is the emergence of a foreign audience for artistic creations, but other modern forces bear upon it.

215

20. See Geirnaert-Martin (1992); Hoskins (1986); Keane (1997); Kuipers (1990a); Onvlee (1980).

21. This novelty was in the depiction of actual events in natural space, a type of representational field that contrasts with how Marie Jeanne Adams perceived the textiles in the 1960s: "Possibly the unreal quality of many of the Sumba textile forms reflects the supernatural realm to which the designs refer" (1969:68).

In my view, the initial influence toward this view of "actual events in natural space" was likely literacy and the introduction of a specific sequentiality of information and events. This sequentiality, in turn, incited the "reflexive of potentialities of writing" (Goody 1986: 37) in new local ponderings on aesthetics, history, and beliefs. Luka's was the first generation to enroll in state schools established in Sumba by the Indonesian government in the decades after national independence. What is more, the cloth of the Wandi designer also reflected the linear layout his village had taken after its reconstruction following World War Two (discussed in the earlier part of this chapter). The dyadic-triadic fabric designs Adams had noted as generally reflecting Sumbanese village layout and social organization had been "opened up" in Wandi. A particular social and intellectual world was somehow altered by a linear lane through the center of the village, a kind of organized open-endedness of space and movement unique to this particular place. Beyond some basic perceptual shifts in thinking about the world implied by the advent of literacy and an altered social geography, Luka was also influenced by the narrative temple paintings he saw in Bali. Myriad other influences may have affected him, but these are the ones I was able to glimpse.

22. The paintings, which impressed Luka, were in the form of long scrolls, relating narratives of religious tales. Such narratives were influential in Luka's subsequent textile designs.

23. This is a type of fabric produced for tourists; it features large "primitive" human figures that run the length of a cloth (see chapter 3). Because less time is taken in binding the warps of these large designs, they can be created expediently for the tourist market. These types of figures (and also those of large lizards) were likely borrowed in recent times from pictures of fabrics of the Iban from Sarawak and Kalimantan (see plate 13).

24. And also characterize him in the Preface.

25. Barbara Babcock considers that "more than simply reflecting or expressing social structure and worldview, any significant new form reconstructs cultural reality, causing a dislocation in the economy of cultural representations" (1993:75). Thus, revised realities come into being and "an original awareness of existence" (Kaufman 1969:147; cited in Babcock 1993) redirects innovators and others involving new ways of looking at the conditions of their worlds. Themes and formats of Luka's narrative cloths also suggest a new ideology of process associated with the ephemeral importance of persons noted by Hoskins in West Sumba (1993a:138).

26. The term *"umbu"* is a title denoting a man of noble rank. The corresponding title for a noblewoman is *"rambu."* These terms will reappear connected to others of the *maramba* caste throughout this book.

27. Barbara Babcock links gender, discourse, and artistic creativity succinctly: "If we are not attuned to gender dynamics and the politics of discourse in the cultures we are studying, as well as in our own, we will perpetuate such idealistic and projective distortions as the ideas that simpler societies are not contaminated by sexual politics and that potteries and politics have nothing to do with each other" (1993:95).

28. Attending secondary school throughout Indonesia requires students to select on paper a religion (*agama*, I.) accepted by the national government, as Biba discussed doing earlier in this chapter. In most regions, local religions are not recognized by the national government.

29. The latter poster was supplied by the local family planning (*keluarga berencana*) official to encourage the compliance of Wandi village with national policy. The Indonesian government has for a number of years been encouraging people to limit their children to two, with the slogan Dua Anak Cukup! (Two Children Are Enough!). Umbu Ama's display of the poster showed his "compliance" with government policy (although his issue far surpasses the "ideal" family size). The prominent display of the gynecological poster seemed odd, however, as Sumbanese (and Indonesians in general) are not given to speaking openly about sexual matters and are certainly modest in revealing their anatomies publicly. Yet the poster on the front wall of the house followed a certain political logic: it proclaimed (visibly) an alliance with state government while employing a sort of transformation of an indigenous gender motif. In East Sumba, an iconography of the female organ has existed for at least a century and can be seen in textiles and in omega-shaped gold items called *mamuli*, given by a man's family as part of marriage exchange. Ironically, however, a *mamuli* represents fertility and wholeness through an aesthetic, stylized symbol, while the family planning poster advertises sterility in starkly scientific, pragmatic terms. The implications of this suggest Foucault's notion of "bio-power" (1978), that is, the control over bodies that he considers to have been indispensable to the development of capitalism. Yet such control has likely been deployed for centuries in Sumba—using a visual, gendered lexicon. What is recent are connections with the state, science, and global media.

30. This exhibit was indicative of the increased value Jakartan authorities have given, in recent years, to "traditional societies" throughout Indonesia, partly as a result of realizing their great international appeal. However, as Picard (1990a, 1990b) has demonstrated in Bali (and which echoes earlier points by Hobsbawm, 1983), increased government "sponsorship" of representations of the "cultures" of ethnic groups also facilitates their

incorporation into a state system. And as Kipp (1993) argues, the celebration of local cultures (largely in nationalized, urban settings) can also be a government strategy to mask social and political inequities and the general dominance of the Javanese and Chinese (respectively) in political and economic realms of Indonesian nationhood. Pemberton (1994) also gives a compelling account of this.

31. See Pemberton (1994:152–161) for history and political implications of the origins of this park with the establishment of New Order Indonesia under Suharto.

Chapter 5: Parai Mutu

1. This is a structural similarity between village spatial organization and textile designs in Sumba discussed at length by M. Adams (1980).

2. Forth (1981) mentions this general social atmosphere in the region, which he characterizes as "taciturn," although he does acknowledge the assistance given him by villagers in the 1970s.

3. This is one of the numerous conceptual dualisms common in Sumba, as mentioned in chapter 2, the most salient of which is male and female. I use these particular concepts in this section because they resonate with the current nature of tensions between the local and the foreign as well as between the historical and the contemporary for people of Parai Mutu. This rooted sense of place and desire for strategic social alliances both resound and conflict with current realities in East Sumba.

4. Benedict Anderson's (1972) ideas of power in Java as emanating from a spiritually potent center out to peripheries established a basic conceptual model for societies and political power in regions of the Southeast Asian world. See also Errington (1989); C. Geertz (1980); Reid (1983, 1988).

5. Within these divisions, there are further distinctions—such as major nobility (*maramba bokulu*) and minor nobility (*maramba kudu*), with the other two castes hierarchically divided as well. In fact, people often told me of situations (in present times) in which the lowest level slaves served slaves higher up on the social hierarchy who were themselves indentured to the yet more elevated slaves of the nobility.

6. The population of the extended domain of Parai Mutu, which includes the surrounding villages and hamlets, numbers more than a thousand, according to the 1993 government census report.

7. In time, and on later visits, I also became better acquainted with other people in the village and was able to arrive at a sense of the various directions individual lives in Parai Mutu had taken and some of the factors that had influenced these directions. Interacting with a variety of Parai Mutu people had taken some perseverance and dexterity on my part. As mentioned above, the residents of this village are not easily given to gregariousness and intermingling. Nevertheless, people did eventually seem to come to an understanding and (at least a partial) acceptance of the fact that my study necessitated interviewing individuals from a number of households, and thus any protests gradually subsided. I was, however, always chided about who my "first friends and family" in the village had been and continued to maintain a relatively central social connection with this family of textile creators and traders. Ana Humba became my closest confidant among them.

8. Ana Humba told me of how such proscriptions applied to even short visits that did not involve spending the night. She explained that even though she had also befriended a certain European schoolteacher (who was working in Sumba through an international volunteer agency), she could not accept the woman's invitation to visit her at her Waingapu home because it was an *uma hewa* (rented house) and thus outside the constraints and morality of her affinal network. As such, it was forbidden to her in any social sense.

217

9. This was a frequent explanation from families with adult, unmarried daughters at home in this region. Forth relates similar situations in some village households of the 1970s, when spinsterhood was not uncommon among noblewomen "who were often said not to have married because a man of the appropriate rank and status could not be found" (1981: 333). As noblemen may marry women of lower caste, but noblewomen must marry a social equal, the result is that more unmarried women than men exist in villages.

10. Forth states that the major axiom of eastern Sumbanese religion is that people cannot communicate directly with God (1981:88). The possibility of doing so, as promised by Christianity, appealed to many converts I spoke with.

11. I purposely use "identity" here in a plural sense, as Ana Humba had any number of situational identities and was dexterous at shifts in self-presentation and behavior as circumstances called for them. Dorinne Kondo (1990) has written of the inseparability of identity and context as each are crafted within possible fields predicated on gender and power. Ana Humba, however, ostensibly complied with such fields, while attempting to circumvent them. By frequently altering her contexts, she was able to transmute restrictions on her own gender and power—trading upon marginal zones and continually reformulating her identity in the process. See also Moore's (1994) discussion of female "fantasies of identity" and how they relate to power and agency in a wider world. Mills (1997) illustrates this in a Thai setting, also drawing from Moore's analysis.

12. Ironically, her own family avoided selling to this particular Chinese family any of the pieces produced in their compound, as the merchants and hoteliers were notorious copiers and reproducers. The hotel "art shop" was filled with many high-priced pieces produced in the shophouse behind it, in which several local women labored. Such fabrics borrowed liberally from a range of village motifs, and the hotel staff always assured tourists that the pieces were actually produced in the villages, that they were authentic, and often that they were antiques.

13. Marie Jeanne Adams noted that the eastern Sumbanese say the visible world is a *maou*, 'shadow' of the heavenly world (1969:28). Yet to me, people in Parai Mutu often referred to the afterworld as one of shadows.

14. As mentioned in chapter 2, it was the availability of these yarns from (Dutch-implemented) Javanese factories that M. Adams (1969) credits with facilitating the upsurge in textile production in the earlier part of this century. Indeed, for decades most fabrics of Sumba have been woven from imported yarns, yet some households (such as the one above) have continued to produce a few handspun pieces, for both ceremonial use and for the external market. A typical, fairly good quality *hinggi* was generally selling to foreigners in Sumba for about 300,000 rupiah in 1994 (about a hundred fifty U.S. dollars), while a handspun piece could bring in five to ten times that amount, depending upon quality. After the Indonesian currency crisis of 1998, many people in East Sumba adjusted the selling price of their cloth in relation to the U.S. dollar.

15. Many of the older patterns found in Sumbanese *pahikung* cloth are recreated by reference to such guides, which do not exist for *ikat* weaving. Holmgren and Spertus suggest that this may be a reason why women's *lau* (generally made of such fabric) "in particular may be an unrecognized source of information about the visual appearance of textiles during the precolonial period precisely because they follow old pattern guides and therefore discourage iconographic information" (1989:38).

16. This same hotel lobby was frequently the scene for numerous "stagings" and intrigues for a number of Sumbanese villagers. In fact, village gossip was often framed within this particular setting. Tales would begin with something like, "A friend of mine saw so-and-so at the Hotel Orchid the other night, and here's what he was up to . . . "

17. This was again the hotel in which he had been publicly taken to task a couple of years earlier.

18. See Edgar Keller's (1993) description of the variously expressive ways Sumbanese men might wrap and fashion their headcloths.

19. In the earlier part of this century, Mia might typically be clad in only pounded bark (*kambala*), the clothing of the *ata* caste.

20. Needham (1983) gives a concise history of warfare and slave trading in Sumba. Forth (1981) discusses the social position of slaves in the region, and M. Adams (1969) speaks of the symbolic functions of such people in village rituals throughout East Sumba.

21. M. Adams (1969); Forth (1981); and Wielenga (1913) also have noted this.

22. As Louis Dumont (1980) has asserted, an ideology of "liberty" and "equality" is a construct of a Western humanistic essentialism, one that emphasizes individuality. Although Dumont's argument perhaps re-essentializes the West and non-West, the social and ideological contrasts it includes could be applied to Sumbanese sociality as compared to modern, democratic values.

23. I knew of others in the caste-based service of higher-ranking people who were treated harshly, sometimes beaten, and generally regarded as lesser beings. People living under such conditions are often trapped by their circumstances, with little means by which to change their condition, although some eventually do. And, as described above in Mia's case, many lower-caste people greatly fear leaving the social familiars and landscapes they have always lived with.

Chapter 6: Hawewa

1. This means "to put in between" in the local language and describes the method of inserting thin wooden strips (*lidi*) between warp threads, to create a distinct pattern to be elevated by the weft, as described in chapter 3.

2. This she expressed as *terikat,* ironically from the Indonesian root *ikat,* which also gives Sumba's cloth its name internationally.

3. Women who engaged in illicit sexual relations (*njuraku*) were almost always regarded in this way by Sumbanese I spoke to—as victims rather than perpetrators. Yet I did hear of men beating their wives for infidelities. Although a pregnant woman suspected of adultery would sometimes be pressured to publicly confess to a Marapu priest (as part of purification rites), she would not be formally punished under customary law for sexual offenses. Conversely, a guilty man would be called upon to pay a fine in livestock or else face possible physical violence from a woman's family (see Mitchell 1982a for a sense of how punishments for sexual offenses differ throughout regions of the island).

4. Comparable figures (in various forms) are found in fabrics of other Indonesian islands, such as Kalimantan, Sulawesi, Timor, and Sumatra, and have been generally interpreted as representations of ancestors by researchers (M. Adams 1969; Gittinger 1979; Hitchcock 1991; Holmgren and Spertus 1989; Maxwell 1990a; Solyom and Solyom 1979). Some consider the human forms to have originated from ancient Dongson motifs, although Ruth Barnes (1989) links them to *patola* designs with origins in Inner Asia (see chapter 2). Older examples of these figures from Sumba contain female figures as well, and Holmgren and Spertus (1989) illustrate this. Male figures tend to predominate in textile collections, however, and in recent times in eastern Sumba such figures in *lau* were almost exclusively male.

5. Indeed, a particularly female discourse often underscores "meaning" attached to fabric designs, and frequently contested and multiple meanings become apparent in the discrepancies between men's and women's commentaries. Furthermore, an ongoing discourse is embedded in certain textile motifs, a discourse that in turn elicits a kind of controversy among the people who view them.

6. Greg Dening reminds us that history cannot be divorced from the circumstances of its telling (1996:50) and that its telling often reveals a poetics in the relationships people have with texts that suffuse their lives (36). Social relations and tensions can be glimpsed in

219

diverse "tellings" of the gendered motif described above, as can its empowerment and disempowerment in responses to an ongoing "text" of representation—images in cloth.

7. Representations abroad stimulated multiple conflicts for eastern Sumbanese. Threats of appropriation by national political concerns merged with resentments against those Sumbanese who determined and spoke about arts from Sumba on exhibit. As Hoskins (1987c) relates of a situation of appropriation in western Sumba of a local warrior into nationalist rhetoric, the cousins in Hawewa were especially irked because exported representations of their culture had been "gotten wrong" in Jakarta.

8. Marapu followers sometimes allude to an ultimate deity, in recent times called Tuhan, as God is referred to by Indonesians following monotheistic faiths.

9. The abstraction of the adjunctive creatures to inanimate, geometric shapes was not exclusively Martha's invention; it can be seen in some older cloths of this sort and in some of the recent ones produced by Marapu women. As noted in chapter 2, triangular and diamond shapes within or conjunctive to human forms may have ancient antecedents. Martha, however, insisted upon her own reasons for creating such figures.

10. Here Martha used the Indonesian word "*kafir*," which is a generally derogatory term applied to those who have not converted to a world faith.

11. A certain local discourse of "authenticity" has emerged in regions of eastern Sumba as village textile producers have realized that outsiders have appropriated their techniques and designs for a foreign market. Villagers' harsh critiques of these reinvented textiles focus upon the arbitrary and slipshod recombination of motifs and dyes, as well as on the social displacement and ignorance of the women who produce them.

12. Foucault considers that "space is fundamental in any form of community life; space is fundamental in any exercise of power" (1994:168). It becomes evident that the organization of space in the Sing Ha workshop—by walls—structures a community life it contains while articulating an exercise of power.

13. Sing Ha's abnormal daughter had generated extensive lore among local villagers, and some claimed that the ancestors on his Sumbanese mother's side had been angry at her marriage to an ethnic Chinese and had put a curse upon her first-born because of this. Among Marapu followers, birth defects or poor health in the young are often said to be the results of offended ancestors.

14. The Bethel Church was imported from the United States and has ongoing connections with churches there. Several times a year, American missionaries affiliated with the denomination arrive in Sumba and sermonize at the numerous evangelical churches on the island.

15. The appeal of this church for the indigenous Sumbanese also relates to prosperity and fosters a certain ethic attributing material success to individual initiative (as in the case of Martha). But Sumbanese appear more concerned with mystical interventions causing sudden cures from illness or financial windfalls. By most accounts, this "antidote" to looming calamities in Sumbanese life discussed by Kuipers (1990a) is what draws them to convert to evangelical Protestantism.

Part Three: Shuttling between Worlds
Chapter 7: Worlds Converge

1. Regarding the Toraja region of Sulawesi, Volkman accounts for how tourism proceeds as a process (in combination with other modern pressures and ideological changes). This process involves local people as elements of the tourist "sights" and as interpreters and critics of the incoming foreigners. Thus, just as locals are objectified by tourism, they come to objectify tourists and, ultimately, aspects of their own "culture" that they display for those tourists.

220

2. This location was at the end of the central village yard, the *talora*, at some distance from the graves.

3. The *pameran* brings to mind what Dean MacCannell (1976) refers to as the staging of "authenticity," an imagined (and ever elusive) reality the tourists (themselves disenchanted by postindustrial life) are seeking—in this case by visiting a "primitive" isle such as Sumba. Although such authenticity can never be defined, it persists as a wistful figment for something lost in the modern world. The *terrain of the authentic* is an imaginative, utopian realm, often beckoning from colonial-era narratives. Echoing Goffman's (1959) concepts of front-stage and back-stage in presentations of self (developed by MacCannell in a sociological theory of tourism), the *pameran* promises a back-stage, intimate glimpse at indigenous "culture" by its very situation within a Sumbanese village. Within such stagings, however, interactions are not necessarily "unreal" (or purely what Boorstin [1975] would call "pseudo-events") but are reflective of the myriad viewpoints and desires of participants. Recent literature (Bruner 1996; Dening 1996; Gewertz and Errington 1991; Myers 1994) urges the analysis of such encounters ethnographically, putting aside concerns centering only on "representation." In Sumba, performances, behaviors, and arts displayed at *pameran*s were not devoid of value or meaning for local people. That is, local "culture" was not supplanted but was rearticulated by the influx of foreigners.

4. This generates an ongoing "play" that confounds everyone's ideas of reality at such an event, as people alternately become performers and audiences, players and non-players, within constantly shifting frames of experience (cf. Goffman 1974).

5. Eastern Sumbanese people often characterized and "graded" tourists by the extent of their awareness of the quality of local cloth. Luka also commented upon a group on this day who were only looking at "dirty cloth" (*kain kotor*, I.), in this case meaning poorly dyed, muddy-colored fabrics, adding that these particular tourists must be really "stupid" (*bodoh*, I.). From among such Philistines, the rare foreign connoisseur was a valued acquaintance among sellers of the more carefully made or distinctive pieces.

6. Umbu Pari's posture suggested a cross-cultural analog to what Christopher Steiner describes as a general attitude among Western ethnic art dealers. This attitude involves avoiding overt, commercial behavior that would betray an "inelegance of economic speculation" (1994:159). Because blatant discussion of prices and engaged haggling are low-status behaviors in Sumbanese villages, high-caste people often adopt demeanors of cool detachment during textile transactions (whether with locals or foreigners). Luka's irate, emotional response to the Dutchman above was noted by several local people at the *pameran* as being "rough" (*haladiku*)—indicative of his less-than-high-caste status.

7. Business cards are sought-after emblems of powerful connections for Sumbanese traders. Having one's own card indicates seriousness and competence in commerce and one's links to a technologically sophisticated world of production, as embodied by the cards themselves.

8. Social class is not the issue for Americans living in Indonesia that it is for Indonesians, by the accounts of numerous people in Sumba who have had dealings with them—probably because Americans living in Jakarta have a more transparently democratic ideology and often tend to romanticize peoples living in distant areas of Indonesia, much as do Western tourists in general. In addition, resident Americans are frequently seekers and collectors of arts from remote regions of Indonesia, and some even adopt a philanthropic attitude toward outer-island people, hosting and sponsoring them when they travel to Jakarta.

9. This reference to "models" largely grew out of his experience in observing Balinese entrepreneurs producing "lines" of fashions for foreign consumption. Unlike Luka, Umbu Taniku was not emphasizing singularity in each of his cloths, but was speaking of them as being part of a *koleksi* (I.; collection), denoting a particular designer (himself) and specific design trends, issuing through a number of cloths. Igor Kopytoff (1988) discusses the eternal tension between commodification and singularity in produced objects. Umbu

221

Taniku had come to perceive commodification as a stylishly modern and prestigious mode of exchange. Singularity was achieved within this state through the connection to one prestigious source. Umbu Taniku was attempting to establish himself as such a source.

10. The late Dutch monarch has appeared iconographically as a regal presence in East Sumba's fabrics since colonial times and persists in modern renditions.

11. Jameson comments on the increasing primacy and isolation of the human form in postmodern art of the West (1994). What appears to be compelling in such forms is a kind of essentialism of the subject denied in most aspects of postindustrial life. The popularity of the figure for Western collectors of non-Western art suggests a kind of "double essentialism" —that of Man and that of the Other. Thus, the "primitive" human figures in textiles such as Sing Ha's function as a leitmotif for foreign seekers, one recognized and promoted by savvy producers.

12. As mentioned in the previous chapter, the half-Chinese entrepreneur is also a follower of the evangelical Bethel Church. Yet Sing Ha's religious zeal, unlike that of the Sumbanese convert Martha, imposed no restrictions on his fabric designs. Less hampered by the church's censures on sexual explicitness than he was stimulated by its emphasis upon worldly enterprise, Sing Ha employed a pragmatic capitalism in ascertaining and mass producing what would sell to the outside world. This strategy was effective in luring certain seekers (such as the podiatrist above) to his products.

13. Sally Price discusses how "sexual attributes affect an object's chances of being both collected and appreciated in Western circles" (1989:47). Sexual orientation does confer intrigue and value for collectors of objects from Sumba. Sexually explicit motifs often appear to appeal to an acknowledged prurient interest among tourists, itself lodged in a self-conscious "worldliness" and "liberalism" toward the foreign. Marianna Torgovnick has commented on how "gender issues always inhabit Western versions of the primitive. Sooner or later those familiar tropes for primitives become the tropes conventionally used for women. Global politics, the dance of colonizer and colonized, becomes sexual politics, the dance of male and female" (1990:17). This view may be too deterministic. The tropes of primitivism wielded in the encounters between tourists and locals described in these pages often convolute notions of conventionality for men or women all around, as well as for colonized and colonizer. Whether the podiatrist was "colonizing" in his quest for non-Western artifacts depicting genitals or whether he was himself being "colonized"—by wily locals exploiting his naiveté regarding indigenous culture—is a matter of interpretation. Thus it is no longer especially useful to consider these encounters only in terms of postcolonial power relations. Torgovnick's further point, however, that the influences of Freud, Malinowski, and other Western thinkers "have assured that how we conceive of the primitive helps form our conception of ourselves as sexual, gendered beings" (1990:18) is worth bearing in mind— especially in some of the sexually charged discourses and encounters involving Westerners and locals in Indonesia. See Daniel Rosenblatt for a discussion of how certain "modern primitives" in the United States might focus on sexuality to "experience a liberation from their own society and to become human rather than Western" (1997:320).

14. The situation in Sumba reflects to some degree Laura Nader's (1989) notion that the control of women is an ingredient in Orientalism and Occidentalism (building upon ideas of Said 1978), through the mutual construction of negative stereotypes. While Western observers might construe the women weaving on village porches as quaint but servile examples of third-world underdevelopment, the weaving women often imagine that their Western counterparts lead immoral lives, dangerously singular and unescorted, and are in frequent peril of earthly or supernatural violence.

15. The weave of the *hinggi*, however, was far too regular to have been created with handspun yarns, which are thick and thin in their lengths and produce a characteristically nubby texture in finished fabrics.

16. Villagers often derided the cloth and commercial tactics of Arab and Chinese merchants. Sumbanese inauthenticated certain types of textiles, such as the one above, by

simply attaching an ethnic adjective to a piece, calling it *hemba mangu Arab* (Arab-owned cloth) or *hemba mangu Hina* (Chinese-owned cloth). This definitively labeled the fabrics as inferior facsimiles of Sumbanese textiles.

17. Many of the poorest vendors had no cloth of their own to sell, but worked as agents for other villagers or for merchants in Waingapu, reselling textiles (at *pamerans* or hotels) to tourists and adding a commission for themselves. Textile sellers at the hotels occupied spaces that illustrate a stratified society of middlemen—a kind of core-periphery in terms of prestigious areas and margins and the contacts with tourists these facilitated. The upper caste or most clever sellers made it into restaurant areas, while those with lower status waited on the margins of hotel grounds. Although he was among those usually admitted to the hotel restaurant, Luka may have unwittingly enacted his dubious social rank by sitting at the threshold of the establishment.

18. The demotion did not affect the man's official position, but it created new "discursive" conditions within the region. That is, rather than being discussed by locals as a corrupt and exploitative person (in which he had held a certain power through his effectiveness), the man was now the subject of a frequently and widely told tale of ridicule. Moreover, the sullied official was aware of this, a recognition that (by many accounts) had a humbling effect upon his demeanor and confidence from then on.

Chapter 8: Village Encounters

1. The term "*mandari*" means "alone," but it can also mean "selfish," something implied in an asserted singularity.

2. Schoolchildren in Wandi now usually speak the national language to each other in public places and often to their parents as well. Some parents lament the reduced use of Kambera and insist upon speaking it in the home with their children; others seem to accept their children's linguistic shift as a process of becoming Indonesian citizens.

223

3. The ground (*tana*) in certain areas of Sumba is considered "hot" (*mbana*), which is an attribute of something spiritually dangerous. In ceremonies, the ground often has to be "cooled" (*pamaringu*) through the blood of animal sacrifice. Moreover, Sumbanese widely believe that one is especially vulnerable to malevolent spirits during sleep. Many people therefore fear sleeping alone or in total darkness, as noted in chapter 4.

4. Such convention parallels what Kuipers notes in a western region of Sumba: "A common Weyéwa image of happiness is noise and movement inside a house full of people. To be outdoors, and furthermore to be alone, is a devastating image of loss and desolation" (1990b:169).

For the European woman to reject lodging in a household in favor of sleeping upon the earth was a travesty of human well-being in the eyes of the village onlookers, some of whom pronounced the woman *katoba* (insane).

5. Villagers usually bathe at least twice a day, in the morning and late afternoon. Commonly, people keep water in rain barrels or cement cisterns and splash it over themselves with a dipper. It was surprising for villagers to encounter a Westerner, such as the Danish tourist, who was apparently not concerned with personal cleanliness. Sumbanese assume that Westerners stay at hotels (as opposed to in village homes, as guests) because of the modern bathrooms.

6. Marapu followers in eastern Sumba often associated the presence of spirits with odors (as did the nearly drowned Mia in chapter 4, who identified the sex of her assailant by the smell of indigo). A strong odor surrounding a long-dead corpse signifies that the spirit (*ndewa*) of the deceased still lingers (an auspicious condition if the corpse has yet to be buried). Villagers often remarked that foreigners smelled quite unlike locals. Often Europeans were described as "smelling like cheese" (*wau keju*), an olfactory attribute explained by their diets. An unusually rank body odor from a living person suggests uncleanliness,

disease, or a malign spirit. See Classen (1992) for a discussion of odor as a category applied to the Other.

7. I had remained at some distance from the tourist during her Wandi visit, but she had seen me passing by Luka's home on the way to the home of Rambu Hamu. From there, I had observed the erection of her tent and had witnessed the watchful and alarmed behavior of the neighboring households, which included the one I was visiting. I often avoided approaching foreign tourists, not because of a superior sense of myself as "anthropologist," but because I frequently had become unwillingly drafted as a broker between locals and foreigners. To some extent, this was unavoidable, as I participated in the lives of people around me. But I did try to limit the extent to which I acted as an intermediary. Although this role could at times be enlightening, it more often created problematic jealousies among other villagers toward me and those I was assisting.

8. In *Primitive Art in Civilized Places,* Sally Price depicts the Western stereotyping and romanticizing of "the primitive" to the point of "casting Primitive societies into the mold of an artistic counterculture or bohemian community in the Western sense" (1989:47). This casting of primitivism has begun to be realized by some eastern Sumbanese, who play into such stereotypes with interesting results. Evident in Balinese tourist regions is the phenomenon of a peculiar type of ethnic chic arising out of an awareness of international fashion trends and consumer demands on the part of informed and inventive local entrepreneurs. The Balinese have been adept at this for years now; Sumbanese are more recently engaging in the self-conscious reformulation of their images for outsiders, following a cosmopolitan sense of "style." In this reformulation, there is tension between remaining "traditional" while appearing to also be sophisticated in a contemporary and worldly manner. Hence the possibility of following someone dressed as Luka was in the Preface of this study.

9. The house took on its long-standing role as a center for crucial concerns and passages of the living, sacred in its own power as "ritual attractor" (see Fox 1993).

10. As noted in chapter 1, ideal feminine demeanor in Sumba involves a kind of bodily lassitude in movement and restraint in facial expression.

11. After staying for several days with Rambu Hamu in Wandi, Jane moved on to the village of Hawewa, confiding to me that Rambu Hamu was too listless for her.

12. My rented home near Waingapu had been an exception because it was owned by a kinsman of Ana Humba, as noted in chapter 5.

13. This reaffirms findings of M. Adams (1969) and Forth (1981, 1991b) in eastern Sumba, and Hoskins (1993a); Keane (1997); Kuipers (1990a); and I. Mitchell (1981) regarding western regions of the island.

Chapter 9: On Other Islands

1. Research in Bali in recent years reflects the presence of tourism as a constant phenomenon. See McKean (1989); Picard (1990a, 1990b, 1996); and Vickers (1989, 1996) for studies that chronicle tourism's development on Bali and some of the resulting effects. Moreover, numerous tourist guidebooks (in various languages) are devoted entirely to the 2,175-square-mile island. An ongoing theme in many of these books—reflecting an evident concern with "authenticity" that underlies much Western tourism (see MacCannell 1976)—addresses what parts of Bali have been "spoiled" by tourism and what parts are still the "real Bali." Bali is an international trope for romance, exoticism, and adventure—immanently available to the world. Exploits of Western tourists in Balinese settings are at the center of recent English-language novels (see Baranay 1992; Lee 1990; and Messud 1994). See also Iyer's impressions of the tourist scene in Bali, as one of several travel tales (1988).

2. Alice Walker summarizes: "In Bali, of course, everyone paints. After the rice is harvested and the long rainy season sets in, painting, sculpting, making music and fine

cloths and dancing and making exquisite offerings to the gods seems all that the people do. And I agree with all my heart that it's enough" (1988:xiv). Unni Wikan notes that "Bali seems to entice everyone into ignoring the commonplace except when it is transformed into dramatic delights, an onlooker's feast" (1990:xvi).

3. Fred Myers cites the emergence of "New Age contexts" as a genre in which to observe cultural elaboration (1994:691). This follows a growing recognition of the multiplicity of views and phenomena that might fall under the rubric of "the West."

4. I use the term "postmodern" here to characterize regions of Bali given to an international commerce based in tourism. The global mixture of peoples and cultural influences in a highly commercial Balinese setting suggests a "cultural logic of late capital" (following Jameson 1994). As becomes evident in this chapter, however, various "cultural logics" and "capital" are employed in Balinese tourist zones, reflecting the diversity of forces such regions draw together. Daniel Miller critically notes that "academic approaches to modern diversity are almost always condemnatory. Diversity is taken to represent a new superficiality and an aliented form of existence, lacking both authenticity and depth. A number of these versions of this critique have recently come together through the development of the term 'post-modernism', which has become a means of both defining and condemning this feature of modernity (e.g. Jameson 1984)" (1987:10). I concur with Miller's argument, particularly as it impels serious study of diversified, contemporary environments of regions such as the tourist zones of Bali.

5. For a range of foreign seekers, Bali is a kind of orientalist crossroads in which they can reconstruct their identities through partaking of an idealized, exotic culture. See Boon's (1990) critique of the history of written depictions of Bali. Boon considers such representations—from colonial narratives through anthropological ones—as exaggerating excesses and creating romanticized cultural caricatures of the Balinese. The description by Walker (n. 2), which interprets the "culture" experienced (in areas strongly affected by foreign influences) as being essentially and universally Balinese, is such a depiction. Such descriptions carry on what Boon calls an "intertextual chain of reading" (1990:14), an ever-elaborating body of literature that continues the allure of the island to foreigners.

225

The long-term residence of numerous Westerners in Bali and the growth in transnational business links, however, has led to a less romanticized and more cynical attitude. Indeed, foreigners who have been engaged with the Balinese for extended periods often adopt a self-distancing, critical stance suggestive of former Dutch colonial positions.

At this point, the academic literature regarding Bali has evolved into "depictions of depictions of" the island's culture. This literature includes critiques of ethnographic texts (most often those of Gregory Bateson and Margaret Mead written in the 1930s) as well as of the packaging and selling of Bali in commercial advertisements (see Boon 1990; Picard 1990a, 1990b, 1996; Vickers 1989, 1996).

6. See Bagus (1976); Francillon (1974–75); Picard (1990a, 1990b, 1996); and Vickers (1989, 1996) for some history of the development of tourism in the region. Although Bruner correctly points out that Bali has been a tourist destination for more than seventy years (1996:157), before the 1970s tourism involved only a basically elite or adventurous international set. The numbers of tourists to the island multiplied exponentially after increased air service in the 1970s. In the 1980s, yet more foreign carriers began providing service to Bali, and tourism burgeoned enormously.

7. Covarrubias (1937); H. Geertz (1995); Holt (1967); McKean (1989); Picard (1996); and Vickers (1989, 1996) have discussed this inventiveness in detail, through various historical periods.

8. McKean (1989) considers this elaboration in Bali, brought about by tourism, as a "cultural involution," borrowing from Clifford Geertz's (1963) concept of "agricultural involution" in Java resulting from colonial plantation pressures. Vickers characterizes the extent to which tourism has affected social realities in Bali: "Tourism has created a new middle class of hoteliers, Artshop owners, and tour guides—groups with access to the con-

sumer symbols of success, such as Mercedes Benzes and video recorders. Tourism has also provided a living for thousands of other Balinese, to the point where poverty in Bali is associated with lack of access to tourist income" (1989:200).

9. I borrow this term from Appadurai (1991).

10. Lombok, an island roughly the size of Bali, is just east of it in the archipelago. Because of Lombok's proximity (a four-hour ferry ride or a half-hour plane trip), many tourists to Bali also include a jaunt to Lombok on their itinerary. A new tourism industry has thus developed on Lombok's western coast. The island is largely Islamic, with a considerable number of Balinese-Hindus in its western region. Neither the Hindu-Balinese nor the Muslim Lombokese would likely ever conceive of themselves as "primitive," yet this term has been enthusiastically promoted by entrepreneurs on both islands in products that appeal to tourists.

11. Adrian Vickers makes note of this (1989:193), citing Australian press reports. Compared to other areas I have visited in Southeast Asia, I consistently saw a much higher proportion of female tourists in Bali, not infrequently accompanied by Indonesian men.

12. As Walter Benjamin notes, "The public is an examiner, but an absent-minded one" (1969:243). While Benjamin was speaking about the lack of attention required by moviegoers due to the continuous motion of the images before them, a similar absentmindedness appears among many tourists in Bali, who browse a phantasmagoria of goods, people, and events.

13. Phillip Curtin (1984) discusses trade diasporas in a world historical context and their function in maintaining the disparate commodity systems of various societies they drew in. Within Indonesia the Balinese trade diaspora has stimulated the commodification of goods from a number of other islands, often introducing a new eclecticism that ultimately impinges upon the disparateness of systems and products. Objects become entangled (cf. Thomas 1991) in trade zones such as Bali, and exported back to producing societies. These societies then adopt new forms—such as might be produced by Biba—that eventually alter those produced in the past. See Van Esterik (1994) for a discussion of similar phenomena involving textiles (as described in the text above) in a Thai context.

14. Raymond Williams (1989) discusses an increased "border-crossing" by European artists in the early twentieth century as they gravitated to metropolitan centers such as Paris. This mobility affected a new "modernism" in experiences and themes, and although such shifts in places and perceptions developed within very different historical circumstances than I present here, a comparison can be made with the transnational "art worlds" and trade encounters in Bali. This comparison includes, drawing from Williams, "the experience of visual and linguistic strangeness, the broken narrative of the journey and its inevitable accompaniment of transient encounters with characters whose self-presentation was bafflingly unfamiliar raised to the universal myth the intense, singular narrative of unsettlement, homelessness, solitude, and impoverished independence" (51).

For Sumbanese fabric designers and traders in Bali, all of the above situations might apply, with consequently individual responses and interpretations of experience. As we will see, these interpretations include accounts of what is "modern" and how the "modern" relates to subjective notions of ethnicity, social class, and gender roles. Moreover, such "modernism" becomes a kind of superior stance one might assume upon returning to village homes in Sumba and carries its own authority in new self-positionings.

15. Biba was referring to the Jakarta theme park depicting ethnic groups across Indonesia, visited by Rambu Hamu in chapter 3.

16. Edward Bruner has recently argued succinctly for the validity of such regions for anthropological study (and in this case specifically in reference to Bali): "The touristic borderzone is a creative space, a site for the invention of culture on a massive scale, a festive liberated zone, one that anthropology should investigate, not denigrate" (1996:159).

226

17. This shop, which is like numerous up-scale establishments in Bali catering to an elite and discriminating set of foreigners, reflects what Appadurai characterizes as an "aesthetics of decontextualization that is at the heart of the [currently prestigious] display, in highbrow Western homes, of the tools and artifacts of the 'other': the Turkman saddlebag, Masai spear, Dinka basket" (1988:28)—and, I might add, the Sumba textile.

18. Because non-Indonesians may not legally own property, many foreigners living and doing business in Bali have similar arrangements with Balinese locals. There is a semi-permanent community of Westerners living in or near tourist regions of the island, carrying on enterprises of their own that cater to tourists or exporting ethnic arts or local fashions to their home countries. Often these same Westerners dictate designs to Balinese producers of goods. In this way, they take advantage of a cheap labor market of Balinese artisans and workers.

19. Bourdieu analyzes at length the role of "taste" in the West as an elite concept or device with which to define and wield an "aristocracy of culture"—a distinction from the commonplace (1984).

20. This, in turn, offers an ultimate, aesthetic overview, resulting in another kind of colonization of Indonesian creations. Graburn remarks that "tourism is rife with snobbery", relying upon "hierarchies of rank and prestige that illustrate the continuum and the contrast between the ordinary/nonordinary" (1989:34). Nonordinary status is achieved in Olga's shop by the inclusion, framing, and positioning of disparate, exotic cultural artifacts within a space that promises prestige. Steiner notes how African art objects are framed to appeal to foreigners, a process he calls *encadrement*, which "encodes appropriated context by unequivocally announcing to its viewers that 'this is art' " (1994:120). Such announcements are continually made in spaces such as the gallery described above.

21. Baudrillard claims that "what society seeks [in this case the "society" that seeks is one composed of foreign tourists] through production, and overproduction, is the restoration of the real which escapes it" (1988:180). If this is so, the "real" likely becomes even more elusive in a foreign setting.

22. Marcus and Myers characterize a dilemma for the anthropologist that I see as also one for the international tourist: "Swamped with automobiles, televisions, popular music, and Western clothes, those once formulated as 'primitives' who inhabited a different world, so to speak, will no longer work as a trope of 'difference' from which a credible imaginative grasp of 'our world' can occur" (1995:19).

23. This follows Graburn's (1989) concept of tourism as a "sacred journey"—a modern-day pilgrimage in which souvenirs such as ethnic arts become sought as "Holy Grails." Indeed, many tourists I encountered in Bali and in Sumba sought fabrics and artifacts with an intensity that often appeared religious. This search was undoubtedly stimulated by their very elusiveness in the context described above. As Simmel notes regarding the phenomenon of purchasing, "We desire objects . . . to the extent to which they resist our desire" (1978:66).

24. This situation in Bali seems to be a kind of gendered inversion of a phenomenon that has been the focus of considerable research in Thailand: that of a type of tourism involving foreign men seeking young local women (see Cohen 1982, 1988; Enloe 1990; Graburn 1983; Lenze 1979; Richter 1989; Truong 1990). Tsing (1996) also discusses this in an Indonesian context.

25. Umbu's emphasis on such "heroics" in his fabric design may have unwittingly played into a certain contemporary Western yearning noted by Huyssen (1990), involving art's relationship to society. As modernist, apocalyptic themes have replaced subjective heroics in the visual arts of the West, a predicament has emerged. This lack of heroics is a more specific type of loss than Jameson's "waning of affect" (1994:10), creating an emotional, experiential need. The implication of such loss is that heroics are hungered for, sought elsewhere, and often seen within the exotic or the primitive by Euro-Amer-

227

icans. Heroics, in Umbu Taniku's textile designs and sales pitches, were a resonant combination of his own self-actualization and his awareness of what was compelling to Westerners.

26. Diasporas have come to the attention of a number of scholars in recent years, contributing to a paradigm that often falls under the label of "transnationalism." While characterized as "hybrid" (Lavie and Swedenburg 1996) and "deterritorialized" (Appadurai 1991), these regions are also discrete localities, despite the global populations and influences they contain. I agree with Visweswaran's (1994) assessment that we should all the more consider such communities as they are actually lived in and not merely as regions of displacement.

27. *"Andung"* means "skull tree" in the language of eastern Sumba.

28. In a number of Indonesian urban settings, American fast-food restaurants are well defined status domains of young elites. In Jakarta, well-dressed, dating couples frequent McDonald's. In Kuta Beach, Indonesians dining at such franchises often demonstrate a certain savoir faire in ordering and eating Western food. Moreover, the bright lights and sterile, plasticized interiors of these restaurants are indicative of an international standard of modernity.

29. In Bourdieu's (1984) discussion, this is considered a privileged cultural code acquired through elite ("legitimate"), Western education—establishing a "pure gaze" within which to appreciate the aesthetic, ostensibly in a "disinterested" manner. Such an "aesthetic disposition" then becomes a kind of hegemonic overview—mastering (by naming, including, or excluding) all within its purview. Yet any such "gaze" is met and reinterpreted by people in eastern Sumba, who then construct knowledges and images to appeal to outsiders from whom they might benefit. There is an endless volley of taxonomies at work here, as producers and sellers of fabrics "read" others' classifications of "arts," classify foreigners according to their tastes, and create goods that then become reclassified by international consumers. The dynamism occurs in the infinity and mutability of tastes, meanings, and encounters.

30. I borrow phrasing from Lavie and Swedenburg (1996:11).

31. The Indonesian government has recently acknowledged AIDS as a public health problem. Posters featuring silhouettes of a man and a woman facing each other and written warning against the disease, *Penyakit AIDS*, are now common along the roads of Balinese tourist zones. I had wondered when a Sumbanese would contract AIDS through casual sexual encounters in Bali. Doctors in Sumba told me that as of 1994 there had not been a diagnosed case of AIDS among the Sumbanese they had examined, although few had actually submitted to an AIDS test.

32. This is in contrast to Foster's (1965) idea of "limited good" in peasant societies mentioned earlier. Because many Sumbanese I knew traveled and formed social and business relationships away from their island, their notions of a boundless prosperity often developed disproportionately to reality.

33. Hasan had sold a *hinggi* to this woman at a *pameran* in Sumba months earlier and at that time had obtained her business card. After their arrival in Jakarta, Luka had telephoned the American, who had congenially invited the three Sumbanese to her home in an exclusive Jakarta neighborhood.

34. After marriage, men and women in Sumba have traditionally acquired tattoos marking distinct passages, such as the birth of children.

35. Sanur is a generally more up-scale area than Kuta, with more costly beach accommodations and less of the traffic and brashness of Kuta Beach. Hasan and Biba preferred it because of the relative peacefulness and the connections they had secured with a couple of gallery owners in the area. Luka, however, eager for independence and adventure, had been attracted to the liveliness of Kuta Beach.

Chapter 10: Unfolding Passages

1. We spoke but once about his experiences months earlier in Bali. Luka had taken to wearing a colorful "friendship bracelet" (made of braided cotton threads). These bracelets were popular among young tourists in Bali; they were often exchanged between young men (Indonesian) and women (tourists) as signifying a romantic relationship. I asked Luka how his time had gone in Bali, hedging on whether or not he had acquired a foreign *pacar* (sweetheart). Luka replied (evasively) that he had enjoyed himself immensely in Bali and planned to go at least twice annually. I asked whether such visits might disturb his new wife, and he answered that she would have no effect on his travel plans, that his marriage was a separate issue.

2. Such linguistic shifts between Kambera and Bahasa Indonesia frequently mark older and newer conceptual references in East Sumba. A bitterness of spirit is an emotional state long accounted for in the local language. Gaining monetary prosperity is a more recent phenomenon, often involving relations with people other than indigenous Sumbanese, and is thus expressed in Indonesian terms.

3. Despite this debt, Kata's father had permitted her to reside in Umbu Taniku's household, although customarily he would have been within his rights to insist she live at her natal family home until at least an acceptable portion of the bride debt was settled. Such debts were often paid in installments, but Umbu Taniku had long been remiss in giving his father-in-law any such payment.

4. It may be remembered from chapter 5 that this was primarily a household of women.

5. To most adult villagers in Parai Mutu, foreign tourists were mainly interesting in commercial terms. If the visitors showed no intention to examine or buy textiles, villagers often all but ignored them.

6. This was the arch-rival of Ibu Ana, proprietress of the Sumba Primitive Art Shop described in chapter 8.

229

Chapter 11: Conclusion

1. See Acciaoli (1985); K. Adams (1999); Errington (1994a); Taylor (1994); and Volkman (1990).

2. As Philip Dark concludes of art in general, "It often produces for man a crystallization of some emotion in a concrete form; of a fear felt which is realized by some artist and given form, causing tension to be released and relieved, or reinforcement and greater agony, the stuff of ecstasy, the boost to esteem or pride, the fulfillment of a creative self which all have to a greater or lesser degree" (1973:49).

3. Heidegger (1977:134), quoted in de Certeau (1988:234–35).

BIBLIOGRAPHY

Abrahams, Roger D.
    1986   "Ordinary and Extraordinary Experience." In *The Anthropology of Experience,* ed. Edward W. Turner and Edward M. Bruner, pp. 45–72. Urbana and Chicago: University of Illinois Press.

Abu-Lughod, Lila.
    1993   *Writing Women's Worlds: Bedouin Stories.* Berkeley, Los Angeles, and Oxford: University of California Press.

Acciaioli, Greg.
    1985   "Culture as Art: From Practice to Spectacle in Indonesia." *Canberra Anthropology* 8(1&2):148–172.

Adams, Kathleen M.
    1985   " 'Come to Tana Toraja: Land of Heavenly Kings': Travel Agents as Brokers in Ethnicity." *Annals of Tourism Research* 12(3):469–485.
    1999   "Taming Traditions: Torajan Ethnic Imagery in the Age of Tourism." In *Converging Interests: Traders, Travelers, and Tourists in Southeast Asia*, ed. Jill Forshee with Christina Fink and Sandra Cate, pp. 249–263. Berkeley: Center for Southeast Asia Studies, University of California.

Adams, Marie Jeanne.
    1969   *System and Meaning in East Sumba Textile Design: A Study in Traditional Indonesian Art*. Cultural Report 16. New Haven, Conn.: Southeast Asia Studies, Yale University.
    1970   "Myths and Self-Image among the Kapunduk People of Sumba." *Indonesia* 10:81–106.
    1971a "Designs in Sumba Textiles: Local Meanings and Foreign Influence." *Textile Museum Journal* 3:28–37.
    1971b "Work Patterns and Symbolic Structures in a Village Culture, East Sumba, Indonesia." *Southeast Asia* 5:320–329.
    1972   "Classic and Eccentric Elements in East Sumba Textiles: A Field Report." *Needle and Bobbin Bulletin* 55:1–40.
    1974   "Symbols of the Organized Community in East Sumba, Indonesia." *Bijdragen tot de Taal- , Land- , en Volkenkunde* 130:324–347.
    1979   "The Crocodile Couple and the Snake Encounter in the Tellantry of East Sumba, Indonesia." In *The Imagination of Reality: Essays in Southeast Asian Coherence Systems*, ed. A. L. Becker, pp. 87–104. Norwood, N.J.: ABLEX.
    1980   "Structural Aspects of East Sumbanese Art." In *The Flow of Life: Essays on Eastern Indonesia,* ed. James J. Fox, pp. 208–220. Cambridge, Mass., and London: Harvard University Press.
    1981   *Threads of Life: A Private Collection of Textiles from Sarawak and Indonesia.* Katonah, N.Y.: Katonah Gallery.

Alexander, Jennifer.
    1987   *Trade, Traders, and Trading in Rural Java*. Singapore: Oxford University Press.

Allende, Isabel.
    1989   *Eva Luna*. New York: Bantam Books.

Anderson, Benedict.
    1972   "The Idea of Power in Javanese Culture." In *Culture and Politics in Indonesia,* ed. Claire Holt, Benedict Anderson, and James Siegel, pp. 1–69. Ithaca, N.Y.: Cornell University Press.
    1983   *Imagined Communities*. London and New York: Verso.

Anderson, Richard.
    1979   *Art in Primitive Societies*. Englewood Cliffs, N.J.: Prentice-Hall.
    1993   "Art that Really Matters." In *Art in Small-Scale Societies: Contemporary Readings,* ed. Richard L. Anderson and Karen L. Field, pp. 445–452. Englewood Cliffs, N.J.: Prentice-Hall.

Anderson, Richard L., and Karen L. Field.
    1993   *Art in Small-Scale Societies: Contemporary Readings*. Englewood Cliffs, N.J.: Prentice-Hall.

Appadurai, Arjun.
    1988   "Introduction: Commodities and the Politics of Value." In *The Social Life of Things: Commodities in Cultural Perspective,* ed. Arjun Appadurai, pp. 3–63. Cambridge: Cambridge University Press.
    1991   "Global Ethnoscapes: Notes and Queries for a Transnational Anthropology." In *Recapturing Anthropology: Working in the Present,* ed. Richard G. Fox, pp. 191–210. Santa Fe, N.M.: School of American Research.
    1992   "Putting Hierarchy in Its Place." In *Rereading Cultural Anthropology,* ed. George E. Marcus, pp. 34–47. Durham, N.C., and London: Duke University Press.
    1997   *Modernity at Large: Cultural Dimensions of Globalization*. Minneapolis: University of Minnesota Press.

Aronson, Lisa.
    1991   "African Women in the Visual Arts." *Signs: Journal of Women in Culture and Society* 16(3):550–574.

Atkinson, Jane Monnig.
    1983   "Religions in Dialogue: The Construction of an Indonesian Minority Religion." *American Ethnologist* 10:684–696.
    1990   "How Gender Makes a Difference in Wana Society." In *Power and Difference: Gender in Island Southeast Asia,* ed. Jane Monnig Atkinson and Shelly Errington, pp. 59–93. Stanford, Calif.: Stanford University Press.

Atkinson, Jane Monnig, and Shelly Errington, eds.
    1990   *Power and Difference: Gender in Island Southeast Asia*. Stanford, Calif.: Stanford University Press.

Babcock, Barbara A.
    1993   "At Home, No Women Are Storytellers: Ceramic Creativity and the Politics of Discourse in Cochiti Pueblo." In *Creativity/Anthropology,*

232

ed. Smadar Lavie, Kirin Narayan, and Renato Rosaldo, pp. 70–99. Ithaca, N.Y., and London: Cornell University Press.

Bagus, G. N.
1976 *The Impact of Tourism upon the Culture of the Balinese People,* pp. 8–10. Washington, D.C.: UNESCO/IBRD.

Bakhtin, Mikhail.
1968 *Rabelais and His World.* Cambridge, Mass.: Harvard University Press.

Baranay, Inez.
1992 *The Edge of Bali.* Pymbly, Australia: Angus and Robertson.

Barnes, R. H.
1988 "Moving and Staying Space in the Malay Archipelago." In *Time Past, Time Present, Time Future: Essays in Honour of P. E. de Josselin de Jong,* ed. David S. Moyer and Henri J. M. Claessen, pp. 117–135. Dordrecht, Holland: Foris Publications.
1995 "Being Indigenous in Eastern Indonesia." In *Indigenous Peoples of Asia,* ed. R. H. Barnes, Andrew Gray, and Benedict Kingsbury, pp. 307–322. Monograph and Occasional Paper Series, no. 48. Ann Arbor, Mich.: Association for Asian Studies.

Barnes, Ruth.
1989a *The Ikat Textiles of Lamalera: A Study of an Eastern Indonesian Weaving Tradition.* Leiden: E. J. Brill.
1989b "The Bridewealth Cloth of Lamalera, Lembata." In *To Speak with Cloth: Studies in Indonesian Textiles,* ed. Mattiebelle Gittinger, pp. 43–55. Los Angeles: Museum of Cultural History, University of California.
1992 "Textile Design in Southern Lembata: Tradition and Change." In *Anthropology, Art, and Aesthetics,* ed. Jeremy Coote and Anthony Shelton, pp. 160–178. Oxford: Clarendon Press.
1994 "Without Cloth We Cannot Marry." In *Fragile Traditions: Indonesian Art in Jeopardy,* ed. Paul Michael Taylor, pp. 13–27. Honolulu: University of Hawai'i Press.
1997 "Women as Headhunters: The Making and Meaning of Textiles in a Southeast Asian Context." In *Dress and Gender: Making and Meaning in Cultural Contexts,* ed. Ruth Barnes and J. B. Eicher, pp. 29–43. Oxford: Berge Publishers.

Barth, Fredrik.
1993 *Balinese Worlds.* Chicago and London: University of Chicago Press.

Barthes, Roland.
1982 *Mythologies.* Trans. Annette Lavers. New York: Hill and Wang.

Bateson, Gregory.
1972 "Style, Grace, and Information in Primitive Art." In *Steps to an Ecology of the Mind*, pp. 128–152. New York: Ballantine Books.

Baudrillard, Jean.
1988 "Simulacra and Simulations." In *Jean Baudrillard: Selected Writings,* ed. Mark Poster, pp. 166–184. Stanford, Calif.: Stanford University Press.

233

Baxandall, Michael.
  1972 *Painting and Experience in Fifteenth-Century Italy: A Primer in the Social History of Pictorial Style.* Oxford: Oxford University Press.

Bayley, C. A.
  1988 "The Origins of *Swadeshi* (Home Industry): Cloth and Indian Society." In *The Social Life of Things: Commodities in Cultural Perspective,* ed. Arjun Appadurai, pp. 285–321. Cambridge: Cambridge University Press.

Becker, Howard.
  1982 *Art Worlds.* Berkeley: University of California Press.

Bellwood, Peter S.
  1997 *Prehistory of the Indo-Malaysian Archipelago.* Honolulu: University of Hawai'i Press.

Ben-Amos, Paula.
  1977 "Pidgin Languages and Tourist Arts." *Studies in the Anthropology of Visual Communication* 4:128–139.

Benjamin, Walter.
  1969 "The Work of Art in the Age of Mechanical Reproduction." In *Illuminations,* trans. Harry Zohn, ed. Hannah Arendt, pp. 217–251. New York: Schocken Books.

Berger, John.
  1973 *Ways of Seeing.* New York: Viking Press.

Blum-Shevill, Margot.
  1993 *Maya Textiles of Guatemala: The Gustavus A. Eisen Collection.* Austin: University of Texas Press.

Bolland, Rita.
  1956 "Weaving a Sumba Woman's Skirt." In *Bali and a Sumba Loom: Royal Tropical Institute Bulletin* 119:49–56. Amsterdam.

Boon, James A.
  1990 *Affinities and Extremes: Crisscrossing the Bittersweet Ethnology of East Indies History, Hindu-Balinese Culture, and Indo-European Allure.* Chicago and London: University of Chicago Press.

Boorstin, Daniel.
  1975 *The Image: A Guide to Pseudo-events in America.* New York: Atheneum.

Bourdieu, Pierre.
  1984 *Distinction: A Social Critique of the Judgement of Taste.* Cambridge, Mass.: Harvard University Press.
  1989 *Outline of a Theory of Practice.* Cambridge, Mass.: Harvard University
  [1977] Press.
  1993 *The Field of Cultural Production: Essays on Art and Literature.* Cambridge: Polity Press.

Bruner, Edward M.
  1986a "Ethnography as Narrative." In *The Anthropology of Experience,* ed. Victor W. Turner and Edward M. Bruner, pp. 139–155. Urbana and Chicago: University of Illinois Press.

1986b "Experience and Its Expressions." In *The Anthropology of Experience,* ed. Victor W. Turner and Edward M. Bruner, pp. 3–30. Urbana and Chicago: University of Illinois Press.

1993 "Epilogue: Creative Persona and the Problem of Authenticity." In *Creativity/Anthropology,* ed. Smadar Lavie, Kirin Narayan, and Renato Rosaldo, pp. 321–334. Ithaca, N.Y., and London: Cornell University Press.

1996 "Tourism in the Balinese Border Zone." In *Displacement, Diaspora, and Geographies of Identity,* ed. Smadar Lavie and Ted Swedenburg, pp. 157–179. Durham, N.C., and London: Duke University Press.

Bühler, Alfred.
1959 "Patola Influences in Southeast Asia." *Journal of Indian Textile History* 4:4–46.

Burnham, Dorothy.
1980 *Warp and Weft: A Textile Terminology.* Toronto: Royal Ontario Museum.

Certeau, Michel de.
1988 *The Writing of History.* Trans. Tom Conley. New York: Columbia University Press.

Clamagirand, Brigitte.
1980 "The Social Organization of the Ema of Timor." In *The Flow of Life: Essays on Eastern Indonesia,* ed. James J. Fox, pp. 134–151. Cambridge, Mass., and London: Harvard University Press.

Classen, Constance.
1992 "The Odor of the Other: Olfactory Symbolism and Cultural Categories." *Ethos* 20(2):133–166.

Clifford, James.
1985a "Histories of the Tribal and the Modern." *Art in America* 72(April): 164–177, 215.

1985b "Objects and Selves—An Afterword." In *Objects and Others: Essays on Material Culture,* ed. George W. Stocking, Jr., pp. 236–246. Madison: University of Wisconsin Press.

1988 *The Predicament of Culture: Twentieth-Century Ethnography, Literature, and Art.* Cambridge, Mass., and London: Harvard University Press.

1991 "Four Northwest Coast Museums: Travel Reflections." In *Exhibiting Cultures: The Poetics and Politics of Museum Display,* ed. Ivan Karp and Steven D. Lavine, pp. 212–254. Washington, D.C., and London: Smithsonian Institution Press.

1993 "On Collecting Art and Culture." In *The Culture Studies Reader,* ed. Simon During, pp. 49–73. London and New York: Routledge.

1997 *Routes: Travel and Translation in the Late Twentieth Century.* Cambridge, Mass., and London: Harvard University Press.

Cohen, Erik.
1982 "Thai Girls and Farang Men: The Edge of Ambiguity." *Annals of Tourism Research* 9:403–428.

1988   "Tourism and AIDS in Thailand." *Annals of Tourism Research* 30: 467–486.

Coote, Jeremy.
1992   " 'Marvels of Everyday Vision': The Anthropology of Aesthetics and the Cattle-Keeping Nilotes." In *Anthropology, Art, and Aesthetics,* ed. Jeremy Coote and Anthony Shelton, pp. 245–273. London: Clarendon Press.

Coote, Jeremy, and Anthony Shelton.
1992   Introduction. In *Anthropology, Art, and Aesthetics,* ed. Jeremy Coote and Anthony Shelton, pp. 1–11. Oxford: Clarendon Press.

Coote, Jeremy, and Anthony Shelton, eds.
1992   *Anthropology, Art, and Aesthetics.* Oxford: Clarendon Press.

Covarrubias, Miguel.
1937   *The Island of Bali.* New York: Alfred A. Knopf.

Crystal, Eric.
1979   "Mountain Ikats and Coastal Silks: Traditional Textiles in South Sulawesi." In *Threads of Tradition: Textiles of Indonesia and Sarawak,* ed. Joseph Fischer, pp. 53–62. Berkeley: Lowie Museum of Anthropology, University Art Museum, University of California.
1985   "The Soul That Is Seen: The *Tau Tau* as Shadow of Death, Reflection of Life in Toraja Tradition." In *The Eloquent Dead: Ancestral Sculpture of Indonesia and Southeast Asia,* ed. Jerome Feldman, pp. 129–146. Los Angeles: Museum of Cultural History, University of California.
1989   "Tourism in Toraja." In *Hosts and Guests: The Anthropology of Tourism,* ed. Valene Smith, pp. 109–125. Philadelphia: University of Pennsylvania Press.

Cunningham, Clark.
1964   "Order and Change in an Atoni Diarchy." *Southwestern Journal of Anthropology* 21:349–383.

Curtin, Philip D.
1984   *Cross-Cultural Trade in World History.* Cambridge: Cambridge University Press.

Damische, Hubert.
1994   *The Origin of Perspective.* Cambridge: M.I.T. Press.

Dark, Philip.
1973   "Kilenge Big Man Art." In *Primitive Art and Society*, ed. Anthony Forge, pp. 49–69. London: Oxford University Press.

Dening, Greg.
1996   *Performances.* Chicago: University of Chicago Press.

Dewey, Alice.
1962   *Peasant Marketing in Java.* New York: Free Press of Glencoe.

Douglas, Mary.
1966   *Purity and Danger: An Analysis of the Concepts of Pollution and Taboo.* London and New York: Ark.

Drake, Richard Allen.
1989   "Construction Sacrifice and Kidnapping Rumor Panics in Borneo."
        Oceania 59:269–279.

Dumont, Louis.
1980   *Homo Hierarchicus: The Caste System and Its Implications.* Chicago
        and London: University of Chicago Press.

Durkheim, Emile.
1965   *The Elementary Forms of Religious Life.* New York: Free Press.
[1912]

Durkheim, Emile, and Marcel Mauss.
1963   *Primitive Classification.* Trans. Rodney Needham. Chicago: University
        of Chicago Press.

Edgerton, Samuel Y., Jr.
1975   *The Renaissance Rediscovery of Linear Perspective.* New York: Basic
        Books.

Enloe, Cynthia.
1990   *Bananas, Beaches, and Bases: Making Feminist Sense out of Interna-
        tional Politics.* Berkeley: University of California Press.

Erb, Maribeth.
1991   "Construction Sacrifice, Rumors, and Kidnapping Scares in Manggarai:
        Further Comparative Notes from Flores." *Oceania* 62:114–127.

Errington, Shelly.
1989   *Meaning and Power in a Southeast Asian Realm.* Princeton, N.J.:
        Princeton University Press.
1990   "Recasting Sex, Gender, and Power: A Theoretical and Regional Over-
        view." In *Power and Difference: Gender in Island Southeast Asia,* ed.
        Jane Monnig Atkinson and Shelly Errington, pp.1–58. Stanford, Calif.:
        Stanford University Press.
1994a   "Unraveling Narratives." In *Fragile Traditions: Indonesian Art in
        Jeopardy,* ed. Paul Michael Taylor, pp. 138–164. Honolulu: University
        of Hawai'i Press.
1994b   "What Became Authentic Primitive Art?" *Cultural Anthropology* 9(2):
        201–226.
1998   *The Death of Authentic Primitive Art and Other Tales of Progress.*
        Berkeley, Los Angeles, and London: University of California Press.

Ewen, Stuart.
1988   *All-Consuming Images: The Politics of Style in Contemporary Cul-
        ture.* New York: Basic Books.

Fabian, Johannes.
1983   *Time and the Other: How Anthropology Makes Its Object.* New York:
        Columbia University Press.

Feld, Steven, and Keith H. Basso, eds.
1996   *Senses of Place.* Santa Fe, N.M.: School of American Research Press.

Fischer, Joseph, ed.
1979   *Threads of Tradition: Textiles of Indonesia and Sarawak.* Berkeley:
        Lowie Museum of Anthropology, University Art Museum, University of
        California.

Forge, Anthony, ed.
  1973   *Primitive Art and Society*. London: Oxford University Press.

Forshee, Jill.
  1999   "Domains of Pedaling: Souvenirs, *Becak* Drivers, and Tourists in Yogya-
          karta, Java." In *Converging Interests: Traders, Travelers, and Tourists
          in Southeast Asia,* ed. Jill Forshee with Christina Fink and Sandra
          Cate, pp. 293–317. Berkeley: Center for Southeast Asia Studies, Uni-
          versity of California.

Forster, E. M.
  1973   *Howards End*. London: E. Arnold.

Forth, Gregory.
  1981   *Rindi: An Ethnographic Study of a Traditional Domain in Eastern
          Sumba*. The Hague: Martinus Nijhoff.
  1985   *The Language of Number and Numerical Ability in Eastern Sumba*.
          Center for Southeast Asia Occasional Paper, no. 9. Hull: University of
          Hull.
  1988   "Fashioned Speech, Full Communication: Aspects of Eastern Sumba-
          nese Ritual Language." In *To Speak in Pairs: Essays on the Ritual
          Languages of Eastern Indonesia,* ed. James J. Fox, pp. 129–160. Cam-
          bridge: Cambridge University Press.
  1991a   "Construction Sacrifice and Head-hunting Rumours in Central Flores
          (Eastern Indonesia): A Comparative Note." *Oceania* 61:257–266.
  1991b   *Place and Space in Eastern Indonesia*. Centre of Southeast Asian
          Studies Occasional Paper, no. 16. Canterbury, U.K.: University of Kent
          at Canterbury.

Foster, George M.
  1965   "Peasant Society and the Image of Limited Good." *American Anthro-
          pologist* 67:293–315.

Foucault, Michel.
  1977   *Discipline and Punish: The Birth of the Prison*. Trans. Alan Sheridan.
          New York: Pantheon Books.
  1978   *The History of Sexuality.* Vol.1: *An Introduction*. Trans. Robert Hurley.
          New York: Pantheon.
  1984   "The Subject and Power." In *Art After Modernism: Rethinking Repre-
          sentation,* ed. Brian Wallis, pp. 417–432. Boston and New York: David
          R. Godine/New Museum of Contemporary Art.
  1994   "Space, Power, and Knowledge." In *The Cultural Studies Reader,* ed.
          Simon During, pp. 161–169. London and New York: Routledge.

Fox, James J.
  1973   "On Bad Death and the Left Hand: A Study of Rotinese Symbolic In-
          version." In *Right and Left: Essays on Dual Symbolic Classification,*
          ed. Rodney Needham, pp. 342–368. Chicago: University of Chicago
          Press.
  1975   "On Binary Categories and Primary Symbols: Some Rotinese Per-
          spectives." In *The Interpretation of Symbolism,* ed. R. Willis, pp.
          99–132. Association of Social Anthropologists Studies 3. London:
          Malaby Press.

1979 "Figure Shark and Pattern Crocodile: The Foundation of Textile Tra-ditions of Roti and Ndao." In *Indonesian Textiles: Irene Emory Round-table on Museum Textiles, 1979 Proceedings,* ed. Matiebelle Gittinger, pp. 39–55. Washington, D. C.: Textile Museum.

1980a Introduction. In *The Flow of Life: Essays on Eastern Indonesia,* ed. James J. Fox, pp. 1–18. Cambridge, Mass., and London: Harvard Uni-versity Press.

1980b "Models and Metaphors: Comparative Research in Eastern Indonesia." In *The Flow of Life: Essays on Eastern Indonesia,* ed. James J. Fox, pp. 327–333. Cambridge, Mass., and London: Harvard University Press.

1988 Introduction. In *To Speak in Pairs: Essays on the Ritual Languages of Eastern Indonesia,* ed. James J. Fox, pp. 1–28. Cambridge: Cambridge University Press.

1997 "Place and Landscape in Comparative Austronesian Perspective." In *The Poetic Power of Place: Comparative Perspectives on Austrone-sian Ideas of Locality,* ed. James J. Fox, pp. 1–21. Canberra: Research School of Pacific and Asian Studies, Australian National University.

———, ed.

1980 *The Flow of Life: Essays on Eastern Indonesia.* Cambridge, Mass., and London: Harvard University Press.

1988 *To Speak in Pairs: Essays on the Ritual Languages of Eastern Indo-nesia.* Cambridge: Cambridge University Press.

1993 *Inside Austronesian Houses: Perspectives on Domestic Designs for Living.* Canberra: Research School of Pacific and Asian Studies, Aus-tralian National University.

1997 *The Poetic Power of Place: Comparative Perspectives on Austrone-sian Ideas of Locality.* Canberra: Research School of Pacific and Asian Studies, Australian National University.

Francillon, G.

1974 *Bali: Tourism, Culture, and Environment.* Report no. SHC-75/WS/17.
–1975 Denpasar, Indonesia; and Paris: Universitas Udayana and UNESCO.

Geertz, Clifford.

1963 *Peddlers and Princes: Social Development and Economic Change in Two Indonesian Towns.* Chicago and London: University of Chicago Press.

1973a "The Balinese Cockfight." In *The Interpretation of Cultures.* New York: Basic Books.

1973b "Religion as a Cultural System." In *The Interpretation of Cultures,* pp. 87–125. New York: Basic Books.

1980 *Negara: The Theatre State in Nineteenth-Century Bali.* Princeton, N.J.: Princeton University Press.

1983 "Art as a Cultural System." In *Local Knowledge: Further Essays in Interpretive Anthropology,* pp. 94–120. New York: Basic Books.

Geertz, Hildred.

1963 "Indonesian Cultures and Communities." In *Indonesia,* ed. Ruth T. McVey, pp. 5–84. New Haven, Conn.: Human Relations Area File Press.

1995 *Images of Power: Balinese Paintings Made for Gregory Bateson and Margaret Mead.* Honolulu: University of Hawai'i Press.

Geirnaert, Danielle.
　1989　"Textiles of West Sumba: Lively Renaissance of an Old Tradition." In *To Speak with Cloth: Studies in Indonesian Textiles,* ed. Mattiebelle Gittinger, pp. 57–79. Los Angeles: Museum of Cultural History, University of California.

Geirnaert-Martin, Danielle.
　1992　*The Woven Land of Laboya: Socio-Cosmic Ideas and Values in West Sumba, Eastern Indonesia.* Leiden: Centre of Non-Western Studies, Leiden University.

Gell, Alfred.
　1988　"Newcomers to the World of Goods: Consumption among the Muria Gonds." In *The Social Life of Things: Commodities in Cultural Perspective,* ed. Arjun Appadurai, pp.110–138. Cambridge: Cambridge University Press.
　1994　"The Technology of Enchantment and the Enchantment of Technology." In *Anthropology, Art, and Aesthetics,* ed. Jeremy Coote and Anthony Shelton, pp. 40–63. Oxford: Clarendon Press.

George, Kenneth.
　1991　"Headhunting, History and Exchange in Upland Sulawesi." *Journal of Asian Studies* 50(3):536–564.

Gewertz, Deborah, and Frederick Errington.
　1991　*Twisted Histories, Altered Contexts: Representing the Chambri in a World System.* Cambridge, New York, Port Chester, Melbourne, Sydney: Cambridge University Press.
　1996　"On Pepsico and Piety in a New Guinea 'Modernity.' " *American Ethnologist* 23(3):476–493.

Giddens, Anthony.
　1992　"Modernity and Self-Identity: Self and Society in the late Modern Age." In *Art in Modern Cultures: An Anthology of Critical Texts,* ed. Francis Frascina and Jonathan Harris, pp. 17–22. London: Phaidon Press.

Gittinger, Mattiebelle.
　1979　*Splendid Symbols: Textiles and Tradition in Indonesia.* Washington, D.C.: Textile Museum.
　1980　*Master Dyers to the World: Technique and Trade in Early Indonesian Dyed Cotton.* Washington, D.C.: Textile Museum.
　1989　"A Reassessment of the Tampan of South Sumatra." In *To Speak with Cloth: Studies in Indonesian Textiles,* ed. Mattiebelle Gittinger, pp. 225–239. Los Angeles: Museum of Cultural History, University of California.

———, ed.
　1989　*To Speak with Cloth: Studies in Indonesian Textiles.* Los Angeles: Museum of Cultural History, University of California.

Goh, Taro.
　1991　*Sumba Bibliography.* Canberra: Department of Anthropology, Australian National University.

Goffman, Irving.
  1959 *The Presentation of Self in Everyday Life*. New York: Doubleday.
  1974 *Frame Analysis: An Essay on the Organization of Experience*. Cambridge, Mass.: Harvard University Press.

Gombrich, E. H.
  1969 *Art and Illusion: A Study in the Psychology of Pictorial Representation*. Princeton, N.J.: Princeton University Press.

Goody, Jack.
  1986 *The Logic of Writing and the Organization of Society*. Cambridge: Cambridge University Press.

Graburn, Nelson H. H.
  1976 "Introduction: The Arts of the Fourth World." In *Ethnic and Tourist Arts: Cultural Expressions from the Fourth World,* ed. Nelson H. H. Graburn, pp. 1–32. Berkeley: University of California Press.
  1978 " 'I Like Things to Look More Different than That Stuff Did': An Experiment in Cross-Cultural Art Appreciation." In *Art in Society: Studies in Style, Culture, and Aesthetics,* ed. Michael Greehalgh and Vincent Megaw, pp. 51–70. London: Duckworth.
  1983 "Tourism and Prostitution." *Annals of Tourism Research* 10(3): 437–442.
  1984 "The Evolution of Tourist Arts." *Annals of Tourism Research* 11(3): 393–419. Special issue on "Tourism and Ethnicity," ed. Pierre L. vanden Berghe and Charles F. Keyes.
  1989 "Tourism: The Sacred Journey." In *Hosts and Guests: The Anthropology of Tourism,* ed. Valene Smith, pp. 21–36. 2d ed. Philadelphia: University of Pennsylvania Press.
  1995 "Tourism, Modernity, and Nostalgia." In *The Future of Anthropology,* ed. Akbar S. Ahmed and Chris N. Shore, pp. 158–178. London and Atlantic Highlands, N.J.: Athlone.

————, ed.
  1976 *Ethnic and Tourist Arts: Cultural Expressions from the Fourth World*. Berkeley: University of California Press.

Groeneveldt, Willem Pieter.
  1877 "Historical Notes on Indonesia and Malaya Compiled from Chinese Sources." *Verhandelingen van het Bataviaasch Genootschap der Kunsten en Wetenschappen* (Batavia), 39.

Gupta, Akhil, and James Ferguson.
  1992 "Beyond Culture: Space, Identity, and the Politics of Difference." *Cultural Anthropology* 7(1):6–23.

Hamilton, Roy W.
  1994a "Textile Technology." In *Gift of the Cotton Maiden: Textiles of Flores and the Solor Islands,* ed. Roy W. Hamilton, pp. 59–77. Los Angeles: Museum of Cultural History, University of California.

————, ed.
  1994b *Gift of the Cotton Maiden: Textiles of Flores and the Solor Islands*. Los Angeles: Museum of Cultural History, University of California.

Handler, Richard.
    1985   "On Having a Culture: Nationalism and the Preservation of Quebec's *Patrimoine.*" In *Objects and Others: Essays on Museums and Material Culture,* ed. George W. Stocking, Jr. Madison: University of Wisconsin Press.

Handler, Richard, and Jocelyn Linnekin.
    1984.   "Tradition, Genuine or Spurious." *Journal of American Folklore* 97: 890–902.

Hart, Lynn M.
    1995   "Three Walls: Regional Aesthetics and the International Art World." In *The Traffic in Culture: Refiguring Art and Anthropology,* ed. George E. Marcus and Fred R. Myers, pp. 127–150. Berkeley, Los Angeles, and London: University of California Press.

Heidegger, Martin.
    1977   "The Age of the World Picture." In *The Question Concerning Technology and Other Essays,* p. 134. New York: Harper and Row.

Hefner, Robert W., ed.
    1998   *Market Cultures: Society and Morality in the New Asian Capitalisms.* Boulder, Colo., and Oxford: Westview Press.

Heine-Geldern, Robert.
    1937   "L'art Prebouddhique de la Chine et de l'Asie Sud-est et son Influence en Oceanie." *Revue des Arts Asiatiques* 11:177–206.
    1945   "Prehistoric Research in the Netherlands Indies." In *Science and Scientists in the Netherlands Indies*, ed. P. Honig and F. Verdoon, pp. 129–167. New York: Foris.

Heringa, Rens.
    1989   "Dye Process and Life Sequence: The Coloring of Textiles in an East Javanese Village." In *To Speak with Cloth: Studies in Indonesian Textiles,* ed. Mattiebelle Gittinger, pp. 107–130. Los Angeles: Museum of Cultural History, University of California.

Hitchcock, Michael.
    1991   *Indonesian Textiles.* New York: Harper Collins.

Hobsbawm, Eric.
    1983   "Mass-Producing Traditions: Europe, 1870–1914." In *The Invention of Tradition,* ed. Eric Hobsbawm and Terence Ranger, pp. 263–307. Cambridge: Cambridge University Press.

Holmgren, Robert J., and Anita E. Spertus.
    1989   *Early Indonesian Textiles from Three Island Cultures: Sumba, Toraja, Lampung.* New York: Metropolitan Museum of Art.

Holt, Claire.
    1967   *Art in Indonesia: Continuities and Change.* Ithaca, N.Y.: Cornell University Press.

Hoskins, Janet.
    1986   "So My Name Shall Live: Stone Dragging and Grave Building in Kodi, West Sumba." *Bijdragen tot de Taal-, Land-, en Volkenkunde* 142: 31–51.

242

1987a   "Complementarity in This World and the Next: Gender and Agency in Kodi Mortuary Ceremonies." In *Dealing with Inequality: Analysing Gender Relations in Melanesia and Beyond,* ed. Marilyn Strathern, pp. 174–206. Cambridge: Cambridge University Press.

1987b   "Entering the Bitter House: Spirit Worship and Conversion in West Sumba." In *Indonesian Religions in Transition,* ed. Rita Smith Kipp and Susan Rodgers, pp. 136–160. Tucson: University of Arizona Press.

1987c   "The Headhunter as Hero: Local Traditions and Their Reinterpretation in National History." *American Ethnologist* 14(4):605–622.

1988   "Etiquette in Kodi Spirit Communication: The Lips Told to Speak, the Mouth Told to Pronounce." In *To Speak in Pairs: Essays on the Ritual Language of Eastern Indonesia,* ed. James J. Fox, pp. 29–63. Cambridge: Cambridge University Press.

1989   "Why Do Ladies Sing the Blues? Indigo Dyeing, Cloth Production, and Gender Symbolism in Kodi." In *Cloth and Human Experience,* ed. Annette B. Weiner and Jane Schneider, pp. 141–173. Washington and London: Smithsonian Institution Press.

1990   "Doubling Deities, Descent, and Personhood: An Exploration of Kodi Gender Categories." In *Power and Difference: Gender in Island Southeast Asia,* ed. Jane Monnig Atkinson and Shelly Errington, pp. 273–306. Stanford, Calif.: Stanford University Press.

1993a   *The Play of Time: Kodi Perspectives on Calendars, History, and Exchange.* Berkeley, Los Angeles, and London: University of California Press.

1993b   "Violence, Sacrifice, and Divination: Giving and Taking Life in Eastern Indonesia." *American Ethnologist* 20(1):159–178.

1996a   "The Heritage of Headhunting: History, Ideology, and Violence on Sumba, 1890–1990." In *Headhunting and the Social Imagination in Southeast Asia,* ed. Janet Hoskins, pp. 216–248. Stanford, Calif.: Stanford University Press.

1996b   "Introduction: Headhunting as Practice and as Trope." In *Headhunting and the Social Imagination in Southeast Asia,* ed. Janet Hoskins, pp. 1–49. Stanford, Calif.: Stanford University Press.

1998   *Biographical Objects: How Things Tell the Stories of People's Lives.* New York and London: Routledge.

———, ed.

1996   *Headhunting and the Social Imagination in Southeast Asia.* Stanford, Calif.: Stanford University Press.

Huyssen, Andreas.

1990   "Mapping the Postmodern." In *Feminism/Postmodernism,* ed. Linda L. Nicholson, pp. 234–277. New York and London: Routledge.

Iyer, Pico.

1988   *Video Night in Kathmandu.* London: Bloomsbury.

Jacobson, Mark Ivan, and Ruth Marie Yaeger.

1995   *Traditional Textiles of West Timor: Regional Variations in Historical Perspective.* Jacksonville, Ill.: Batuan Baru Productions.

Jameson, Fredrik.
  1984   " 'Postmodernism,' the Cultural Logic of Late Capital." *New Left Review* 146:53–90.
  1994   *Postmodernism: or, The Cultural Logic of Late Capital*. Durham, N.C.: Duke University Press.

Jolly, Margaret.
  1992   "Custom and the Way of the Land: Past and Present in Vanuatu and Fiji." *Oceania* 62(4):330–354.

Jolly, Margaret, and Nicholas Thomas.
  1992   Introduction. *The Politics of Tradition in the Pacific*. Special edition of *Oceania. Oceania* 62(4):241–248.

Jules-Rosette, Bennetta.
  1985   *The Messages of Tourist Art: An African Semiotic System in Comparative Perspective*. New York: Plenum Press.

Kahlenberg, Mary Hunt, ed.
  1977   *Textile Traditions of Indonesia*. Los Angeles: Los Angeles County Museum of Art.

Kantor Statistik Kabupaten Sumba Timur (Statistics Office of the District of East Sumba).
  1993a   *Penduduk: Kabupaten Sumba Timur Hasil Sensus Penduduk 1990* (Population: Results of the 1990 census of the population of East Sumba). Waingapu, Sumba: Kantor Statistik Kabupaten Sumba Timur.
  1993b   *Rindi Umalalu dalam Angka 1992* (Rindi Umalalu region statistically in 1992). Waingapu, Sumba: Kantor Statistik Kabupaten Sumba Timur.
  1993c   *Statistik Hotel Losmen Kabupaten Sumba Timur 1992* (Statistics on hotels and small hotels in the District of East Sumba 1992). Waingapu, Sumba: Kantor Statistik Kabupaten Sumba Timur.
  1993d   *Sumba Timur dalam Angka 1992* (East Sumba statistically in 1992). Waingapu, Sumba: Kantor Statistik Kabupaten Sumba Timur.

Kapita, Oe. H.
  n.d.   "Latar Belakang Historis Gareja Kristin Sumba" (The historical background of the Sumbanese Christian Church). Manuscript.
  1976a   *Masyarakat Sumba dan Adat Istiadatnya* (Sumbanese society and customs). Waingapu, Sumba: Gareja Kristen Sumba.
  1976b   *Sumba di dalam Jangkuan Jaman* (Sumba in times past). Waingapu, Sumba: Gareja Kristen Sumba.
  1982   *Kamus Sumba/Kambera—Indonesia* (Dictionary of Sumbanese Kambera—Indonesian). Waingapu, Sumba: Gareja Kristen Sumba.

Karp, Ivan, and Steven D. Lavine, eds.
  1991   *Exhibiting Cultures: The Poetics and Politics of Museum Display*. Washington and London: Smithsonian Institution Press.

Kartiwa, Suwati.
  1987   *Tenun Ikat: Indonesian Ikats*. Jakarta: Djambatan.
  1989   *Kain Songket Indonesia: Songket Weaving in Indonesia*. Jakarta: Djambatan.

Kasfir, Sidney.
1992   "African Art and Authenticity: A Text with a Shadow." *African Arts* 25(3):40–53, 96–97.

Kaufman, Fritz.
1969   "Art and Phenomenology." In *Essays in Phenomenology,* ed. W. Natanson, pp. 144–156. The Hague: Martinus Nijhoff.

Keane, Webb.
1991   "Delegated Voice: Ritual Speech, Risk, and the Making of Marriage Alliances in Anakalang." *American Ethnologist* 18:311–330.
1995a   "Religious Change and Historical Reflection in Anakalang, West Sumba." *Journal of Southeast Asia Studies* 26:289–306.
1995b   "The Spoken House: Text, Act, and Object in East Indonesia." *American Ethnologist* 22(1):102–124.
1996   "Materialism, Missionaries, and Modern Subjects in Colonial Indonesia." In *Conversion to Modernities: The Globalization of Christianity,* ed. Peter van der Veer, pp. 137–170. New York: Routledge.
1997   *Signs of Recognition: Power and Hazards of Representation in an Indonesian Society.* Berkeley, Los Angeles, and London: University of California Press.

Keesing, Roger M.
1990   "Ta'a geni: Women's Perspectives on Kwaio Society." In *Dealing with Inequality: Analysing Gender Relations in Melanesia and Beyond,* ed. Marilyn Strathern, pp. 33–62. Cambridge: Cambridge University Press.

Keller, Edgar.
1993   "Barkcloth Production and Dress in Laboya, West Sumba." In *Weaving Patterns of Life: Indonesian Textile Symposium 1991,* ed. M. Nabholz-Kartaschoff, R. Barnes, and D. Stuart-Fox, pp. 247–270. Basel: Museum of Ethnology.

Kipp, Rita Smith.
1993   *Disassociated Identities: Ethnicity, Religion, and Class in an Indonesian Society.* Ann Arbor: University of Michigan.
1995   "Conversion by Affiliation: The History of the Karo Batak Protestant Church." *American Ethnologist* 22(4):868–882.

Kipp, Rita Smith, and Susan Rodgers, eds.
1987   *Indonesian Religions in Transition.* Tucson: University of Arizona Press.

Kirshenblatt-Gimblett.
1991   "Objects of Ethnography." In *Exhibiting Cultures: The Poetics and Politics of Museum Display,* ed. Ivan Karp and Steven D. Lavine, pp. 127–150. Washington and London: Smithsonian Institution Press.
1994   "Spaces of Dispersal." *Cultural Anthropology* 9(3):339–344.

Kondo, Dorinne K.
1990   *Crafting Selves: Power, Gender, and Discourses of Identity in a Japanese Workplace.* Chicago and London: University of Chicago Press.

Kopytoff, Igor.
1988 "The Cultural Biography of Things: Commoditization as Process." In *The Social Life of Things: Commodities in Cultural Perspective,* ed. Arjun Appadurai, pp. 64–91. Cambridge: Cambridge University Press.

Kruyt, Albert.
1922 "De Soembaneezen" (The Sumbanese). *Bijdragen tot de Taal-, Land-, en Volkenkunde* 78:466–608.

Kubovy, Michael.
1986 *The Psychology of Perspective and Renaissance Art.* Cambridge, New York, Port Chester, Melbourne, and Sydney: Cambridge University Press.

Kuipers, Joel.
1988 "The Pattern of Prayer in Weyéwa." In *To Speak in Pairs: Essays on the Ritual Languages of Eastern Indonesia,* ed. James J. Fox, pp. 104–128. Cambridge: Cambridge University Press.
1990a *Power in Performance: The Creation of Textual Authority in Weyéwa Ritual Speech.* Philadelphia: University of Pennsylvania Press.
1990b "Talking about Troubles: Gender Differences in Weyéwa Ritual Speech Use." In *Power and Difference: Gender in Island Southeast Asia,* ed. Jane Monnig Atkinson and Shelly Errington, pp. 153–175. Stanford, Calif.: Stanford University Press.

Lambooy, P. J.
1926 "Een Scheppingsverhaal bij de Soembaneezen" (A creation story by the Sumbanese). *De Macedonier* 30:231–233.

Langewis, Laurens, and Frits A. Wagner.
1964 *Decorative Art in Indonesian Textiles.* Amsterdam: Van der Peet.

Lavie, Smadar; Kirin Narayan; and Renato Rosaldo, eds.
1993 *Creativity/Anthropology.* Ithaca, N.Y., and London: Cornell University Press.

Lavie, Smadar, and Ted Swedenburg.
1996 "Introduction." In *Displacement, Diaspora, and Geographies of Identity,* ed. Smadar Lavie and Ted Swedenburg, pp. 1–25. Durham, N.C., and London: Duke University Press.

Lavine, Steven D., and Ivan Karp.
1991 "Introduction: Museums and Multiculturalism." In *Exhibiting Cultures: The Poetics and Politics of Museum Display,* ed. Ivan Karp and Steven D. Lavine, pp. 1–9. Washington and London: Smithsonian Institution Press.

Layton, Robert.
1992 "Traditional and Contemporary Art of Aboriginal Australia: Two Case Studies." In *Anthropology, Art, and Aesthetics,* ed. Jeremy Coote and Anthony Shelton, pp. 137–159. Oxford: Clarendon Press.

Leach, Edmund R.
1954 *Political Systems of Highland Burma.* Boston: Beacon Press.

Lee, Gerard.
1990 *Troppo Man.* Australia: University of Queensland Press.

246

Leibrick, Fiona.
    1994   *Binding Culture into Thread: Textile Arts of Biboki, West Timor*.
           Darwin: Centre for Southeast Asian Studies, Northern Territory
           University, and Museum and Art Galleries of the Northern
           Territory.

Lenze, Ilse.
    1979   "Tourism Prostitution in Asia." *ISIS International Bulletin* 13.

Leur, J. C. van.
    1955   *Indonesian Trade and Society*. The Hague: Van Hoeve.

Levi-Strauss, Claude.
    1966   *The Savage Mind*. Chicago: University of Chicago Press.
    1969   *The Elementary Structures of Kinship*. Boston: Beacon Press.
    1978   *Myth and Meaning*. New York: Schocken Books.

Linnekin, Jocelyn.
    1992   "On the Theory and Politics of Cultural Construction in the Pacific."
           Oceania 62(4):249–263.

Loeber, J.
    1901   "Soemba-Doeken" (Sumba cloths). *Niuew Rotterdamsche Courant*
           4(9).
    1902   "Het 'Ikatten' in Nederlandsch-Indie" (The "ikats" of the Dutch
           Indies). *Onze Kunst* 1:17–33.

Losche, Diane.
    1997   "What Do Abelam Images Want from Us?: Plato's Cave and Kwatbil's
           Belly." *Anthro/Aesthetics: The Cultural Construction of Aesthetic*
           Objects. Special Issue 8. *Australian Journal of Anthropology* 8(1):
           35–49.

———, ed.
    1997   *Anthro/Aesthetics: The Cultural Construction of Aesthetic Objects*.
           Special Issue 8. *Australian Journal of Anthropology*.

MacCannell, Dean.
    1976   *The Tourist: A New Theory of the Leisure Class*. New York: Schocken
           Books.
    1984   "Reconstructed Ethnicity: Tourism and Cultural Identity in Third
           World Communities. *Annals of Tourism Research* 11:375–391.
    1992   *Empty Meeting Grounds: The Tourist Papers*. London and New York:
           Routledge.

Mackie, J. A. C., ed.
    1976   *The Chinese in Indonesia*. Melbourne: Monash University.

Maher, Vanessa.
    1987   "Sewing the Seams of Society: Dressmakers and Seamstresses in Turin
           between the Wars." In *Gender and Kinship: Essays toward a Unified*
           Analysis, ed. Jane Fishburne Collier and Sylvia Junko Yanagisako, pp.
           132–159. Stanford, Calif.: Stanford University Press.

Maquet, Jacques.
    1986   *The Aesthetic Experience: An Anthropologist Looks at the Visual Arts*.
           New Haven, Conn., and London: Yale University Press.

247

Marcus, George E.
 1995 "Ethnography in/of the World System: The Emergence of Multi-Sited Ethnography." *Annual Review of Anthropology* 24:95–117.

Marcus, George E., and Fred R. Myers.
 1995 "The Traffic in Art and Culture: An Introduction." In *The Traffic in Culture: Refiguring Art and Anthropology,* ed. George E. Marcus and Fred R. Myers, pp. 1–51. Berkeley, Los Angeles, and London: University of California Press.

Marcus, George E., and Michael M. J. Fischer, eds.
 1986 *Anthropology as Cultural Critique: An Experimental Moment in the Human Sciences.* Chicago and London: University of Chicago Press.

Mauss, Marcel.
 1990 *The Gift.* Trans. W. D. Halls. New York and London: W. W. Norton.

Maxwell, Robyn.
 1987 *Southeast Asian Textiles: The State of the Art.* Working Paper no. 42. Clayton, Australia: Centre of Southeast Asian Studies, Monash University.
 1990a *Textiles of Southeast Asia: Tradition, Trade, and Transformation.* Canberra: The National Gallery.
 1990b "The Tree of Life in Indonesian Textiles: Ancient Iconography or Imported Chinoiserie?" *Ethnologia* (Cologne), 14.

Maxwell, Robyn J., and John R. Maxwell.
 1989 "Political Motives: The Batiks of Mohamad Hadi of Solo." In *To Speak with Cloth: Studies in Indonesian Textiles,* ed. Mattiebelle Gittinger, pp. 131–150. Los Angeles: Museum of Cultural History, University of California.

McKean, Philip Frick.
 1989 "Towards a Theoretical Analysis of Tourism: Economic Dualism and Cultural Involution in Bali." In *Hosts and Guests: The Anthropology of Tourism,* ed. Valene L. Smith, pp. 119–138. Philadelphia: University of Pennsylvania Press.

McKinnon, Susan.
 1989 "Flags and Half-Moons: Tanimbarese Textiles in an 'Engendered' System of Valuable." In *To Speak with Cloth: Studies in Indonesian Textiles,* ed. Mattiebelle Gittinger, pp. 27–42. Los Angeles: Museum of Cultural History, University of California.

Metcalf, Peter.
 1996 "Images of Headhunting." In *Headhunting and the Social Imagination in Southeast Asia,* ed. Janet Hoskins, pp. 249–290. Stanford, Calif.: Stanford University Press.

Mehta, Gita.
 1993 *A River Sutra.* New York: Vintage Books.

Messud, Claire.
 1994 *When the World Was Steady.* New York: Granta Books.

Mies, Maria.
 1982   *The Lace Makers of Narsapur: Indian Housewives Produce for the World Market.* London: Zed Press.

Milgram, Lynne, and Penny Van Esterik, eds.
 1994   *The Transformative Power of Cloth in Southeast Asia.* Toronto: Canadian Council for Southeast Asian Studies.

Miller, Daniel.
 1987   *Material Culture and Mass Consumption.* London: Basil Blackwell.

Mills, Mary Beth.
 1997   "Contesting the Margins of Modernity: Women, Migration, and Consumption in Thailand." *American Ethnologist* 24(1):37–61.

Mitchell, David.
 1979a   "For Humans, Animals, and Spirits." *Hemisphere* 23(6):362–365.
 1979b   "Which Doctor Is the Witch Doctor?" Paper delivered at the First International Conference on Traditional Asian Medicine, Canberra, Australia.
 1982a   "Endemic Gonorrhea in Sumba." Paper presented to the Fourth National Conference of the Asian Studies Association of Australia, Melbourne, May 10–14, 1982.
 1982b   "Folk Medicine in Sumba, A Critical Evaluation." In *Indonesian Medical Traditions: Bringing Together the Old and the New,* ed. David Mitchell, pp.1–13. Melbourne: Monash University.
 1988   "Method in the Metaphor: The Ritual Language of Wanukaka." In *To Speak in Pairs: Essays on the Ritual Languages of Eastern Indonesia,* ed. James J. Fox, pp. 64–86. Cambridge: Cambridge University Press.

Mitchell, Istutiah Gunawan.
 1981   "Hierarchy and Balance: A Study of Wanokaka Social Organization." Ph.D. Thesis. Monash University, Melbourne.

Mohanty, Chandra.
 1988   "Under Western Eyes: Feminist Scholarship and Colonial Discourse." *Feminist Review* 30:61–88.

Moore, Henrietta.
 1994   *A Passion for Difference: Essays in Anthropology and Gender.* Bloomington: Indiana University Press.

Morley, David, and Kevin Robins.
 1995   *Spaces of Identity: Global Media, Electronic Landscapes, and Cultural Boundaries.* London and New York: Routledge.

Morphy, Howard.
 1991   *Ancestral Connections: Art and an Aboriginal System of Knowledge.* Chicago and London: University of Chicago Press.

Munn, Nancy.
 1973   *Walbiri Iconography: Graphic Representation and Cultural Symbolism in a Central Australian Society.* Ithaca, N.Y.: Cornell University Press.

Myers, Fred.
1992   "Representing Culture: The Production of Discourse(s) for Aboriginal Acrylic Paintings." In *Rereading Cultural Anthropology,* ed. George E. Marcus, pp. 319–355. Durham, N.C., and London: Duke University Press.
1994   "Culture-making: Performing Aboriginality at the Asia Society Gallery." *American Ethnologist* 21(4):679–699.

Nabholz-Kartaschoff, Marie-Louise; Ruth Barnes; and David J. Stuart-Fox, eds.
1993   *Weaving Patterns of Life: Indonesian Textile Symposium 1991.* Basel: Museum of Ethnology.

Nader, Laura.
1989   "Orientalism, Occidentalism, and the Control of Women." *Cultural Dynamics* 11(3):323–355.

Needham, Rodney.
1980   "Principles and Variation in the Structure of Sumbanese Society." In *The Flow of Life: Essays on Eastern Indonesia,* ed. James J. Fox, pp. 21–47. Cambridge, Mass., and London: Harvard University Press.
1983   *Sumba and the Slave Trade.* Working Paper no. 31. Melbourne: Centre of Southeast Asian Studies, Monash University.
1984   "The Transformation of Prescriptive Systems in Eastern Indonesia." In *Unity in Diversity: Indonesia as a Field of Anthropological Study,* ed. P. E. Josselin de Jong, pp. 221–233. Dordrecht, Holland: Foris Publications.
1988   "Makasarese/Endehnese/Sumbanese." In *Time Past, Time Present, Time Future: Essays in Honour of P. E. de Josselin de Jong,* ed. David S. Moyer and Henri J. M. Claessen, pp. 42–54. Dordrecht, Holland: Foris Publications.

Niessen, Sandra.
1994   *Batak Cloth and Clothing: A Dynamic Indonesian Tradition (The Asia Collection).* Oxford: Oxford University Press.

Nieuwenkamp, W. O. J.
1920   "Soemba-Weefsels" (Sumba textiles). *Tijdschrift van het Koninklijk Nederlandsche Aardrijkskundig Genootschap* 37:374–378, 503–513.
1927   *"Eenige Voorbeelden van het Ornament op de Weefsels van Sumba"* (Some examples of cloth designs from Sumba). *Nederlandisch-Indië Oud and Nieuw* 11(9):259–290.

Nooteboom, Charles.
1940   *Oost Soemba, een Volkenkundige Studie* (East Sumba, an ethnographic study). The Hague: Martinus Nijhoff.

Nooy-Palm, Hetty.
1989   "The Sacred Cloths of Toraja: Unanswered Questions." In *To Speak with Cloth: Studies in Indonesian Textiles,* ed. Mattiebelle Gittinger, pp. 163–180. Los Angeles: Museum of Cultural History, University of California.

Ong, Aiwa.
1987   *Spirits of Resistance and Capitalist Discipline: Factory Women in Malaysia.* Albany: SUNY Press.

1991   "The Gender and Labor Politics of Postmodernity." *Review of Anthropology* 20.

Onvlee, L.
1977   "The Construction of the Mangili Dam: Notes on the Social Organization of Eastern Sumba." In *Structural Anthropology in the Netherlands*, ed. P. E. de Josselin de Jong, pp. 150–163. The Hague: Martinus Nijhoff.
1980   "The Significance of Livestock in Sumba." In *The Flow of Life: Essays on Eastern Indonesia,* ed. James J. Fox, pp. 195–207. Cambridge, Mass., and London: Harvard University Press.

Pannel, Sandra.
1992   "Traveling to Other Worlds: Narratives of Headhunting, Appropriation, and the Other in the Eastern Archipelago." *Oceania* 62:162–178.
1997   "From the Poetics of Place to the Politics of Space: Redefining Cultural Landscapes on Damer, Maluku." In *The Poetic Power of Place: Comparative Perspectives on Austronesian Ideas of Locality,* ed. James J. Fox, pp. 163–173. Canberra: Research School of Pacific and Asian Studies, Australian National University.

Peacock, James L.
1979   "Dahlan and Rasul: Indonesian Muslim Reformers." In *The Imagination of Reality: Essays in Southeast Asian Coherence Systems,* ed. A. L. Becker, pp. 245–268. Norwood, N.J.: ABLEX.

Panofsky, Irwin.
1991   *Perspective as Symbolic Form*. Trans. Christopher Wood. New York: Zone Books.

Pemberton, John.
1994   *On the Subject of "Java."* Ithaca, N.Y., and London: Cornell University Press.

Phillips, Herbert P.
1969   "The Scope and Limits of the 'Loose Structure' Concept." In *Loosely Structured Social Systems: Thailand in Comparative Perspective,* ed. Hans Dieter-Evers, pp. 25–38. Cultural Report Series no. 17. New Haven, Conn.: Yale University Southeast Asia Program.
1992   *The Integrative Art of Modern Thailand*. Seattle: University of Washington Press.

Picard, Michel.
1990a   " 'Cultural Tourism' in Bali: Cultural Performance as Tourist Attraction." *Indonesia* 49:37–74.
1990b   "Kebalian Orang Bali: Tourism and the Uses of 'Balinese Culture' in New Order Indonesia." *Review of Indonesian and Malaysian Affairs* 24:1–38.
1996   "Dance and Drama in Bali: The Making of an Indonesian Art Form." In *Being Modern in Bali: Image and Change,* ed. Adrian Vickers, pp. 115–157. New Haven, Conn.: Yale University Southeast Asia Studies.

Price, Sally.
1989   *Primitive Art in Civilized Places*. Chicago and London: University of Chicago Press.

Purcell, Victor.
  1951   *The Chinese in Southeast Asia*. London: Oxford University Press.
Radin, Paul.
  1933   *The Method and Theory of Ethnology*. New York: McGraw Hill.
Reid, Anthony.
  1983   *Slavery, Bondage, and Dependency in Southeast Asia*. With the assistance of Jennifer Brewster. St. Lucia and New York: University of Queensland Press.
  1988   *Southeast Asia in the Age of Commerce 1450–1680*. Vol. 1: *The Lands below the Winds*. New Haven, Conn., and London: Yale University Press.
  1993   "Introduction: A Time and a Place." In *Southeast Asia in the Early Modern Era*, ed. Anthony Reid, pp. 1–19. Ithaca, N.Y., and London: Cornell University Press.
  1994   "Early Southeast Asian Categorizations of Europeans." In *Implicit Understandings: Observing, Reporting, and Reflecting on the Encounters between Europeans and Other Peoples in the Early Modern Era*, ed. Stuart B. Schwartz, pp. 268–294. Cambridge, New York, and Melbourne: Cambridge University Press.
——, ed.
  1996   *Sojourners and Settlers: Histories of Southeast Asia and the Chinese*. Sydney: Allen and Unwin.
Renard-Clamagirand, Brigette.
  1988   "Li'i Marapu: Speech and Ritual among the Wewewa of West Sumba." In *To Speak in Pairs: Essays on the Ritual Languages of Eastern Indonesia*, ed. James J. Fox, pp. 87–103. Cambridge: Cambridge University Press.
Richter, Linda K.
  1989   *The Politics of Tourism in Asia*. Honolulu: University of Hawai'i Press.
Ricklefs, M. C.
  1993   *A History of Modern Indonesia Since c. 1300*. Stanford, Calif.: Stanford University Press.
Robinson, Kathryn.
  1997   "History, Houses, and Regional Identities." *Anthro/Aesthetics: The Cultural Construction of Objects*. Special Issue 8. *Australian Journal of Anthropology* 8(1):71–88.
Rodgers, Susan, ed.
  1995   *Telling Lives, Telling History: Autobiography and Historical Imagination in Modern Indonesia*. Berkeley and Los Angeles: University of California Press.
Rodman, Margaret.
  1992   "Empowering Place: Multilocality and Multivocality." *American Anthropologist* 94(3):640–656.
Roo van Alderwerelt, J. de.
  1906   "Historische Aanteekeningen over Soemba" (Historical notes about Sumba). *Tijdschrift voor Indische Taal-, Land-, en Volkenkunde* 48: 185–316.

Rosaldo, Michelle Z.
   1980   *Knowledge and Passion: Ilongot Notions of Self and Society.* New
            York: Cambridge University Press.

Rosaldo, Renato.
   1989a *Culture and Truth: The Remaking of Social Analysis.* Boston: Beacon
            Press.
   1989b "Imperialist Nostalgia." *Representations* 29:107–122.
   1993   "Ilongot Visiting: Social Grace and the Rhythms of Everyday Life." In
            Creativity/Anthropology, ed. Smadar Lavie, Kirin Narayan, and Renato
            Rosaldo, pp. 253–269. Ithaca, N.Y., and London: Cornell University
            Press.

Rosenblatt, Daniel.
   1997   "The Antisocial Skin: Structure, Resistance, and 'Modern Primitive'
            Adornment in the United States." *Cultural Anthropology* 12(3):
            287–334.

Rybczynski, Witold.
   1987   *Home: A Short History of an Idea.* New York: Penguin Books.

Sahlins, Marshall.
   1985   *Islands of History.* Chicago: University of Chicago Press.
   1994   "Cosmologies of Capitalism. The Trans-Pacific Sector of 'the World
            System.' " In *Culture/Power/History: A Reader in Contemporary
            Social Theory,* ed. Nicholas B. Dirks, Geoff Eley, and Sherry Ortner,
            pp. 412–55. Princeton, N.J.: Princeton University Press.

Said, Edward.
   1978   *Orientalism.* New York: Pantheon.

Sears, Laurie J., ed.
   1996   *Fantasizing the Feminine in Indonesia.* Durham, N.C., and London:
            Duke University Press.

Schneider, Jane.
   1987   "The Anthropology of Cloth." *Annual Review of Anthropology* 16:
            409–448.
   1989   "Rumpelstiltskin's Bargain: Folklore and the Mercantile Capitalist In-
            tensification of Linen Manufacture in Early Modern Europe." In *Cloth
            and Human Experience,* ed. Annette B. Weiner and Jane Schneider,
            pp. 177–213. Washington and London: Smithsonian Institution Press.

Schneider, Jane, and Annette B. Weiner.
   1989   "Introduction." In *Cloth and Human Experience,* ed. Annette B.
            Weiner and Jane Schneider, pp. 1–29. Washington and London:
            Smithsonian Institution Press.

Schulte Nordholt, H. G.
   1980   "The Symbolic Classification of the Atoni of Timor." In *The Flow of
            Life: Essays on Eastern Indonesia,* ed. James J. Fox, pp. 231–247.
            Cambridge, Mass.: Harvard University Press.

Sexton, Lorraine D.
   1982   " 'Wok Meri': A Women's Savings and Exchange System in Highland
            Papua New Guinea." *Oceania* 52:167–198.

253

Sheldon, Anthony.
  1992 "Predicates of Aesthetic Judgement: Ontology and Value in Huichol
        Material Representations." In *Anthropology, Art and Aesthetics*, ed.
        Jeremy Coote and Anthony Sheldon, pp. 209–244. Oxford: Clarendon
        Press.

Siegel, James.
  1969 *The Rope of God*. Berkeley and Los Angeles: University of California
        Press.

Simmel, Georg.
  1965 "The Handle." In *Essays on Sociology, Philosophy and Aesthetics*, ed.
        Kurt H. Wolff. New York: Harper and Row.
  1978 *The Philosophy of Money*. Trans. T. Bottomore and D. Frisby. London,
        Henley, and Boston: Routledge and Kegan Paul.

Solyom, Bronwen, and Garrett Solyom.
  1979 "Notes and Observations on Indonesian Textiles." In *Threads of Tradi-
        tion: Textiles of Indonesia and Sarawak*, ed. Joseph Fischer, pp.
        15–33. Berkeley: Lowie Museum of Anthropology, University of
        California.

Spivak, Gayatri.
  1988 "Can the Subaltern Speak?" In *Marxism and the Interpretation of
        Culture*, ed. Carey Nelson and Lawrence Greenberg, pp. 271–313.
        Urbana: University of Illinois Press.

Spooner, Brian.
  1986 "Weavers and Dealers: The Authenticity of an Oriental Carpet." In *The
        Social Life of Things: Commodities in Cultural Perspective*, ed. Arjun
        Appadurai, pp. 195–235. Cambridge: Cambridge University Press.

Steedly, Mary Margaret.
  1993 *Hanging without a Rope: Narrative Experience in Colonial and
        Postcolonial Karoland*. Princeton, N.J.: Princeton University Press.

Steinberg, David Joel, ed.
  1987 *In Search of Southeast Asia: A Modern History*. Honolulu: University
        of Hawai'i Press.

Steiner, Christopher.
  1990 "Worlds Together, Worlds Apart: The Mediation of Knowledge by
        Traders in African Art." *Society for Visual Anthropology Review* 6(1):
        45–49.
  1994 *African Art in Transit*. Cambridge: Cambridge University Press.

Stewart, Kathleen.
  1990 "Backtalking the Wilderness: 'Appalachian Engenderings.' " In *Uncer-
        tain Terms: Negotiating Gender in American Culture*, ed. Anna Tsing
        and Faye Ginsberg, pp. 43–56. Boston: Beacon Books.
  1996 *A Space on the Side of the Road: Cultural Poetics in an "Other" Amer-
        ica*. Princeton, N.J.: Princeton University Press.

Stocking, George W., Jr.
  1985 "Philanthropoids and Vanishing Cultures: Rockefeller Funding and the
        End of the Museum Era in Anglo-American Anthropology." In *Objects*

and Others: Essays on Museums and Material Culture, ed. George W. Stocking, Jr., pp. 112–145. Madison: University of Wisconsin Press.

Strathern, Marilyn.
1990   *The Gender of the Gift.* Berkeley, Los Angeles, and London: University of California Press.

———, ed.
1987   *Dealing with Inequality: Analyzing Gender Relations in Melanesia and Beyond.* Cambridge: Cambridge University Press.

Swain, Margaret Byrne.
1989   "Gender Roles in Indigenous Tourism: Kuna *Mola*, Kuna Yala, and Cultural Survival." In *Hosts and Guests: The Anthropology of Tourism,* ed. Valene L. Smith, pp. 83–104. Philadelphia: University of Pennsylvania Press.

Taylor, Paul Michael, ed.
1994   *Fragile Traditions: Indonesian Art in Jeopardy.* Honolulu: University of Hawai'i Press.

Taylor, Paul Michael, and Lorraine V. Aragon.
1991   *Beyond the Java Sea: Art of Indonesia's Outer Islands.* Washington, D.C.: National Museum of Natural History, Smithsonian Institution (in Association with Harry N. Abrams, New York).

Thomas, Nicholas.
1991   *Entangled Objects: Exchange, Material Culture and Colonialism in the Pacific.* Cambridge, Mass.: Harvard University Press.
1995   "A Second Reflection: Presence and Opposition in Contemporary Maori Art." *Journal of the Royal Anthropological Institute* 1(1):23–46.
1998   "Hybrid Histories: Gordon Bennett's Critique of Purity." *Communal Plural: Journal of Transnational and Crosscultural Studies* 6(1): 107–116.
1999   *Possessions: Indigenous Art/Colonial Culture.* London: Thames and Hudson.

Torgovnick, Marianna.
1990   *Gone Primitive: Savage Intellects, Modern Lives.* Chicago: University of Chicago Press.

Traube, Elizabeth G.
1986   *Cosmology and Social Life: Ritual Exchange among the Mambai of East Timor.* Chicago and London: University of Chicago Press.

Trinh, T. Minh-Ha.
1991   *When the Moon Waxes Red: Representation, Gender and Cultural Politics.* New York and London: Routledge.

Truong, Thanh-Dam.
1990   *Sex, Money and Morality: Prostitution and Tourism in Southeast Asia.* London and New York: Zed Books Ltd.

Tsing, Anna Lowenhaupt.
1993   *In the Realm of the Diamond Queen.* Princeton, N.J.: Princeton University Press.

255

1996   "Telling Violence in the Meratus Mountains." In *Headhunting and the Social Imagination in Southeast Asia,* ed. Janet Hoskins, pp. 184–215. Stanford, Calif.: Stanford University Press.

Turner, Victor.
1967   "Betwixt and Between: The Liminal Period in Rites of Passage." In *The Forest of Symbols,* ed. Victor Turner, pp. 93–111. Ithaca, N.Y.: Cornell University Press.
1969   *The Ritual Process.* Harmondsworth, England: Penguin Books.

Valeri, Valerio.
1980   "Notes on the Meaning of Marriage Prestations among the Huaulu of Seram." In *The Flow of Life: Essays on Eastern Indonesia,* ed. James J. Fox, pp. 178–192. Cambridge, Mass., and London: Harvard University Press.

Van Der Kroef, J. M.
1954   *Indonesia in the Modern World.* Bandung, Indonesia: Masa Baru.

Van Esterik, Penny.
1994   "Cutting Up Culture: Colonizing Costume." In *The Transformative Power of Cloth in Southeast Asia,* ed. Lynne Milgram and Penny Van Esterik, pp. 39–52. Toronto: Canadian Council for Southeast Asian Studies.

Velden, A. J. H. van der.
1894   "De plechtigheid de Eerste H. Communie voor de eerste maal gevierd op het eiland Soemba" (The ceremony of first Holy Communion at the first time given on the island Sumba). *Berichten uit Nederlandsch Oost-Indie ten Dienste der Eerwaarde Directeuren van den St. Claver-Bond* 1894(2):91–95.

Veldhuisen-Djajasoebrata, Alit.
1988   *Weavings of Power and Might: The Glory of Java.* Rotterdam: Museum voor Volkenkunde.

Vickers, Adrian.
1989   *Bali: A Paradise Created.* Berkeley and Singapore: Periplus Editions.
1996   "Modernity and Being 'Moderen': An Introduction." In *Being Modern in Bali: Image and Change,* ed. Adrian Vickers, pp. 1–36. Monograph 43. New Haven, Conn.: Yale University Southeast Asia Studies.

———, ed.
1996   *Being Modern in Bali: Image and Change.* Monograph 43. New Haven, Conn.: Yale University Southeast Asia Studies.

Visweswaran, Kamala.
1994   *Fictions of Feminist Ethnography.* Minneapolis and London: University of Minnesota Press.

Volkman, Toby Alice.
1985   *Feasts of Honor: Ritual and Change in the Toraja Highland.* Urbana: University of Illinois Press.
1990   "Visions and Revisions: Toraja Culture and the Tourist Gaze." *American Ethnologist* 17:91–110.

Walker, Alice.
　　1988　Introduction. In Made Kertonegoro, *The Spirit Journey: Stories and Paintings of Bali,* pp. xiii–xv. Navarro, Calif.: Wild Trees Press.

Waterson, Roxana.
　　1997　"The Contested Landscapes of Myth and History in Tana Toraja." In *The Poetic Power of Place: Comparative Perspectives on Austronesian Ideas of Identity,* ed. James J. Fox, pp. 63–90. Canberra: Research School of Pacific and Asian Studies, Australian National University.

Weber, Max.
　　1958　*The Protestant Ethic and the Spirit of Capitalism.* New York: Charles Scribner's Sons.

Weiner, Annette B.
　　1976　*Women of Value, Men of Renown: New Perspectives on Trobriand Exchange.* Austin: University of Texas Press.
　　1985　"Inalienable Wealth." *American Ethnologist* 12(2):210–227.
　　1994　"Cultural Difference and the Density of Objects." *American Ethnologist* 21(2):391–403.

Weiner, Annette B., and Jane Schneider, eds.
　　1989　*Cloth and Human Experience.* Washington and London: Smithsonian Institution Press.

Wielenga, Douwe K.
　　1913　"Soemba voorheen en thans" (Sumba past and present). *Indisch Genootschaap,* Vergadering van 18 Februari 1913:121–148.
　　1931　"De Godsnaam op Soemba" (The name of God in Sumba). *De Macedonier* 35:14–20.
　　1937　*Marapoe: Een Verhaal uit Soemba* (Marapu: A Story from Sumba). The Netherlands: Uitgave J. H. Kok, n.v. Tekampan.

Wiener, Margaret J.
　　1995　*Visible and Invisible Realms: Power, Magic, and Colonial Conquest in Bali.* Chicago and London: University of Chicago Press.

Wikan, Unni.
　　1990　*Managing Turbulent Hearts: A Balinese Formula for Living.* Chicago: University of Chicago Press.

Williams, Raymond.
　　1976　*Keywords: A Vocabulary of Culture and Society.* New York: Harper and Row.
　　1989　"When Was Modernism?" *New Left Review* 175:48–52.

Wolf, Diane L.
　　1992　*Factory Daughters: Gender, Household Dynamics, and Rural Industrialization in Java.* Berkeley: University of California Press.

Wolf, Eric R.
　　1982　*Europe and the People without History.* Berkeley, Los Angeles, and London: University of California Press.

Wolters, O. W.
　　1982　*History, Culture, and Region in Southeast Asian Perspectives.* Singapore: Institute of Southeast Asian Studies.

Wouden van, F. A. E.

1935 *Sociale Structuurtypen in de Groote Oost* (Types of social structure in the Greater East). Leiden: Ginsburg.

1968 *Types of Social Structure in Eastern Indonesia.* Trans. Rodney Needham. Koninklijk Instituut voor Taal-, Land-, en Volkenkunde Translation Series, vol. 11. The Hague: Martinus Nijhoff.

1977 "Social Groups and Double Descent in Kodi, West Sumba." In *Structural Anthropology in the Netherlands,* ed. P. E. Josselin de Jong, pp. 183–222. The Hague: Martinus Nijhoff.

258

INDEX

Pages containing illustrations are in boldface type.

263

ABOUT THE AUTHOR

Jill Forshee is a research fellow at the Centre for Southeast Asian Studies of Northern Territory University, Darwin, Australia. She holds a Ph.D. in Social and Cultural Anthropology from the University of California, Berkeley. Her previous publications include *Converging Interests: Traders, Travelers, and Tourists in Southeast Asia* (editor) and numerous articles about eastern Sumba. She is presently working on a book about contemporary arts and folklore of the eastern Indonesian islands of Sumba and Timor.